Table of Contents

THE

PERIPHERAL

AMERICANS

BY

FRANK J. CAVAIOLI AND SALVATORE J. LaGUMINA

— 8668535

Draw

508-653-3151

ROBERT E. KRIEGER PUBLISHING COMPANY
MALABAR, FLORIDA 1984

Original Edition 1983
BASED UPON *THE ETHNIC DIMENSION IN AMERICAN SOCIETY*

Printed and Published by
ROBERT E. KRIEGER PUBLISHING COMPANY, INC.
KRIEGER DRIVE
MALABAR, FL 32950

Copyright © 1984
ROBERT E. KRIEGER PUBLISHING COMPANY, INC.

Printed in the United States of America

Library of Congress Cataloging in Publication Data

Cavaioli, Frank J.
  The peripheral Americans.

  Bibliography: p.
  Includes index.
  1. United States—Ethnic relations. 2. United
States—Emigration and immigration. 3. Ethnicity—
United States—History. 4. United States—Ethnic
relations—Sources. 5. United States—Emigration
and immigration—History—Sources. 6. Ethnicity—
United States—History—Sources. I. LaGumina,
Salvatore John, 1928-   . II. Title.
E184.A1C346 1983   305.8'00973   82-14019
ISBN 0-89874-542-X

Introduction

Until recently ethnic diversity has been minimized because true Americanism seemed to signify assimilation, that to be loyal to the nation the citizen had to be melted down into a completely new person, just as the immigrant was physically severed from the old country. The "melting pot" idea provided the rational for explaining the American identity and the source of American nationality. The Frenchmen Crevecoeur said as early as 1782 that "here individuals of all nations are melted into a new race of men."[1] He was not entirely correct because he disregarded the durability of the immigrants' cultural baggage.

Another major theory that sought to explain the uniqueness of the American civilization was "Anglo-conformity." It suggests that the immigrants must be made to conform to the mold of the English-speaking people because of the superiority of their culture. The nativist Madison Grant, who came from an old-line established colonial family that traced its roots to the Anglo-Saxon heritage, witnessed the millions of southern and eastern Europeans entering the United States at the turn of the twentieth century, and he concluded that this "alien invasion" was corrupting the superior "Nordic race." Grant stated in his influential book, *The Passing of the Great Race*, written in 1916 that

> These new immigrants were no longer exclusive members of the Nordic race as were the earlier ones. . . . The new immigration. . .contained a large and increasing number of the weak, the broken, and the mentally crippled of all races drawn from the lowest stratum of the Mediterranean basin and the Balkans, together with hordes of the wretched, submerged population of Polish Ghettos. Our jails, insane asylums, and almshouses are filled with human flotsam, and the whole tone of American life, social, moral, and political, has been lowered and vulgarized by them.[2]

Finally, the contemporary prevailing theory of cultural pluralism accepts ethnic diversity as beneficial to the entire society as well as the ethnic groups themselves. The intent of the current emphasis is not to achieve a fragmentation or "balkanization" of American society, to use Kevin Phillips's term, nor is it to separate Americans into disparate segments concerned only with their own well-being. Rather its intent is to require little more than the use of the English language and the embracing of democratic principles in order to gain acceptance in American society. Whether the immigrant adapted to American society by his external actions (behavioral assimilation) to survive and at the same time remained an ethnic deep in his soul, or whether he merged in the institutional life (structural assimilation) of American society, should be the choice of the immigrant or his forebears. "Democracy involves. . .the perfection and conservation of differences. . . .It involves a give and take between radically different types, and a mutual respect and mutual cooperation," stated Horace Kallen in his insightful examination of American culture and democracy.[3] Ethnicity persists today just as ethnic subcultures existed in colonial times. Monsignor Geno Baroni, president of the National Center for Urban Ethnic Affairs, stated that "America is the most ethnically, radically, religiously, and culturally pluralistic nation in the world." And Michael Novak, author of *The Rise of the Unmeltable Ethnics*, (New York: Macmillan, 1972), said "to be American is to come from somewhere."

The resurgence of ethnicity emphasizes the pluralistic nature of society and the free choice of the individual and the group. Ethnic homogenization violates individualism and the fredom of choice. Ethnic affirmation points up group solidarity for social, economic, and political reasons, particularly for the white ethnics who feel they have been overlooked by government officials and ignored by society. Group power is an essential reality in modern times. Additionally, ethnic consciousness provides a sense of value identification and security for the individual. Michael Novak has said that

> If you explore your own ethnic identity, the effort will not blind you to the subtle, provocative ways in which others differ from you. To understand what is means to be a Jew or an Italian-American is to gain some insight into the difference implicit in being Afro-American, into black pride, into black politics, and the reverse . . . persons who are secure in their identity act with greater freedom, greater flexibility, greater openness to others. People who feel inferior or unacceptable lash out in anger.[4]

Jane Addams, the social worker at the turn of the twentieth century, described how American patriotism should not be taught.[5] She addressed a Greek audience on the founding of Plymouth colony and the Anglo-Saxon achievements. Afterward one Greek approached her and said, "I wish I could describe my ancestors." Another Greek said his ancestors could surpass the achievements of the Anglo-Saxons. In another example she recounted how a public-spirited organization got leading citizens to speak to children in the public schools. One Civil War veteran spoke about a Civil War battle in Tennessee to an audience of Italian immigrant children. An Italian student went up to the veteran and proudly described his father's campaigning under Garibaldi. The veteran was not impressed and admonished the student to forget that because he was no longer an Italian but an American.

Some scholars have asserted that neo-ethnicity represents a new tribalism and a new apartheid triggered by the black movement. Joshua A. Fishman explained that "it brought about a massive redefinition of the WASP category, to such an extent that few wanted to be included in the "soulless" group devoted to material comfort, middle-class values, environmental pollutants, and Vietnamization with which it was variously identified."[6]

Robert F. Hill, Orlando Patterson, Howard F. Stein, and Stephen Steinberg have indicated that neo-ethnicity is a manifestation of ethnicity at its worst, since it is based on the opposition of the lower middle-class ethnics who resent the achievements of the nonwhite minorities.[7] They feel that the special programs for nonwhite minorities have come at their expense, and argue therefore for attention for themselves.

Many critics say that neo-ethnicity threatens the foundation of democracy by weakening individualism, equality, and due process. They contend that it leads to balkanization of society because of the resultant divisiveness which places one group against another, all selfishly fighting for their own benefit.

These reservations notwithstanding, ethnicity in contemporary American life remains. It perdures not only in the familiar settings of the Little Italys, Little Tokyos, Little Manilas, Chinatowns, Polishtowns, and Harlems, but also manifests a staying power within suburban communities. Americans have paid too little attention to the latter, but it would be instructive to cite an example of ethnicity in suburbia by reference to Nassau and Suffolk counties, Long Island, New York. Constituting perhaps the nation's archetypical suburbia, with a heavy overlay of surface middle-class homogenization replete with split-level homes, two-car garages, and well-manicured lawns, one has only to scratch the surface to acknowledge that the ethnic phenomenon has indeed moved to the suburbs and is manifest in the resurgence of ethnic organizations such as the Ancient Order of Hibernians, the building of nationality clubs such as that of the Portuguese Americans in Mineola, and the revival of Italian feasts in various parts of Long Island. Clearly ethnicity is not limited to the urban demographic contest.[8]

In a similar manner, a recent study by Russel L. Gerlach revealed the variegated ethnic cultures of the Ozark Highlands region, which are quite different from the stereotyped uniform culture of Appalachia. Thus in the Ozarks in addition to the major groups of English and Scots, there are numerous smaller groups of Italians, French, Germans, Poles, Belgians, Swedes, Swiss, Yugoslavs, Austrians, Hungarians, Bohemians, and smaller ethnic religious sects such as Dunkards, Amish, and Mennonites. German ethnicity is strong today in architecture, housing, language, and religion. The open display of German culture is equally prominent through the Maifest and Oktoberfest. In fact, German festivals have increased in recent years, and Gerlach points out that the Catholic Church remains an ethnic church in the rural Ozarks, with French, Germans, Poles, and Italians comprising the bulk of membership. "The French at Old Mines, the Italians at Rosati, and the Poles at Pulaskifield represent the few non-German European settlements where ethnic identity has been retained. . . .the old hypothesis that the United States is an ethnic melting pot is not applicable in the rural Ozarks."[9]

Moreover, the contemporary ethnic festivals of such major cities as Detroit, Chicago, New York, and Kansas City reflect the real and psychic value of such events. The period of mass migration may be long gone, and the Americanization process has taken its toll, but the need for people to identify themselves along ethnic lines becomes imperative. It leads to the strenghtening of one's sense of ethnicity. The leaders of the contemporary ethnic revival are not recently arrived immigrants, but people who are several or more generations removed from the Old World.

It is our contention that diversity in American life has been an ever-recurring theme. Whether one speaks about the competition between various immigrant groups in the early period of American history or about contemporary manifestations of racial and ethnic unrest, it is evident that ethnic diversity has played and continues to play a major role in the weaving of the unique American social fabric. Blacks and other minority groups are now aware of their own ethnicity and the need to articulate it. While many deplore the negative reaction of ethnic power in the context of competition for jobs, housing, and political power, not enough attention has been given to the positive aspects of ethnicity. The simple fact is that out of the crucible of American pluralism a unique and effective, if somewhat unsteady, unity has resulted. The ethnic factor persists with astonishing tenacity as an important element in American society in spite of the seemingly growing assimilation.

Ethnic subcultures appeared as far back as the early colonial times as the new immigrants attempted to reconstruct replications of the old World societies from which they emerged. For the most part this endeavor to conserve indigenous systems of accumulated beliefs, customs, styles, solutions, and practices failed with important exceptions. The record shows that most immigrant groups became acculturated by the second or third generation. Notwithstanding this acculturation, true assimilation often did not follow. One scholar astutely observed that Americanization of an ethnic group "says little about its social relations with the host society."[10]

In sociological terms an ethnic group is defined as a group of people racially and historically related, having a common and distinctive culture. Further, such a group is described as a "foreign-stock segment of the population which preserves in some degree a distinctive way of life, in language, mannerism, habit, loyalty and the like."[11] However, sociologists also acknowledge that some individuals are ethnics even though their attitudes and behavior are indistinguishable from the majority. Nor is birth location a certain indicator or identifier of ethnic group attachment. "The essense of minority group membership has today become not so much observable differences in appearances and behavior. . .as it is the extent to which one's group-identified forbears are held to be socially unacceptable by the majority or other minorities."[12]

Another researcher finds that ethnic stratification is virtually inevitable so long as ethnocentrism, competition, and power differential are brought into play. Competition provides motivation for stratification, while ethnocentrism channels the competition along ethnic lines, and the power differential determines whether one group will be able to subordinate the other.[13]

Statistically, about 20 percent of Americans are in the "foreign stock" category, which is defined by the Census Bureau as either foreign born or having at least one foreign-born parent. By using the widest possible latitude, the term "ethnic" can also be defined as any individual who differs from the white Anglo-Saxon settlers by religion, language, and culture.[14] This would account for up to 65 percent of the total population and thus further enhance the validity of the assumption that the various ethnic and nationality groups bear studying. The following statement underscores this point:

> Ethnic differences, even in the second half of the twentieth century, proved far more important to men than did differences in philosophy or economic system. Men who would not die for a premise or a dogma or a division of labor would more or less cheerfully die for a difference rooted in ethnic origins.[15]

The existence of ethnicity ought not to be regarded as a remnant of immigration; rather it must be acknowledged that group differences form an enduring part of social life. This principle was given ringing affirmation in 1972 as Congress and the President approved the Ethnic Heritage Studies Act. As Pennsylvania Senator Richard S. Schweiker, sponsor of the bill in the U.S. Senate, put it:

> America's melting pot has not melted. . . .More and more, we see throughout society a new pluralism in America. I feel this is healthy and constructive. It can help all persons to break down the prejudices and divisiveness of the past, so that communities can begin to work together to solve mutual problems. . . .Now is the time to give equal time to the "many" ethnic groups and to recognize that only through cultural diversity can we achieve the harmonious society that the "one" is designed to achieve.
> The "new Pluralism" is not really a new concept. It is merely a recognition that we have ignored a great American resource: ethnicity and cultural diversity.[16]

If we are to appraise and evaluate the nation in which they form an integral part, it behooves us to know more about our various ethnic and nationality groups. We have an urgent obligation to become acquainted with the history and culture of all American peoples and their reaction to the problems of adjustment and accomplishment in American society.

This volume is an effort to understand America's history and development as a nation through the eyes of "peripheral Americans." In the sense that we are all ethnics (since, as the readings will show, each group had to come to terms with a new life in America), the experience of all groups can be instructive toward the attainment of a greater understanding of American civilization. To the extent that today's problems of vital national concern are racial and ethnic problems, then meaningful studies directed toward the solution of these problems will be indispensable to an interpretation of contemporary society. A study of ethnic group dynamics is of immense importance to a greater appreciation of the problems faced by victims of discrimination. As the United States is the classic country of immigration, it is also the classic ethnic country. It is a land of many and varied cultures which give it the richness of diversity as well as the danger of divisiveness. Today, as never before, it is imperative that every effort be undertaken to preserve the former and prevent the latter.

This study is an endeavor to fill a gap in the long-neglected area of ethnic America. It is an appraisal, an observation, and a commentary on the development of this nation's history unlike usual readers in the analysis of American society. The focus will be on selections from those individuals who were on the periphery of American life or who spoke for the peripheral Americans or interpreted their experience in America. The emphasis will be on the hopes and aspirations, and the laments and disappointments, or representative of typical individuals or various ethnic groups who, although residents of the United States, tended to be looking in on American life from the outside. This will be seen in the writings of the peripheral Americans and sometimes in the writings of those who harbored little goodwill toward them.

To look at the ethnic constellation is to learn something important about American society problems. It is also to learn that the melting pot concept not only is inadequate to an understanding of contemporary problems and issues but also has always been, at any period, inaccurate as an explanation of group interrelationships. From the very beginning of recorded American history to the present, group interests, group power, and group aspirations have affected American civilization. Although checkered and subject to modification according to local conditions, the responses of different groups, and conflicts between these responses, have been different in given situations.

To emphasize the role of ethnicity in American life is not to make a value judgment. It is not to say that this role is positive or negative. In fact, it can be either or both. But even more basic is the recognition of it as a phenomenon making a significant impact on American life. It exists; that is sufficient reason for studying it.

ONE

The Pre-Civil War Period:
The English, French, Dutch,
Scotch-Irish, Scots, and Welsh

The early immigrants who settled in the colonial period laid the foundation of ethnic diversity. Population figures in the first census of 1790 reflect an English pervasiveness with 82.1 percent of the total white population. But the rest of the population was made up of other ethnic groups: Germans and Scotch-Irish along the frontier, Swedes and Dutch in the Atlantic seaboard colonies, French Huguenots in South Carolina and New England, and some Spanish and Portuguese Jews in the Atlantic port towns, and Scots scattered about. Of the total population in 1790, which amounted to 4 million, 757,208 or 19.27 percent comprised blacks. Furthermore, a sizeable population of American Indians was present, but the exact number is not known. Here and there were scattered small numbers of Italians, Finns, and other nationalities. The fact remains that the population was ethnically diverse.

The large number of nationalities that entered into American life in the pre-Civil War period necessarily precludes coverage of each group at this point. Therefore, the groups that were predominant will be given attention while other ethnic groups will be examined later. This chapter will include the English, French, Dutch, Scotch-Irish, Scots, and Welsh, in focusing in on the role, the extent, and the impact of ethnic group response to the earliest days of the American experience.

THE ENGLISH

There can be little doubt that American civilization has been the recipient of much in the English culture: language, law, religion, architecture. Nevertheless, English immigrants in the opening stage of colonization demonstrated an ethnic consciousness that indicated both uncertainty and confidence because of their national background.

The first selection that follows includes excerpts from William Bradford, *Of Plymouth Plantation, 1620-1647*. Bradford, first governor of Plymouth colony, was an English yeoman farmer (a freeman farmer below the landed gentry class) who exercized extraordinary perseverance as a colonial leader. His classic chronicle contains early expressions of English immigrants as ethnically conscious people. For example, although the Pilgrims were prepared to flee England in order to practice their religion without interference, they found it impossible to live in Holland, a tolerant country which, nevertheless, proved to be insensitive to the needs of an English ethnic minority. The consequence was emigration to America.

Of Their Setting in Holland, and Their Manner of Living, and Entertainment There

Being now come into the Low Countries, they saw many and goodly fortified cities, strongly walled and guarded with troops of armed men. Also, they heard a strange and uncouth language, and beheld the different manners and customs of the people, with their strange fashions and attires, all so far differing from that of their plain country villages (wherein they were bred and had so long lived) as it seemed they were come into a new world. . .

Showing the Reasons and Causes of their Removal

After they had lived in this city about some eleven or twelve years (which is the more observable being the whole time of that famous truce between that state and the Spaniards) and sundry of them were taken away by death and many others began to be well stricken in years (the grave mistress of Experience having taught them many things), those prudent governors with sundry of the sagest members began both deeply to apprehend their present dangers and wisely to foresee the future and think of timely remedy. In the agitation of their thoughts, and much discourse of things hereabout, at length they began to incline to this conclusion: of removal to some other place. Not out of any newfangledness or other such like giddy humor by which men are oftentimes transported to their great hurt and danger, but for sundry weighty and solid reasons, some of the chief of which I will here briefly touch. . . .

As necessity was a taskmaster over them so they were forced to be such, not only to their servants but in a sort to their dearest children, the which as it did not a little wound the tender hearts of many a loving father and mother, so it produced likewise sundry sad and sorrowful effects. For many of their children that were of best dispositions and gracious inclinations, having learned to bear the yoke in their youth and willing to bear part of their parents' burden, were oftentimes so oppressed with their heavy labours that though their minds were free and willing, yet their bodies bowed under the weight of the same, and became decrepit in their early youth, the vigour of nature being consumed in the very bud as it were. But that which was more lamentable, and of all sorrows most heavy to be borne, was that many of their children, by these occasions and the great licentiousness of youth in that country, and the manifold temptations of the place, were drawn away by evil examples into extravagant and dangerous courses, getting the reins off their necks and departing from their parents. Some became soldiers, others took upon them far voyages by sea, and others some worse courses tending to dissoluteness and the danger of their souls, to the great grief of their parents and dishonour of God.[1]

Being thus convinced of the undesirability of residence in Holland, the Pilgrims determined to locate in the New World to carry on their distinctive way of life.

Being thus arrived in a good harbor, and brought safe to land, they fell upon their knees and blessed the God of Heaven who had brought them over the vast and furious ocean, and delivered them from all the perils and miseries thereof, again to set their feet on the firm and stable earth, their proper element. . . .

If they looked behind them, there was the mighty ocean which they had passed and was now as a main bar and gulf to separate them from all the civil parts of the world. If it be said they had a ship to succour them, it is true; . . . of these fathers rightly say: "Our fathers were Englishmen which came over this great ocean, and were ready to perish in this wilderness; but they cried unto the Lord, and He heard their voice and looked on their adversity," etc. "Let them therefore praise the Lord, because He is good: and His mercies endure forever."

The American Revolution did not fundamentally change the preferential feeling that most Americans had for the English heritage. Indeed, Washington Irving, in *The Sketchbook*, responded to the publication of anti-American writers in England by admonishing Americans not to react in kind but to acknowledge that, for Americans, English culture is more worthy of emulation than that of other people.

But above all let us not be influenced by any angry feelings, so far as to shut our eyes to the perception of what is really excellent and amiable in the English character. We are a young people, necessarily an imitative one, and must take our examples and models, in a great degree, from the existing nations of Europe. There is no country more worthy of our study than England. The spirit of her constitution is most analogous to ours. The manners of her people—their intellectual activity, their freedom of opinion, their habits of thinking on those subjects which concern the dearest interests and most sacred charities of private life—are all congenial to the American character; and, in fact, are all intrinsically excellent; for it is in the moral feeling of the people that the deep foundations of British prosperity are laid; and however the superstructure may be timeworn or overrun by abuses, there must be something solid in the basis, admirable in the materials, and stable in the structure of an edifice that so long has towered unshaken amidst the tempests of the world.[2]

The celebrated Alexis de Tocqueville discussed the importance of English origins in American society in his impressive and prophetic classic, *Democracy in America.* In the selection below, he describes the common background of the Anglo-Americans.

If we carefully examine the social and political state of America, after having studied its history, we shall remain perfectly convinced that not an opinion, not a custom, not a law, I may even say not an event is upon record which the origin of that people will not explain. The readers of this book will find in the present chapter the germ of all that is to follow and the key to almost the whole work.

The emigrants who came at different periods to occupy the territory now covered by the American Union differed from each other in many respects; their aim was not the same, and they governed themselves on different principles.

These men had, however, certain features in common, and they were all placed in an analogous situation. The tie of language is, perhaps, the strongest and most durable that can unite mankind. All the emigrants spoke the same language; they were all children of the same people. Born in a country which had been agitated for centuries by the struggles of faction, and in which all parties had been obliged in their turn to place themselves under the protection of the laws, their political education had been perfected in this rude school; and they were more conversant with the notions of right and the principles of true freedom than the greater part of their European contemporaries. At the period of the first emigrations the township system, that fruitful germ of free institutions, was deply rooted in the habits of the English; and with it the doctrine of the sovereignty of the people had been introduced into the very bosom of the monarchy of the house of Tudor.[3]

American nativists in the middle of the nineteenth century and around the turn of the twentieth century felt besieged by the large-influx of non-Anglo-Saxon immigration, and they reacted to defend their pattern of civilization in America. One scholar suggested that "the race-thinkers were men who rejoiced in their colonial ancestry, who looked to England for standards of deportment and taste, who held the great academic posts or belonged to the best clubs or adorned the higher Protestant clergy." Frank Parsons, Albert Shaw, Episcopalian Bishop A. Cleveland Coxe, Woodrow Wilson, Henry Cabot Lodge, Barret Wendell, among others, expressed strong Anglophile sentiments. In 1891 Lodge, the New England brahmin, published a statistical report that included a biographical report to "prove" the English racial superiority in the history of the nation, and therefore the alleged "inferiority" of the non-English ethnic groups.[4]

In this respect, national ethnic pride proved to be a prime motivating force in the expansion of Western imperialism. The desire to spread one's cultural heritage is demonstrated in Rudyard Kipling's *Whiteman's Burden*, written in 1899. Yet in 1848 pride in the Anglo-Saxon "race" is articulated in the following poem which urged Great Britain to go forth to sow the seeds of its advanced civilization. Though well-meaning, the poem embodied ethnic paternalistic superiority.

The New Home

Lo! to every human creature
Born upon this bounteous earth,
Speaks the God of grace and nature,
Speaks for plenty or for death;
Till the ground; if not, thou starvest;
Fear shall drive to duteous toil;
Till the ground; a golden harvest
Then shall wave on every soil!

And behold! the King all-glorious
Unto Britain tythes the world,—
Everywhere her crown victorious,
Everywhere her cross unfurl'd!
God hath giv'n her distant regions,
Broad and rich,; and store of ships;
God hath added homeborn legions
Steep'd in trouble to the lips!

Join then in holy tether
Those whom Man hath put aside
Those whom God would link together,
Earth and Labour well applied:
Ho! thou vast and wealthy nation,
Wing thy fleets to every place,
Fertilizing all Creation
With the Anglo-Saxon race!

England's frank and sturdy bearing,
Scotland's judgment true and tried,
Erin's energetic daring,
And the Welshman's honest pride,—
Send these forth, and tame the savage,
Sow his realm with British homes,
Where till now wild monsters ravage,
Or the wilder Myal roams![5]

THE FRENCH

French immigration to the United States has never been very large. It is estimated that 740,000 French nationals have migrated to this country since 1820, and nearly 40,000 had settled here earlier. With few exceptions the ethnic trait did not in the long run emerge as a readily identifiable factor as the French were assimilated into the American social fabric. As distinct from the French Canadians, there are scarcely any vestiges of "French Americans." This background notwithstanding, ethnic origin shaped their experiences.

The growth of religious intolerance in France in the latter part of the seventeenth century led to the arrival in the colonies of a group of French Huguenots. Although their Protestantism and their industry removed two of the principal prejudices normally lodged against foreigners, they nevertheless were treated with suspicion and even violence. This ill will goes a long way toward explaining their unique amalgamation.

The French Huguenots imparted a high-spirited aristocratic tone to the colony of South Carolina, for example, yet at the same time quickly adopted the English language and joined the Anglican Church. The following selection explains the rapid assimilation that developed over two generations.

The Assimiliation of The Huguenots

The rapid assimilation of the French in Carolina into the Established Church and their intermarriage with other nationalities are remarkable features of their early history. The absorption into the Anglican Church was indirectly coercive, rapid and thorough. The English institutions mastered and overpowered the French. The French became English in language and religion, British in sentiment and policies. The fulcrum by which it was accomplished was economic necessity, the lever was political preferment. We are slow to conclude that the change was made with graceful ease. . . . Only after a conflict, the temper of which is too remote to be easily understood today, did the French Protestants relinquish their church affiliation and embrace Anglicanism. . . .

There seems to have been little effort on the part of the Carolina French Protestants to perpetuate the remembrance of a distinct nationality. Their children, except in the isolated sections, were not encouraged to speak French. Frequent interruptions in the conduct of the French churches, caused by the illness, death and resignations of French pastors, constantly afforded reason for their members to attend the services of churches other than their own. Owing to Dissenter antipathies the step to Anglicanism was sometimes made proportionately easy. By 1706, sufficient time had elapsed since the Revocation to give rise to a younger generation unsatisfied with the adherence to old French forms, a generation adverse to a language not in general use in the province, clamoring for the new and the popular. The rising generation could not be expected to feel the bitterness of the Revocation as did their parents. The children of many of the refugees were even ashamed to bear French names. The idea of remaining foreigners in a land in which they were born and reared was alien to their thought. The establishment of the Church of England by law in the colony in 1700 welded these several links into a chain of necessity. The Bishop of London sagaciously supplied the Huguenots with a ministry of French nativity and Anglican ordination, men proficient in both the French language and the ritual of the Establishment. . . .

But the absorption of the French was more extensive than a mere change in church forms. It extended to proper names, to language, to customs, and even to blood. It has become evident that for several reasons the Huguenots were regarded with disfavor before they were able to rise socially by the accumulation of wealth. However unreasonable that circumstance may have been regarded it was nevertheless a fact and became very unpleasant. Out of it grew the desire to become anglicized. A French name was constantly a bid to disfavor. Therefore some people changed their names completely, others modified them, still others accepted the English equivalent. Jacques Serrurier easily became Smith; for convenience Pasquereau degenerated into Packerow; Villepontoux became Pontoux; Lewis Janvier, a goldsmith, became Lewis Jennings; Timothée was anglicized to Timothy. . . .[7]

In the wake of the French Revolution, immigration to the United States underwent a fascinating phase. The thousands of French aristocrats who came here were the proudeest to enter this land in the late eighteenth and early nineteenth centuries. When they returned to France, as many did, they left hardly a trace on American society. Nevertheless, it is significant to note the intermixture of class and ethnic interests in the pockets of French life that they tried to establish in the United States. This phenomenon is described in the narrative of C.F. Volney, *"Gallipolis, or the French Colony of Scioto,"* in *A View of the Soil and Climate of the United States of America.*

On my arrival in America, in October, 1795, I made some enquiry after these people, but could only hear a vague story that they were buried somewhere in the western wilds, and had not prospered. Next summer I shaped my course through Virginia, and after traveling three hundred miles to Staunton, two hundred more over a rugged desert to the Great Kenhawah, and sixty miles down that river, through a scene still more dreary and desolate, to the Ohio, I at last reached a village called Point Pleasant, four miles from Gallipolis; by this splendid appellation (which means French city) the emigrants denominated their settlement. My eagerness to see the face and hear the language of my countrymen, once more, made me hasten thither without delay.

Colonel Lewis, a kinsman of General Washington, facilitated my journey. I went on, but reflecting that I was going to visit Frenchmen disappointed in their dearest hopes, their vanity mortified, and their mortification likely to be aggravated by the sight of one, who had probably foretold their misfortunes to some of them, my impatience was greatly diminished. It was night-fall before I reached the village, and I could perceive nothing but a double row of small white houses, built on the flat top of a bank of the Ohio, which here laves the foot of a cliff fifty feet high. The water being low, I climbed the bank, by a slope formed in its side, and was conducted to a log house called an inn. It was kept by a Frenchman, who asked me but few questions, and his demeanour evinced the truth of all my prognostics.

Next day I took a view of the place, and was struck with its forlorn appearance; with the thin pale faces, sickly looks, and anxious air of its inhabitants. They were shy of conversing with me. Their dwellings, though made externally cheerful by whitewash, were only log huts, patched with clay, and roofed with shingles, consequently damp, unwholesome, and uncomfortable. The village forms an oblong quadrangle of two rows of contiguous buildings, which a spark would consume altogether. . . .

All the labours of clearing and tillage were imposed on the family itself of the proprietor, labourers not being to be hired but at enormous prices. It may easily be imagined how severe a hardship it was, on men brought up in the ease and indolence of Paris, to chop trees, to plough, to sow, to reap, to labour in the field or the barn, in a heat of 85 or 95 degrees. . . .

Such is the condition of the Scioto colony, which does not altogether realize the pictures of the inland paradise given by American farmers, nor the glories of the future capital of the Ohio and its realms, predicted by a certain writer. . . .

I wished to leave this settlement with a persuasion that they were doing well and would prosper; but, besides the original and incurable error in the choice of situation, I am afraid that their despondency will never be entirely removed, since there will always be some cause for it, and since the French nation are less qualified for settling a new country than the emigrants from England, Ireland, or Germany. Among fifteen instances of farms, cultivated or formed by Frenchmen, which were mentioned to me in America, only two or three were likely to thrive. As to collecting men in villages, such as Gallipolis, those that have been formed on the frontiers of Louisiana or Canada, and have been left to shift for themselves, have generally dwindled, and sooner or later disappeared; while plain men, from the British Isles or Germany, who have pierced the heart of the forest with their families only, and even ventured alone into the Indian territory, have generally made good their footing, and have prospered and multiplied.[8]

For the most part, however, French emigrants to the United States were ethnically little distinguished, except by their surnames, from English settlers. Even those who colonized the French-named New Rochelle had become well assimilated.

The French Protestants who colonized New Rochelle have chiefly, if not wholly, become mere Americans; in no way distinguishable, except by their surnames, from the descendants of the English Colonists. It is a fact, deserving of notice, that a considerable number of these people have been persons of high respectability, and have been elevated to very honorable stations; and many others have acquired ample fortunes, and sustained very desirable characters in private life. A prophet might attribute their prosperity to a particular blessing of God, who on many occasions has been pleased to shower his favour upon the descendants of those who have been persecuted for their piety.

Of all these classes of Colonists it is to be observed, generally, that they will soon be so entirely amalgamated with those from New England as to be undistinguishable.[9]

THE DUTCH

In the latter part of the sixteenth century, the Dutch entered into a successful movement for independence against the Spanish monarchs which simultaneously predisposed the nation to a remarkable period of expansion. This expansion led to important claims in North America, as the colony of New Netherlands was founded. In the wake of that colony's growth, several thousand immigrants came to the New World in the seventeenth century. They remained the predominant strain in the otherwise cosmopolitan character of what later became New York.

Promoters of the Dutch colony were intent on establishing a military and economic base in North America. In the process they gave the Hudson Valley region an indelible Dutch stamp. So strong was the Dutch imprint that as late as the American Revolution, Dutch was one of two foreign tongues apparently firmly rooted in American society.

New Netherlands was never to be a Dutch frontier in the same sense that Jamestown and Plymouth were for England because the Dutch government was apathetic about the settlement in America. Nevertheless, the Dutch who emigrated to New Netherlands had a strong attachment to their ethnic roots. In the following extract Arnold Mulder speculates on what might have been in regard to the implanting of Dutch culture in America.

The folk of New Netherland in terms of the wave of what was their future were far more enlightened than their leaders who tried to govern them with supercilious contempt. An objective examination of the record, honestly allowing for all their faults and weaknesses, shows that they were worthy of becoming the bearers of their country's culture across our continent. The ineptness and short-sightedness of politicians and traders robbed them of that destiny, but their defeat was only partial, as the subsequent story of the life of their nationality in America shows.

There is a footnote to the story of the Dutch colonial episode on the American continent. In less than a decade after the surrender to the English, the Dutch recaptured New York during the war that broke out between England and Holland in 1672. The folk of New Netherland industriously set about restoring their own institutions, even to the extent of wiping out many of the English place names and substituting for them the Dutch words by which they had been known for half a century. It was a last instinctive attempt to impose their culture on America.[10]

One of the first institutions that the Dutch inhabitants of New Netherlands were determined to establish was a schoolhouse. An illustration of their understanding of the value of education, this institution also perpetuated national traits. As the following excerpt shows, after the English replaced the Dutch as rulers of New Netherlands, the Dutch school, taught in the Dutch language and with other concessions to ethnicity, remained.

Under early English rule the schooling of the Dutch children was little interfered with. They were to be instructed in the "Netherlandisch tongue" as of old, and the schoomaster was still to be under the supervision of the Consistory. The school hours were fixed from nine to eleven A.M. in summer, from half-past nine to half-past twelve in winter, while the afternoon session the year round lasted from one to five o'clock. The schools were opened and closed with prayer, twice a week the pupils were examined in the catechism and express stipulation was made that teachers should use "none but edifying and orthodox text-books and such as should meet the approbation of the Consistory."

The control of the schools so wisely conceded by the English continued in the hands of the Dutch long enough to stamp the character which endures to this day in the representative school of the Collegiate Reformed Dutch Church of New York, which with its fine buildings and elaborate equipments is the direct successor of the little school gathered together by Adam Roelantsen under the shadow of the old Fort.

Those of us of Dutch blood have a special right to look with pride upon this steady growth of the educational institution planted and fostered by our forefathers and bearing perpetual testimony to their energy and perseverance, their just valuation of "the things of the spirit," their respect for learning, and their determination to "learn the youth the first principles" and to make them men "who may be able to serve their country in Church and State."[11]

Nearly a century after the English conquest of New Netherlands, perceptive observers noted the strength of ethnic feelings among the

Dutch inhabitants in New York. Peter Kalm, a Swedish naturalist, in
En Resa Til Norra America pa Kongl (Stockholm, 1753-1761), pointed
out that "in Albany the inhabitants are almost all Dutchmen. They
speak Dutch, have Dutch preachers, and the divine service is
performed in that language. Their manners are likewise Dutch. . . ."[12]

In the 1840s, immigration became epidemic as over 1,700,000
newcomers entered the United States. A significant number of Dutch
people participated in this movement because of religious and
economic reasons. They gave evidence of their ethnic loyalties by
establishing a number of settlements in Michigan in the 1840s and
1850s, giving them Dutch names such as Holland and Zeeland.

THE SCOTCH-IRISH AND THE SCOTS

In examining emigration from Scotland, it is important to distinguish the Scotch-Irish from the Scots. The Scotch-Irish came from
Ulster and were almost exclusively of Lowland Scots blood. They settled on the frontier in the South and in the central Appalachians and
played a prominent part in the American Revolution, especially in the
colonies of Pennsylvania and North Carolina. It is estimated that over
50,000 Scotch-Irish arrived in America in the fifty years preceding the
Revolution.

The Scots came from the Highlands of Scotland and followed a
different development. The Scots were not frontiersmen; they remained
loyal to the King during the American Revolution; and they sought to
maintain their ties with the home country. About 25,000 Scots entered
America's ports in the third quarter of the eighteenth century.

In spite of their sober views of America, the emigrants from
Scotland were generally industrious, frugal, and successful in their
endeavors. One Scottish observer criticized his fellow countrymen in
1802 for expressing optimistic hopes of becoming "great of affluent."
The Scottish experiences, as pointed out in the following selections,
reveal persistent ethnic characteristics: deep religious faith, strict moral
code, realistic attitudes, and desire to duplicate life patterns of the Old
Country.

Religion left an indelible mark on the Scotch-Irish, as attested to
in numerous church records in the Scotch-Irish settlements. In the
following, the Reverend Samuel Wilson, pastor of the Big Spring
Church, Cumberland County, Pennsylvania, gives stern moral admon-
ishment in a marriage ceremony around 1800.

From old church records that have been preserved some idea may be obtained of the thoroughness with which religious instruction was diffused through Scotch-Irish settlements. Big Spring congregation, in the western part of Cumberland County, was organized not later than the spring of 1737, for in June of that year a minister was called. This congregation had a succession of pastors, either natives of Ulster or born of Ulster parents. One of these early pastors was the Rev. Samuel Wilson. He was born in 1754 in Letterkenny township, now included in Franklin County, was graduated from Princeton in 1782, licensed by Donegal Presbytery on October 17, 1786, and was installed pastor of the Big Spring Church, June 20, 1787. Some records of his pastorate have been preserved, and they give an instructive view of the workings of the system, the details showing that Ulster traditions were still vigorous after the lapse of over half a century. He used a form of address in the marriage ceremony which illustrates the plainness and directness of speech then still in vogue. After searching inquiry whether or not objections to the marriage existed Mr. Wilson proceeded to address the couple as follows:

The design of marriage is, that fornication may be avoided, and as our race is more dignified than the lower creations, so then, our passions should be regulated by reason and religion. It is likewise intended for producing a legitimate offspring, as a seed for the church. There are duties incumbent upon those who enter this relation, some of them are equally binding upon both parties, some upon one party, some upon the other.

First, it is equally binding upon you both to love each other's persons, to avoid freedom with all others which formerly might have been excusable, to keep each other's lawful secrets, fidelity to the marriage bed, and if God shall give you an offspring, it will be mutually binding upon you both, to consult their spiritual, as well as their temporal concerns.

Secondly, it will be particularly binding upon you, Sir, who is to be the head of the family to maintain the authority which God hath given you. In every society there must be a head, and in families, by divine authority, this is given to the man, but as woman was given to man for an helpmeet and a bosom companion, you are not to treat this woman in a tyrannical manner, much less as a slave, but to love and kindly entreat her, as becomes one so nearly allied to you.

Lastly, it is incumbent upon you, Madam, who is to be the wife, to acknowledge the authority of him who is to be your husband, and for this, you have the example of Sarah, who is commended for calling Abraham, Lord. It seems to be your privilege in matters in which you and he cannot agree, that you advise with him, endeavoring in an easy way by persuasion to gain him to your side; but if you cannot in this way gain your point, it is fit and proper that you submit in matters in which conscience is not concerned. It will be your duty in a particular manner, to use good economy in regard to those things which may be placed in your hands. In a word, you are to be industrious in your place and station.[13]

The Scots assimilated quite readily after they arrived in America. Yet they insisted that a distinction be made between them and other groups from the British Isles, and they chose to regard themselves as "American Scots." The passage below describes the need for ethnic identification felt by Scots. Many of the characteristics of Scottish social and cultural life were continued in the United States.

Among the many immigrants to the United States, those who came from Great Britain on the whole assimilated themselves readily to the American nation, mainly because it has always been hard to think of people speaking the same language as being different nationalities, and they were apt to identify themselves with other Americans of British descent as against those of other national origins. The Scots, in particular, had always had a great gift for assimilation, and most of them readily adopted the American idiom and ways of life, though there were always the representatives of the more angular type of Scot who delights in making himself conspicuous. In general, however, while the Scot became an American he became an American Scot, insistent that he was distinct from English, Welsh and Irish, and where there were Scottish communities they carefully fostered—and sometimes exaggerated—what they could preserve of Scottish life and Scottish ways.

Not least significant was the retention of many of the characteristics of Scottish church life. The rigid discipline of the Presbyterian system was maintained in the United States at least as long as it lasted at home. Antiquated customs in worship survived, like the practice of 'lining out' the metrical psalms, a practice which meant that the precentor (who led the singing when instrumental music of any kind was abhorred) read each line, after which the congregation sang it. In America as in Scotland, church services were provided in Gaelic for highland congregations. One hears of them at Elmira in Illinois, at Boston and elsewhere, but the last Gaelic sermon in North Carolina is said to have been preached in 1860 and the language is now extinct in that area. . . .

The Protestant Episcopal Church in the United States had peculiarly close associations with the Scottish Episcopal Church. In 1784 its first bishop, Samuel Seabury, was consecrated by Scottish bishops in Aberdeen, and an undertaking was given that the American Communion service would follow the pattern of the Scottish Liturgy. Scottish Episcopalians who went to America therefore felt themselves at home, and Scottish immigrants provided some clergy for the American Church: James Bonner, for instance, born in Edinburgh in 1810, was a teacher in Scotland before he emigrated in 1835 to America, where he took orders and ministered in a succession of churches in Pennsylvania, New York, Ohio and Maryland.

In the secular sphere, Scots kept up their festivities at Hogmanay (New Year's Eve) and New Year's Day, and also the traditional 'guising' and other customs connected with Hallowe'en. St. Andrew's Day was observed in the United States in generations when it was almost forgotten in Scotland—a curious example of the triumph of national sentiment over ecclesiastical standards which had at the Reformation renounced the observance of saints' days. Another anniversary which came to be of even greater importance was the birthday of Robert Burns (25th January), which was celebrated in the United States at least as early as 1820, with a banquet in New York. The first Burns Club in America was established in New York in 1847, and now one finds Burns Clubs in places like Akron (Ohio), Atlanta (Georgia), Buffalo (New York), Charlotte (North Carolina), Flint (Michigan) and St. Louis (Missouri). No other Scottish author captured the imagination to quite the same degree, but Sir Walter Scott was not forgotten on the centenary of his birth in 1871. . . .[14]

THE WELSH

Welsh immigrants were the early colonists, first arriving in large numbers late in the seventeenth century, as Baptists and Quakers, settling in Massachusetts, Pennsylvania, and Delaware. Welsh Anglicans and Presbyterians followed later. Immigration figures show that no steady flow of immigrants from Wales was maintained. Nonetheless, in the pre-Civil War period there were enough Welshmen in Pennsylvania who sought to retain their own ethnicity to justify printing some books in Welsh.

When comparing the English, Scottish, Scotch-Irish, and Irish emigration with the Welsh, only a small proportion of the population of Wales went to America. The census recorded only 95,000 persons from Wales between 1820 and 1976. There probably were more than this number because many were counted as British or English, and the census must have missed many.

The Welsh helped to lay the foundation for the United States during the colonial period by making important contributions in all fields of endeavor. Welsh-Americans contributed their share to the success of the American Revolution. Five signers of the Declaration of Independence were of Welsh stock: Francis Lewis, Lewis Morris, Thomas Jefferson, William Floyd, and Button Gwinnett.

After the Revolution economic conditions in Wales became so critical that the lure of free land and a new life drew more Welsh men and women to the United States. Overcoming problems of social and economic adjustment, they sent letters back to the home country that generally extolled the advantages of living in America.

The selections that follow reveal a strong awareness of ethnic identity. Living together, aiding each other, and retaining the old patterns of life gave comfort and security to the Welsh in an alien land.

The religious upheavals sweeping Europe in the seventeenth century penetrated Wales and resulted in strained relations between Welsh religious reformers and the Anglicans. The Baptists and the Quakers were the first two separatist sects that sent Welsh group settlements to the American colonies. The following selection describes Welsh Quakers seeking to establish a religious refuge in Pennsylvania and simultaneously attempting to "maintain a community of their own with their distinctive Welsh language and institutions." It also summarizes their many achievements during the colonial and revolutionary periods. Note the ethnic pride of the author, himself the son of a Welsh-born, Welsh-speaking mother from Pennsylvania.

The Friends made their greatest conquest when they converted the noted William Penn to their beliefs, for it was the latter who furnished them a refuge in America where they might propagate their religion in peace. Penn, so tradition held, was the grandson of a Welshman, John Tudor, who was called Pen-mynydd (of the hilltop) and who took the name Penn when he removed from Wales to Ireland. William's father had been a noted admiral in the English Navy and had loaned King Charles II a considerable sum of money while the latter had been in exile. . . .

Penn's plans for a Quaker refuge became known to the Welsh Friends. They viewed them with enthusiasm as a means of escaping the then current persecution. Furthermore they believed that in the new colony they could purchase a large tract of land and to settle there in a body so that they could maintain a community of their own with their distinctive Welsh language and institutions. Many of them were gentry of considerable means and could meet the liberal terms of purchase offered by Penn. Then, too, the fact that Penn was both a Quaker and a Welshman (so they believed) made the plan ever more attractive. Accordingly, the Welsh Quakers were among the first to take advantage of Penn's liberal terms. A group of prominence among them, led by John ap John, went to London in 1681 to start negotiations with Penn for the proposed purchase. An agreement was later worked out with Penn whereby 40,000 acres in the new colony were purchased by the Welsh Quakers with the oral understanding that the plot would be set aside as a separate "barony" within which the Welsh would have full rights of self-government in order to protect their distinctive language and institutions. Unfortunately, this latter part of the agreement was verbal on Penn's part and was never put into writing. It was to become a cause of controversy between Penn and the Welsh later on.

A special committee of the Welsh Quakers had consummated the purchase, but since considerable time might elapse before the land could be disposed of to settlers, leaders of the enterprise were made trustees for 30,000 acres of the tract and took out patents in their own names with the understanding that they would sell their holdings to other Welsh Quakers. The leaders formed self-constituted heads of seven companies for the division and sale of the land.

The so-called "Welsh Barony" was eventually located on the west side of Schuylkill River to the northwest of Philadelphia. It included what became the townships of Upper Merion, Lower Merion, Haverford, Radnor, Tredyffrin, East Whiteland, West Whiteland, East Goshen, West Goshen, Willistown, East Town, and part of West Town, in the present counties of Montgomery, Chester, and Delaware. It was situated in a magnificently fertile territory and was admirably suited to meet the desires of the Welsh. The "Barony" was not surveyed until 1684, and its exact boundaries were not determined until 1687. . .

Thus by the end of the colonial period, Welsh immigrants and their descendants were to be found not only scattered throughout the thirteen colonies, but also in compact numbers in various key areas. In the north was the smallest of these Welsh settlements, that of Swansea, Massachusetts, consisting of some two hundred settlers. Farther to the south were the extensive Pennsylvania settlements, comprising the so-called Welsh Barony and adjacent Great Valley settlements to the west of the Schuylkill River, the Gwynedd settlement to the north of the city of Philadelphia, the small Lancaster and Berks counties settlements, and a considerable proportion of the inhabitants of the Pennsylvania metropolis itself. It has been estimated that the number of Welsh settlers in these areas amounted to some 6,000. Over the provincial line lay the Delaware Welsh Tract in Newcastle County with a Welsh population estimated around 1,000. Then far to the south were to be found the North Carolina Black River colony of unknown strength and the Welsh Neck settlement of South Carolina with an estimated Welsh population of some 500.

As one might expect, it was in Philadelphia and Pennsylvania that the Welsh exerted a very strong influence socially and politically for here they were most numerous. For over a century, men of Welsh blood occupied prominent positions in the life of the city, and inasmuch as the city and its surrounding counties dominated the life of the province, the Welsh played an equally prominent part in the life of the Pennsylvania province itself. A large proportion of the early city fathers, including mayors, Edward Roberts and Robert Wharton, were Welsh. Such, too, was the case in respect to the fields of justice, the arts, science, business and commerce. For the first quarter of the century, 1682-1730, almost all the physicians were Welshmen including Dr. Thomas Wynne, who attended William Penn during his virst voyage to America. Many of the eminent religious leaders, too, as we have seen were Welshmen.

Here in early Philadelphia were published two momumental books in the Welsh language. The first *Annerch i'r Cymru* (Salutation to the Welsh), was the pietistic work of Ellis Pugh, a humble stonemason and Quaker preacher, who willed the manuscript to the Gwynedd Quaker Meeting. The latter had it printed by Andrew Bradford in 1721. It was subsequently translated and issued in an English version. The other, *Cyd-gordiad Enwyddorawl o'r Scrythurau* (Alphabetical Concordance of the Scriptures), was the work of Able Morgan, the noted Baptist divine, and was the first real Welsh concordance of the Bible. It was published in 1730 by Samuel Keimer and Dafydd Harry, a Welshman, eight years after Morgan's death. Both books rate among the rarest of Americana.

Two other works in Welsh were also published in Philadelphia during these early years. The firm of Benjamin Franklin and Hugh Meredydd published a Welsh translation of an English book by Benjamin Wallin, *Y Dull a Fedyddio a Dwfr* (The Manner of Baptizing with Water), in 1730. Meredydd, a Welshman, later aided Franklin in publishing the noted *Pennsylvania Gazette*. The other work in Welsh entitled simply, *A Welsh Pamphlet*, was a reprint of a British original printed by Andrew Bradford in 1735. It dealt with moral reflections on death, judgment, Heaven and Hell.

It was in Philadelphia that the oldest Welsh-American society was founded in 1729 for the purpose of honoring St. David, the patron saint of Wales. It developed eventually into a benevolent society aiding newly arrived immigrants from Wales, dispensing charity when necessary, and sponsoring interest in Welsh culture. The Welsh Society of Philadelphia is still in existence today, a monument to the durability of self-consciousness of the little ethnic group that made its weight felt so strongly in the early life of the city. It claims the honor of being the oldest existing society of Philadelphia.[15]

"A nation is made up of many parts," stated a Welsh-American editor in 1898, "and each part has to be nurtured and cared for."[16] This statement may have been directed to the following letter, written in 1800 by a group of Welsh settlers in Cambria, Pennsylvania, describing the soil and climate and praising the rich resources in America. Within this context, there emerges evidence of a strong desire to retain the distinct Welsh ethnicity.

Our end in establishing this settlement was for the general good of the Welch, particularly that they may have the privilege of hearing the gospel in their own language. [16] There are in Cambria preachers of different denominations, living together in peace and amity. We have three or four Welch sermons every first day in the week, and there are English preachers in Beula. There are 350 lots in (and some near) the town goven to support a school; more than 1,000 books have been purchased for a general library, and 200 acres of land for the support of the preachers, not of any one particular sect or party, but such as esteemed worthy, of every denomination, and profess that Jesus is the Son of God, and Saviour of Men. We do not mention the above privileges to allure you into this neighbourhood, if you can do better in any other. . .

Though having met with many difficulties, as it is natural to expect the first years, we now increase our stock every year. Within the last four years, upwards of 100 families have come to our neighborhood, and 100 more may get a comfortable livelihood here. Should any of you be disposed to come over here, we would advise you to consult the captain of the vessel with respect to victuals that will be necessary for your voyage, with a sufficient quantity of bread, water, salt, meat, potatoes, oatmeal, and malt liquor.

After landing in America, many sorts of people will be met with; some will say this is the best place, and some another. All who are acquainted with our nation know it is easy to impose upon a Welchman; therefore, we would advise them to be upon their guard. They who have families would do well to get a waggon immediately after their landing, and remove all their goods out of the ship into in, and convey them to the place of their destination without delay. If they come hither (though they abide not), it will be cheaper for them to leave their families with us until they can find a place to their satisfaction, than in the cities, which in the summer are unhealthy to strangers, but the country round is as healthy as any part of Wales. Should any of the poor be disposed to come, and not able to bear the expense of their voyage, if their friends be able to assist them, and can depend on their faithfulness, they will not be long here before they are repaid with thankfulness. . . .[17]

The first official census of 1790 emphasized the overwhelming American population originating from northern Europe, as reflected in the following figure.

Proportion of Total Population Formed by Each Nationality: 1790.

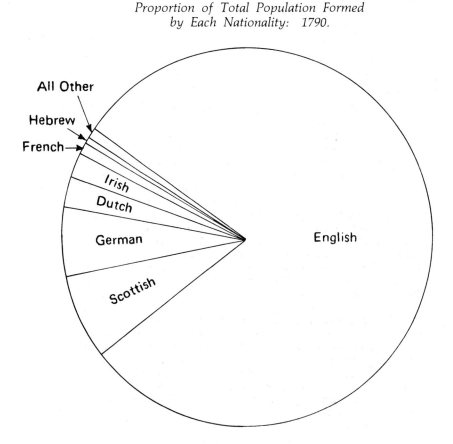

The black population represented the largest non-English segment in the United States in 1790.

Table 1.2
White and Black Population in 1790[19]

	Number	Percent
White	3,172,444	80.73
Black	757,208	19.27
Total	3,929,652	100.00

Population figures of 1790 clearly show the Anglo Saxon dominance, which influenced significantly the institutional development of the United States.

Table 1.3
White Population in 1790 by Nationality[20]

Nationality	Number	Percent
English	2,605,699	82.1
Scotch	221,562	7.0
Irish	61,534	1.9
Dutch	78,959	2.5
French	17,619	.6
German	176,407	5.6
Hebrew	1,243	*
All Other	9,421	.3
Total	3,172,444	100.0

*Less than 1/10 of 1 percent.

1. Reprinted from William Bradford, *Of Plymouth Plantation, 1620-1647,* ed. Samuel Eliot Morison, pp.11-63. Copyright © 1952, by Samuel Eliot Morison, By permission of Alfred A. Knopf, Inc.

2. Reprinted from Washington Irving, *The Sketchbook* (Philadelphia: Henry Altemus, 1895), pp. 80,82.

3. Reprinted from Alexis de Tocqueville, *Democracy in America,* vol. 1 (New York: Alfred A. Knopf, 1961), p. 29.

4. John Higham, *Strangers in the Land,* (New York: Atheneum, 1971) pp. 139-41.

5. Martin F. Tupper, "The New Home," *Sidney's Emigrant's Journal,* (edited by Samuel and John Sidney), (London: W.S. Orr & Co., 1894), p. 54.

6. Australian aborigine.

7. Reprinted from Arthur Henry Hirsh, *The Huguenots of Colonial South Carolina* (Hamden, Conn.: The Shoe String Press, 1962), pp. 90, 95, 100. By permission of the Duke University Press.

8. From Edith Abbot, *Historical Aspects of Immigration Problem,* pp. 30-36. Copyright© 1926 by University of Chicago Press. By permission of Arno Press.

9. Ibid, p. 429.

10. Reprinted from Arnold Mulder, *Americans from Holland* (Philadelphia: J.B. Lippincott Company, 1947) p. 57.

11. Reprinted from Maud Wilder Goodwin et al. (eds.), *Historic New York,* vol. 2 (reprinted ed., Port Washington, N.Y.: Ira J. Friedman, Publishers, Kennikat Press, 1969), pp. 341-342.

12. *This Was America,* edited by Oscar Handlin, (Cambridge, Mass.: Harvard U. Press, 1949), p. 33.

13. Reprinted from Henry Jones Ford, *The Scotch-Irish in America* (New York: Arno Press, Inc., 1969), pp. 286-288.

14. Reprinted from Gordon Donaldson, *The Scots Overseas* (London: Robert Hale, 1966), pp. 124-128.

15. Reprinted from Edward G. Hartmann, *Americans from Wales* (North Quincy, Mass.: The Christopher Publishing House, 1967), pp. 43-44, 54-55.

16. *Harvard Encyclopedia of American Ethnic Groups,* edited by Stephan Thernstrom, (Cambridge, Mass.: Harvard U. Press, 1980), p. 1015.

17. From Abbott, *Historical Aspects of Immigration Problem,* pp. 29-30. Copyright © 1926 by University of Chicago Press. By permission of Arno Press.

18. Reprinted from U.S., Bureau of the Census, *A Century of Population Growth* (Washington, D.C.: Government Printing Office, 1909), p. 117

19. Reprinted from Bennett, *American Immigration Policies,* p. 298; and U.S., Census, *Century of Population Growth,* chap. 11.

20. Reprinted from Marion T. Bennett, *American Immigration Policies* (Washington, D.C.: Public Affairs Press, 1963), p. 298; and U.S., Census, *Century of Population Growth,* chap. 11.

KEY QUESTIONS

1. The American Revolution notwithstanding, could it be said that ethnic affinity between the English and many Americans still persisted in the generation following independence?

2. What conclusions may be drawn from an analysis of the 1790 census report?

3. How strongly did the French Huguenots consciously strive to assert their national traits?

4. To what extent did the Dutch attempt to maintain their ethnic institutions in America?

5. Compare the Scotch-Irish with the Scots concerning origins, settlement patterns in America, and the degree of ethnic maintenance.

6. Explain how and why the Welsh exerted a significant social and political influence on Pennsylvania.

TWO

Immigration and Mid-Nineteenth Century America: The Germans, Irish, and Scandinavians

Mid-nineteenth century America was at once a rich, invigorating, but puzzling and combative society exhibiting all the facets of a variegated peoples. During the period 1861 - 1865, it would be tried by the fire of Civil War, the grisliest and most devastating conflict of its kind in the nation's history. The war was not long over when Americans came to realize that trial by combat, although deadlier, was a simpler means of resolving differences compared to the complexities facing a nation in which one section was victor over another. The post war period was also one in which the nation plunged headlong into the industrial revolution which would propel the country into the world's greatest industrial power.

It was into this tumultuous, sometimes tortured but dynamic environment that millions of Germans, Irishmen, and Scandinavians moved during the 1840 - 1880 period, prompted by a combination of economic, social, and cultural factors, chief of which was economics. Immigrants in this era reflected that Teutonic flavor as described by the seminal immigration historian, Marcus Lee Hansen. "This exodus was Teutonic in blood, in institutions and in the basis of its language, forming the most homogenous of all migrations to America."

THE GERMANS

The first significant immigration of Germans to America developed in the latter part of the seventeenth century with the inauguration of the new colony of Pennsylvania.

A.B. Faust, historian of German emigration to the United States, describes the process by which many became redemptioners. His history also includes a contemporary critical account of the practice by Muhlenbug, as well as some comments regarding Germans who turned the redemption system to their own advantage.

A system was established very early in American colonial history, by which an immigrant could get to the promised land, though not in possession of the means to pay for his passage. He would agree to serve from three to seven years in the colonies until the price of his transportation was paid off to the shipmaster who had advanced it. At the end of his term he was released, given a suit of clothes, sometimes money or land, and awarded all the rights of a free citizen. Hence the term redemptioners [because redeemed] was applied to this class of immigrants, who were also known as "indented servants." At first the system seemed humane and liberal, yielding the poor ultimately the same opportunities as the well-to-do. It had been advocated by Furley, the agent of William Penn, and had been in vogue in Virginia since the first decade of that colony's existence. The system began to be applied extensively to German immigration about 1728. Muhlenberg describes the arrival of a ship in Philadelphia in the following manner:

Before the ship is allowed to cast anchor in the harbor, the immigrants are all examined, as to whether any contagious disease be among them. The next step is to bring all the new arrivals in a procession before the city hall and there compel them to take the oath of allegiance to the king of Great Britain. After that they are brought back to the ship. Those that have paid their passage are released, the others are advertised in the newspapers for sale. The ship becomes the market. The buyers make their choice and bargain with the immigrants for a certain number of years and days, depending upon the price demanded by the ship captain or other "merchant" who made the outlay for transportation, etc. Colonial governments recognize the written contract, which is then made binding for the redemptioner. The young unmarried people of both sexes are very quickly sold, and their fortunes are either good or bad, according to the character of the buyer. Old married people, widows, and the feeble, are a drug on the market, but if they have sound children then their transportation charges are added to those of the children, and the latter must serve the longer. This does not save families from being separated in the various towns or even provinces. Again, the healthiest are taken first, and the sick are frequently detained beyond the period of recovery, when a release would frequently have saved them.

Not only tillers of the soil and artisans became serfs for their passage money, students and schoolmasters also were often sold in this labor market. The Reverend Mr. Kunze naively writes, that he had entertained the thought, if he ever became the owner of twenty pounds, of buying the first German student who would land at Philadelphia, put him into his garret, and there with his help begin a Latin school, which he was sure would quickly pay off the outlay. People of rank, who had lost their money, fared no better than the low-born peasant. There was Frederick Helfenstein, probably a lineal descendant of Count Helfenstein and the Emperor Maximilian, who was compelled to sell himself as a redemptioner in Georgia.[1]

Attachment to German customs and language was constant among German immigrants, especially in Pennsylvania. One effect of this attachment was criticism for allegedly being unable to see the value of education. Faust analyzes the problem in the selection below.

The Pennsylvania Germans have frequently suffered the rebuke of being neglectful in matters of education. It was a charge made during nativistic epochs, and has made by far too strong an impression. The main origin of the charge was the tenacity with which Germans held to their own language and customs. The German settlers brought with them their school-teachers and preachers. Schools were invariably established by them, and sometimes before churches. The schools were, however, rarely separated from the churches, and when a movement began for establishing public schools in their districts, the Germans opposed it. They viewed the movement with suspicion, as if its purpose were to deprive them of their religion, the influence of their preachers, or the use of their language.

Along with that went a degree of pride [Bauernstolz] in their ability to pay for the instruction of their children. They did not wish to inflict this burden upon the state, failing altogether to see the benefits derived from a common school system. It was long before the church school could be replaced by a public school in their counties. An attempt was made to train a body of teachers among the German population, giving instruction in the English language and the rudiments of American law and politics, by the establishment of a college. This foundation was located in Lancaster County, in 1787, and was named after Benjamin Franklin. Henry Muhlenberg was chosen the first head of Franklin College. The charge of ignorance against the Pennsylvania Germans was frequently due to their lack of proficiency in the use of the English language. Education in that day did not go beyond the three R's, or the practical necessities of life, and to the native population the first of these necessities seemed, of course, the ability to use the English language.[2]

Major immigration from Germany took place in the nineteenth century. At first, Germans attempted to transplant Germanism into their new surroundings, but gradually concluded that efforts to create "New Germany" colonies in America were doomed to failure. Nevertheless, until well into the twentieth century, German settlers in the United States exhibited certain social, economic, and political peculiarities which rendered assimilation difficult and at times brought them into conflict with the ideas and mores of earlier comers. German resistance to Americanization was attributable to pride in their own culture and language which tended to leave their communities apart, German islands in a sea of Americanism.

During this period, Germany supplied more immigrants than any other country and the characteristics of German immigration of the pre-Civil War period persisted in the postwar period as well. Yet there were some important differences as more men of culture and refugees from political oppression migrated. During this nineteenth century, interest in retention and perpetuation of the German language in American schools was a proper area of emphasis.

Concern with the retention of the native language in American schools is the subject of the next extract.

The school question, that is, the introduction of the German language into the public schools, was also a cause for which the Germans in various localities brought pressure to bear at the polls. The Germans in Ohio, having given powerful support to the Democratic Party in the election of 1836, began to feel that the party owed them some recognition. The preservation of the German language in the next generation has always been a fond aim of the German immigrant; so it was in Cincinnati. Though there existed a Presbyterian school and a Catholic institution in which German instruction was given, nevertheless a more general opportunity was desired. Since they had paid taxes for the support of the public schools, the Germans considered it their right to exercise some influence on the course of study. According to their idea, English was not to be excluded, but German was to be taught, parallel with the language of the country, in the public schools. The German element turned to the legislature of Ohio, and the latter in 1838 passed a law by which the German language might be taught in the public schools in those districts where there was a large German population and the people desired it. The law was expected to be enforced by the school board, who, however, interpreted the law as advisory and not compulsory. In the succeeding election of 1839 pledges were taken from the candidates that the wording of the law should be revised so as to prevent any possibility of loopholes. Accordingly the law was changed in 1840, which marks the date of introduction of German English public schools in Cincinnati and Ohio. . . .

Within the last decades the Germans have made a successful attempt at uniting all the German clubs of the United States, whether social, musical, gymnastic, military, or political, into one large national organization. The movement began in the original home of Germanism, the state of Pennsylvania and in its ancient stronghold, Philadelphia, where a union of all the German societies of the states was effected in the year 1899. Since then the organization has grown into the so-called "National German-American Alliance," which includes societies of every city, state and territory of the United States where there is a German population. The membership is about a million and a half. . . . The object on the whole is to preserve and unite what is best in German culture and character, and devote it to the best interests of the adopted country. The principle, therefore, which Carl Schurz and Friedrich Muench announced for the Germans in America—namely, that they become American citizens as quickly as possible, without, however, losing their culture and character—has won in our own day.[3]

Carl Schurz was the epitome of the educated, urbane German immigrant to the United States. A storied romantic fighter against tyranny, he was in the forefront of virtually every reform movement of his era. A towering spokesman of progressive American ideals, he was far ahead of most German Americans of his time; nevertheless, he too felt an ethnic sympathy with his Germanic past. In the selections that follow, he champions German-American patriotism and defends as a positive good the persistence of many ethnic features, such as the use of foreign language and the foreign press. He also describes the role of ethnicity in his campaign for a Senate seat against Senator Drake.

I have as much personal experience of the German-born population of the United States, its character, its aspirations, and its American patriotism, as any person now living; and this experience enables me to affirm that the prejudice against the German-American press is groundless. On the contrary, that press does the country a necessary and very important service. In the first place, it fills a real and very urgent want. That want will exist so long as there is a large number of German-born citizens in this republic. There will always be many among them, especially persons of mature years who arrived on American soil without any knowledge of the English language, who may be able to acquire enough of it to serve them in their daily walk, but not enough to enable them to understand newspaper articles on political or similar subjects. Such persons must receive the necessary information about current events questions to be considered and duties to be performed, from journals published in the language they understand, or they will not have it at all. The suppression of the German-American press would, therefore, be equivalent to the cultivation of political ignorance among a large and highly estimable class of citizens.

It is argued that the existence of the German newspaper is apt to render the German immigrant less sensible of the necessity of learning English. This is the case only to a very limited extent. A large majority of the German immigrants of mature age, being farmers or industrial laborers, do not acquire their knowledge of English in this country through regular linguistic instruction, or by reading books or newspapers, but from conversation or attempts at conversation with their neighbors who do not speak German, and that knowledge will, of necessity, remain very imperfect. . . .

The charge that the existence of the German-American press promotes the use of the German language in this country and thus impedes the development of a healthy American patriotism among the population concerned, can be entertained only by those who do not know the German-Americans. I speak from a large personal experience when I say that their love of their new home and their devotion to this republic does not at all depend upon their knowledge of the English language. . . .

The same may be said of the inhabitants of German settlements of more recent date who have come with the bona fide intention to make this country their permanent home. Among them German may long remain the language of social and business intercourse, they may be slow in acquiring easy familiarity with the English tongue, but even if they have come here for the mere purpose of bettering their fortunes, they are as a rule not slow in appreciating the benefits conferred upon them by American conditions, and in conceiving an attachment to this republic which before long ripens into genuine devotion. . . .

That the existence of the German press tells for the preservation in this country of the German language as a language of social and business intercourse is to a limited extent true. But what harm is there in this? While it is of great use to the older immigrants, it does not keep their children from learning English, even in settlements which are preponderantly German, for such settlements are no longer isolated as the original German settlements in Pennsylvania were. But it does give the younger generation the advantage of knowing two languages. That kind of American patriotism which takes umbrage at an American citizen's knowledge of a foreign besides the English—sort of patriotism I have here and there met with—is certainly too narrow-minded, not to say too silly, to be seriously considered. No educated, nay, no soundminded person, will deny, that the knowledge of more than one language tends to widen our mental horizons, to facilitate the acquisition of useful intelligence, and thus to broaden education. . . . [4]

The career of Richard Bartholdt is still another story of a German immigrant who, having become a success in his newly adopted land, yet steadfastly retained a strong attachment to the cultural values of his original nationality. A newspaperman, Bartholdt went on to serve in Congress for over two decades, spanning the years 1893 to 1915. Throughout his career he found himself championing and defending the cultural and social values of his ethnic group. In the excerpts that follow, he judges the prohibition movement as an obvious example of race prejudice, is critical of the effort to Anglo-Saxonize everyone, and deals with the issue of allegiance during the First World War.

As to the prohibition movement it was not difficult to demonstrate that one of its underlying motives, too, was race prejudice because it aimed to undermine the social life of the Germans and to bankrupt the richest men among them. In fact, it is claimed by shrewd observers that the prohibition fire would have died aborning but for the fuel with which race prejudice constantly fed it. The fact that the crusade of professional drys is directed more viciously against the harmless beverage of the Germans than against ardent spirits seems fully to confirm that assertion. . . .

In my editorial opposition to the different fads invented to torment the German element, I believe that I was on solid American ground. My opinion was and is that the form of worship, the customs and racial aspirations of our adopted citizens, as long as they do not conflict with the laws of the land, should be given free play in a democracy. If this be true, then every attempt to make them conform to the social habits, dress, mannerisms, ways of thinking and all other peculiarities of one particular element, even if it be numerically the strongest, must be adjudged undemocratic and unAmerican and is, therefore, intolerable. And I went even further by venturing the assertion that any man incapable of freeing himself from race prejudice which manifests itself in self-exaltation and a domineering attitude toward others, is by nature disqualified from being a real American. . . .

The public mind is now sufficiently composed, I believe, to realize what a cruel outrage was committed against American citizens of German blood by the propaganda press using them as scape-goats to kindle the war passions of the nation. It was done, too, against the better judgment of their assailants, because the latter know them full well and have never, at any other time, so studiedly misunderstood and misjudged them. These same self-styled one hundred percenters were perfectly aware that the hyphen was used innocently, and merely as a racial designation, but they purposely imputed an objectionable meaning to it at a time when they had the ear of the public and when every word of defense was lost in the fury of the storm.

To the Englishman, the Scotchman, the Irishman we habitually do concede the right of devotion to ancient traditions and of affection for the ancestral home. Why not the German? Is it because he speaks a different tongue? God save the mark! If that were the reason, the world's conscience would push us from the high pedestal we occupy, and adjudge such narrow-mindedness a national disgrace. Or is it because his old fatherland was one of the great powers, hence a world factor? Well, I have already shown that the native country of nearly nine-tenths of our citizens of German stock is America. And the last tenth? Suppose they do sing German songs and cherish, become most conversant with them, German literature, art, science, music and philosophy, what on earth has that to do with official Germany? As one who knows whereof he speaks I assert that not even in the innermost recesses of their hearts is a trace to be found of their old political allegiance. . . . Affection for the old home, after all, is only a sentiment, an emotion of the heart while loyalty to the new is a matter of conscience, and no instance is known in history in which men of German blood ever failed to respond to the voice of conscience or the call of duty. Double allegiance? Why, in its only possible meaning, namely in a political sense, it does not exist in America. . . .

The severest test was the one to which the American Germans were put during the last years of the World War. Have they stood it? For an answer I refer to the "rolls of honor," the casualty lists, the records of the War, Treasury and all other departments of the government. Their loyalty to the flag, tried and tested in every crisis, is founded not only on their innate love of freedom and their honest fealty to democratic institutions, but also on a sacred oath of whose sanctity they believe heaven itself to be the guardian.

> Only a short while ago this whole discussion would probably have been denounced as "German Propaganda." Be it so. Propaganda for the truth is a highly meritorious effort and should be welcomed by every honest man. Fortunately, the public has sufficiently recovered to open its eyes and ears to the truth. Therefore, I shall venture a prediction. It is that no danger will ever come to our country, its liberty, security, prosperity, and independence, from so-called "German Propaganda" which, as we shall see later, is largely a myth. . . . [5]

Observers of contemporary German-Americana concluded that descendants from Germany have become so thoroughly assimilated that they no longer need to create protective organizations to defend themselves against slurs as is the case with other ethnic groups. They have all but become invisible as an ethnic group. Even if this assessment were exaggerated, surely it was not always the case. Well into the twentieth century Germans exhibited ethnic traits in varying degrees. Institutions such as beer saloons were part of the American scene into the 1930's and it seemed as if Germanic ethnic life was regulated by the ebb and flow of sources of imbibing—clearly a transference of their ethnic past, especially for those who emigrated from South Germany.

One final aspect of German ethnic life is worthy of mention: the role ethnicity played among German Catholics who struggled with the Irish for control of "the rooftop of the church," as Richard O'Connor puts it.

> The Irish archbishops were being made increasingly aware of the fact that their German coreligionists were displeased at being kept out of places of power. In the number of communicants the Irish had only a slight edge over the Germans, yet the Irish had noticeable monopoly on the episcopal offices. . . .
> The Irish resented the fact that the Germans clung to their mother tongue "Wherever they settled in any numbers the familiar pattern of church, parish school, parish clubs and the German language newspaper soon appeared: Many American Catholics became more sensitive about their German coreligionists' holding on to their native language, for with good reason did they remember the charge of 'foreignism' was one of the constant refrains against Catholics in former times."[6]

The problems between the two transcended language, since the points of dispute really encompassed the full range of cultural differences and opposing temperaments. These temperamental differences became the substance of stereotyping in stage performances for many years as the phlegmatic German was contrasted with his more mercurial Irish neighbor.

The intrareligious bickering between Germans and Catholics had its counterpart in the religious sparring that went on within the ranks of German Lutheranism, specifically the American and the Missouri synods. Indeed this intrareligious controversy is an ongoing phenomenon reflecting the differences between those of German background who had arrived in this country early in its history and had abandoned the German language in its Lutheran expression, and the later German Lutheran immigrants who are intent to retain the language of their ancestry.

For the most part German ethnicity is not now as visible as it once was. As O'Connor has observed, their singular characteristics have all but disappeared or at least become homogenized.

> . . . gone with the little German bands that played on street corners, the German butchers in their sawed-off straw hats and white aprons, the beer gardens, the summer-night festivals, the May wine parades. . . . They are now generally regarded as being part of the conservative element. . . .[7]

THE IRISH

From the first, economic hardship and British oppression provided the background for Irish immigration. This was true of the 15,000 Irish in America before 1830 and in the thirty-year period to follow between 1830-1860 when the great flow left the Emerald Island. In the 1830s the Irish constituted 44 percent of the total immigration to this country, with the figure increasing to 49 percent in the 1840s and finally peaking in the 1850s with 1851 serving as the largest single year as 221,253 entered the United States. By this time the tragedy of the great famine had done its work of separating the Irish from their homeland.

This enormous influx of Catholic immigrants caused Protestant America to overreact against what it considered an "alien" culture. The Irish were Roman Catholic, anti-British, and generally uneducated and unskilled. The most violent native American movement developed in the 1830s and produced an inglorious record of intolerance. "No Irish need apply" appeared in advertisements in Boston and other cities. A convent was burned in Charlestown, Massachusetts, in 1831; a mob attacked a Catholic church in Philadelphia in 1846.

The Irish saw America against this background of flourishing bigotry. The selections in this section illustrate Irish efforts to accommodate to the situation by retaining a high degree of ethnicity.

Irishmen expressed their disappointment at the American experience, while contemporaries criticized them for being clannish and "noisy, turbulent, and intolerant."

The early Irish who came to America engaged in the most menial tasks. In this narrative, the Irish actor Tyrone Power, an ancestor of the Tyrone Power of motion picture fame, relates with awe, pride, and respect the conditions under which his fellow countrymen worked on a canal connecting Lake Ponchartrain with New Orleans.

> I only wish that the wise men at home who cooly charge the present conditions of Ireland upon the inherent lazyness of her population could be transported to this spot, to look upon the hundreds of fine fellows labouring beneath a sun that at this winter season was insufferable fierce, and amidst a pestilential swamp whose exhalations were fetid to a degree scarcely endurable for a few moments; wading amidst stumps of trees, mid-deep in black mud, clearing the spaces pumped out by powerful steam engines; wheeling, digging, hewing, or bearing burdens it made one's shoulders ache to look upon; exposed meantime to every change of temperature in log huts laid down in the very swamps, on a foundation of newly-felled trees, having the waters lying stagnant between the floor-logs, whose interstices, together with those of the side-walls, are open, pervious alike to sun, wind or snow. Here they subsist on the coarsest fare, holding life on a tenure as uncertain as does the leader of a forlorn hope; excluded from all the advantages of civilization; often at the mercy of a hard contractor, who wrings his profits from their blood; and all this for a pittance that merely enables him to exist, with little power to save, or a hope beyond the continuance of the like exertion.[8]

Francis Leiber was a Prussian who had been twice imprisoned for his political views. As political conditions worsened, he fled to England and then to the United States. In the following selection, Leiber draws upon the Irish experience in examining the problems of assimilation in America. Critical of the Irish attitude, he upbraids them for exploiting ethnicity to their advantage.

> The Irish—in spite of what I have said above of their facility in assimilating with the Americans—clan more together than the emigrants of any other nation. They, in fact, openly retain their name, and often, in the very moment that they make use of the highest privileges of citizenship which any country can bestow, they do it under the banner of Irishmen. There is no election in any of the large cities without some previous calls upon the "true-born sons of Ireland," to vote so or so. On the election day itself banners are seen floating from the windows of taverns, some of which, you may be certain, are ornamented with mottos having reference to the Irish alone. They do farther, sometimes; they will bring forward their own candidate, if they feel strong enough. All this is, to speak guardedly, at least impolite

towards the natives, who receive the foreigner with a degree of national hospitality unequalled by any other nation. Every career on the wide field of enterprise which is open to the natural citizens of this republic, is equally open to the naturalized. After the brief period of five years' residence, any alien may take the citizen's oath, and this done, he enjoys every privilege of which a free-born American can boast, an unstinted citizenship, with the single exception that he cannot become a president of the United States. The least that could be expected, in return for such a boon, it should be supposed, would be the frankest and most heartfelt union, in every thing, with the nation which so hospitably makes no difference between its own sons and the new comers. But the Irish are desirous of becoming Americans and yet remaining Irish, and this serving of two masters will not do. Whatever the innermost feelings of an emigrant toward his native country may be, and with every generous heart will be, as a citizen of America, he should be American and American only, or let him remain alien. As the latter, he is protected as much by the law of the land as is a citizen; there is no necessity whatever for his becoming naturalized. It is, therefore, with great concern, that a good citizen must observe that disturbances at elections are not infrequently caused by those who do not enjoy their citizenship by birthright, sometimes by those who do not enjoy at all.

What are the reasons that the Irish in this country can clan more together than the emigrants of any other nation? I believe they are threefold. First, more Irish than people of other countries come to the United States, and as I think I have observed in a previous letter, they have a predilection for large cities, so that they remain in greater numbers together. Secondly, the Irish feel that they have been wronged in their country, they have, in a degree, been driven from it; the feelings with which they look back to it are, therefore, of a more intense character than they would otherwise be; or, if this be not the case, they feel among themselves the strong tie of bearing one common wrong. Thirdly they are encouraged to this clanship by party men; their Irish feelings are flattered and excited, in order to win them; they are called upon as Irish in order to gain their votes, which become, in some quarters of large cities, or indeed in some whole counties, at times, very important, when, otherwise, the parties might be nearly balanced. . . .[9]

At the height of Irish immigration to the United States concern was expressed for their religious welfare in the new Protestant environment. The following selection, offered by a Catholic priest, prescribes guidelines to those intending to emigrate.

It will be a matter of importance for the Irish Catholic emigrant to learn those stations where he will be within reach of a church, and a resident clergyman of his religion. This information can be obtained partially from the *Dublin Catholic Directory* and fully from the *U.S. Catholic Alamanac* for each year, published in Baltimore. In the latter he will find the names, churches, and stations of the Bishops and Priests of each Diocese, together with a full list of educational and religious establishments. . . .

With most Catholic settlers it will be a matter of much regard to discover the proximity of a Catholic church and resident priest to the site of their intended homes. A Catholic school or institution will enhance the value of their location. It should be always considered that, how firm soever in the faith, and however exemplary in the practice of religious duties Catholic parents may be, it will be no easy matter to instill the same principals into the minds, or procure the same observances in the conduct of their children, should they be removed from a church of their persuation or placed without the circle of religious influences. . . .

. . . the dictates of nature, strong in the minds of all men, and especially in the sons of the Green Isle, must ever bring strongly to recollection and heart, the memories, hopes, and interests of the land of our birth. Love of country however must not be rendered exclusive. . . .

No man will suffer in the estimation of native American citizens, for a love of the country of his birth.[10]

A surprisingly moderate view toward the Know-Nothing movement in 1854 is presented in the selection that follows. The writer exhorts Irish Americans to reform their behavior in order to evoke favor among the more tolerant and democratic elements in the United States, thereby presaging victory over bigotry.

An Irish View of "Know-Nothingism"

We have at all times been averse to the course taken by those who fled from Ireland, within the last six years, without taking time to consider maturely the prospects before them, and the dangers and difficulties they would meet within a strange land. They rushed headlong from their native country, instead of battling for land and life, and flung themselves amongst a people who are proverbial for their love of gain, and who welcomed the Irish, not because they sympathized with their sufferings, but because they required them to build their railroads, dig their canals, clear their forests, till their fields, and work in their factories.

We are told now that Jonathan has got more of the Irish than he requires, and lest the Celt should become his master, that he desires to oppress him as the Egyptians oppressed the Israelites in Egypt. A storm of Know-Nothing persecution rages against the Irish and their religion in America, the object of which is to deprive them of many of their civil rights, and if possible make it penal to profess their faith openly.

We cannot believe that this persecution will continue very long. We believe that the good sense of the country will again return, and that the bastard policy of the Know-Nothing will speedily die out. But while censuring the outrageous conduct of the Know-Nothings, let us be impartial and just. Has this persecution been unprovoked? Have all the Irish conducted themselves, as citizens of the Great Republic, in that sober, orderly, and prudent manner becoming a persecuted people who fled from the lash of tyrants and found a home and a refuge in America?

We fear that some of them have been a noisy, turbulent, and intolerant class, who did no credit to the character of their native country, and were of little benefit to the land of their adoption. We fear, too, that some of the ultra-Catholic journals went far beyond the bounds of prudence in writing on religious subjects.

We do not make these remarks to palliate the conduct of the native despots, who assign and malign the Irish. We merely allude to the matter for the purpose of stating that the conduct of some of the Irish emigrants is not what it ought to be, and to counsel them to give up their intemperate habits, their rows, their faction fights, and act in such a manner as to earn the respect of their bitterest enemies.

If they do this they will at once disarm the Know-Nothings, and bring to their aid every good citizen in the United States, those glorious spirits who subscribe to the tolerant views of Washington, Jefferson, and other illustrious fathers of the Republic. But if by their follies they disgrace themselves, can it be wondered at if the Americans declare that such a people are unworthy to share with them the freedom and blessings guaranteed by the constitution of their country?

What, we ask, would the Irish people say, if two millions of Russians, Prussians, or Greeks should come amongst them, and by their conduct set us all by the ears, commence rows in our streets, faction fights on our railways; and in their journals assail our creed, and evince little willingness to respect our best institutions? Would not the native population begin to think it right to exclude them from public offices, and declare them dangerous foes to the country?[11]

Irish immigration in the post-Civil War years continued to be high with the consequence that they constituted one of the largest ethnic groups in the country and accordingly were faced with numerous problems of adjustment in the face of hostility. This adverse environment, notwithstanding, they gradually became esteemed in the eyes of Americans.

John Francis Maguire's *The Irish in America*, orginally published in 1868, is an extensive personal account by an Irish member of Parliament. One of Maguire's concerns was for the Irish crowded in the cities of the eastern seaboard of the United States, a condition which he deplored as a great evil, especially for a people so passionately attached to the soil.

But there is no excuse whatever for his remaining in the cities of America, crowding and blocking them up, when there are at this hour as many opportunities for his getting on in the country—that is, making a home and independence for himself and his children—as there were for millions of all nationalities who went before him, and who now constitute the strength and glory of the Republic.[12]

By contrast, he observed with satisfaction Irish attraction to the West, to the mining region and to land cultivation.

With the pick and the shovel they were a match for any workers under the sun, and their luck was on the average as fortunate as that of others. It was a fair start, and no favour—just what best suits the true Irishman; and the result at this moment is, that one-half, or nearly one-half, of the entire mining property of the country is in the hands of Irishmen or the sons of Irishmen.

. . . Employment was to be had in every direction by those who were willing to work; and none were more willing than the Irish. Everything had to be built up, literally created—cities and towns as well as communities . . . . Happily, the cities and towns did not seduce the Irish from their legitimate sphere, and the dollars made in the mine, or in ditching and digging, or in hard toil of various kinds, were converted into land. . . .

Maguire was also interested in the religious welfare of Irish Catholics.

Whatever religious indifferentism there may be in other parts of America, there is none in San Francisco among its Irish Catholic population. In their hard struggle for the good things of this life they did not forget their interests in the next. . . . Giving Catholics of other nationalities full credit for their liberality, and allowing for the generous assistance afforded by those of different denominations, it is admitted that three-fourths of what has been done for the Church in the city and county of San Francisco has been done by the Irish. In fact, without them little could have been done; but with them everything was possible. . . .

He suggested encouraging further immigration on the part of the Irish.

As this sheet was going through the press, my attention was attracted by an article in the Monitor of San Francisco, from which I quote the concluding passage, written, as I believe, in the right spirit:-
It is our interest to have as many of our countrymen here as possible. . . . Why cannot the Irishmen of this city form a society for diffusing a knowledge of California's resources among our countrymen, and communicating with employers throughout the state, for securing immediate employment on their arrival? We almost feel a scruple about encouraging emigration from poor depopulated Ireland, where the fortunes of our race have yet to be retrieved; but in England and Scotland there are nearly a million of Irishmen from whose ranks we could easily obtain an annual immigration of many thousands by a system such as that we have just proposed. We know by experience the state of feeling existing among our countrymen in Europe, and we believe that by a plan such as we have described, an immense Irish population could be drawn here, to both their own and our advantage. The Irish of California are wealthy and liberal and surely such a society as the one we have proposed could be easily started

among them. We hope our suggestions may turn the attention of some of them to the practical development of Irish immigration from England and the Eastern cities.

Maguire made some meaningful observations on the reasons for and effects of drinking among the Irish.

Were I asked to say what I believed to be the most serious obstacle to the advancement of the Irish in America I would unhesitatingly answer Drink; meaning thereby the excessive use, or abuse, of that which, when taken in excess, intoxicates, deprives man of his reason, interferes with his industry, injures his health, damages his position, compromises his respectability, renders him unfit for the successful exercise of his trade, profession, or employment—which leads to quarrel, turbulence, violence, crime. . . . Were this belief, as to the tendency of the Irish to excess in the use of stimulants, based on the testimony of Americans, who might probably be somewhat prejudiced, and therefore inclined to judge unfavorably, or pronounce unsparingly, I should not venture to record it; but it was impressed upon me by Irishmen of every rank, class, and condition of life, wherever I went, North or South, East or West.

This prevailing custom or habit springs more from a spirit of kindness than from a craving for sensual gratification. Invitations to drink are universal, as to rank and station, time and place, hour and circumstance; they literally rain upon you. . . . To the generous, company-loving Irishman there is something like treason to friendship and death to good-fellowship in refusing these kindly-meant invitations; but woe to the impulsive Irishman who becomes the victim of this custom of the country! The Americans drink, the Germans drink, the Scotch drink, the English drink—all drink with more or less injury to their health or circumstances; but whatever the injury to these, or any of these, is far greater to the mercurial and light-hearted Irish than to races of hard head and lethargic temperament.

The "liquor business" is most pernicious, either directly or indirectly, to the Irish. Requiring little capital, at least to commence with, the Irish rush into it; and the temptation to excess which it offers is often more than the virtue of the proprietor of the business can withstand. If the evil were confined to the individual himself, the result would be a matter of comparatively trifling consequence; but the Irishman attracts the Irishman to his saloon or his bar, and so the evil spreads. Almost invariably the lowest class of groggery or liquor-store—that which supplies the most villainous and destructive mixtures to its unfortunate customers—is planted right in the centre of the densely-crowded Irish quarter of a great city; while too often the name on the sign-board acts as a fatal lure to those who quaff ruin or death in the maddening bowl. . . . The bad liquor of the native American or the Dutchman is far less perilous to poor Pat than what is sold by the bar-keeper whose name has in it a flavour of the shamrock. A feeling of clanship, if not a spirit of nationality, operates as an additional inducement to the Irishman, who probably requires little incentive to excess, beyond his own craving for momentary enjoyment and dangerous excitement.

Residence in a new country did not mean an abandonment of the culture of the old country. Many Irishmen in America deliberately chose to perpetuate their ancient heritage. This aspect of ethnic identification is clearly evident in the following poem by T. D. Sullivan.

The Irish-American

Columbia the free is the land of my birth
And my paths have been all on American earth
But my birth is as Irish as any can be,
And my heart is with Erin afar o'er the sea.

My father, and mother, and friends all around.
Are daughters and sons of the sacred old ground;
They rambled its bright plains and mountains among,
And filled its fair valleys with laugh and with song.

But I sing their sweet music; and often they own
It is true to old Ireland in style and in tones;

I dance their gay dances, and hear them with glee
Say each touch tells of Erin afar o'er the sea . . . .

Dear home of my fathers! I'd hold thee to blame
And my cheeks would at times take the crimson of shame,
Did thy sad tale not show, in each sorrow-stained line,
That the might of thy tyrant was greater than thine.[13]

Abbott's collection also contained the views of Philip H. Bagenal, an Englishman who presents a picture of the Irish as they struggled to achieve a place for themselves in America. He stresses the function and value of politics as the vehicle through which the Irish gained respectability. Concomitantly, he recounts the deadening experience of Irish existence in the tenements of New York City.

Since the final issue of the American war of Rebellion, the position of the Irish in America has in every way changed. They have been acknowledged as a power in politics, in religion, and society. They have not increased in popularity as a section of the American population, principally because they have always persisted, against their own interests, in keeping up their distinctiveness of race and religion in a manner antagonistic to the great mass of the American people. Their bands, their societies, their newspapers, and their foreign politics, all very well when unobtrusive, have from time immemorial been distasteful to the undemonstrative and more Puritanic or native American.

The Irishman has long been taught to look upon America as the refuge of his race, the home of his kindred. His feelings towards her are those of love and loyalty. But when he lands, his great expectations and sometimes checked. He often finds himself slighted as a man, and his people despised as a race, and this not by any means directly, but indirectly. Then he throws himself with all the fervour of his race into party politics, determined to show he is as good as the best. Five years' probation (sometimes less) in electioneering tactics makes him an able auxiliary at the poll, and soon the fierce zeal with which he enters political strife excites the jealousy and dislike of the native American. The most sober and tolerant cannot endure the boisterous patriotism of the newly-fledged citizens, nor feel at ease in seeing those who were a few years ago despised subjects of England acquire per saltum an equality of right with the offspring of home-born Republicans. It is this survival of Native-Americanism which makes the Irish question in America a delicate one from a political point of view. And when the fate of a Presidential election depends upon the votes of a single state, and that state is New York, the empire state of the Union, which is governed almost entirely by the Irish vote, we then see how bitter may be the thoughts of old-fashioned Americans when they find the election of a President virtually in the hands of a race whom for years they had looked upon as alien and inferior.

The more modern Americans, however, have accepted facts, and, with the well-known ingenuity of the race, have turned the Irish population to good advantage. They manipulate Irish nationality, flatter Irish pride and "scoop" the Irish vote with the same aptness that they corner wheat in Chicago or "utilize the margin" on the New York Stock Exchange. But if the Americans are still jealous of the political power of the Irish race that is planted in their midst, there is also in some quarters a religious-born fear and distrust of the Catholic Church which has been built up by means of the Irish population to its present position of wealth and influence. . . . [14]

Students of ethnicity in America have wondered aloud about exhibition of an ethnic sense among Irish Americans of the 1980s. Thus they see St. Patrick's Day celebrations and Irish step dancers, and Irish names prominent in American political life, yet seemingly not manifesting many characteristic Irish traits. Assimilation has indeed seems applicable to these descendant from the Emerald Island. But there are of late signs that Irish ethnicity is on the upswing. One can point to the revival of Irish fraternal associations such as the Ancient Order of Hibernians, the increase in courses on Irish history in American colleges, and growing concern voiced by Irish Americans over the tragic events occuring in Northern Ireland. The latter situation is the most serious and seems to be coalescing Irish-American public opinion in sympathy with their co-religionists in Northern Ireland. In 1981 one sees Irish-American support for the aspirations of Irish Catholics in that country in the form of protests in which Americans of Irish descent march before the United Nations in New York City and in various drives to endorse the actions of the Irish

Republican Army in its militant stance against Northern Irish Protestants and British authorities. Admittedly a delicate issue with complex dimensions defying easy solution, current developments have attracted increasing attention among Irish Americans.

The following selection indicates interest in an Irish-American community in a social event not merely for entertainment purposes, but also because of the desirability to enlist support among Irish Americans for the building of a "New Ireland."

THE WEST CAVAN MEATS CO-OPERATIVE LTD.
Big Get-together Cavan and Leitrim

At Gaelic Park on Friday, November 24th, at 9 p.m. the people from West Cavin and West Leitrim areas will have a get-together. This time it is not just for the sake of dancing but more important business is at hand. The Rev. Phil Brady will address the people supporting his new endeavors to help build a New Ireland.

In a plea to his friends in the United States to aid him in this endeavor he sent the following letter:

Friends: The Giangevlin, Doobally, Blacklion and Dowra Development Association hopes to set up a factory or factories in the near future. We are endeavoring to get people from the above mentioned areas who have emigrated to the United States or England to take shares in these enterprises. We would also hope that the Cavin men's association in New York and in London would also help us out. As well, at home we hope to be able to persuade the people to take shares. We believe that if employment is not provided in the parish within the next two to three years it will disappear off the map. We are confident that if the people at home and away co-operate we can create jobs and so improve the living standards of the people and stem emigration.

We also hope that the people will interest some of their friends in our venture. The shares will be legally established and we would hope that the unit share would be $2.50 or one pound. Accordingly, we are arranging in conjunction with an organising committee in the United States a get-together of Giangevlin people and friends in Gaelic Park on the night of Friday November 24th, 1972. Also the organizing committee will have tickets on sale well in advance for a raffle.

We sincerely hope that you will do all in your power to promote this very worthy cause. As you will appreciate, something needs to be done very quickly to provide jobs for the young people of the area. However, we are all conscious of the fact that Giangevlin is a closely knit community and if we set about doing something together like this, it will definitely succeed.

What we have in mind primarily is a "Meat Processing Plant" which will give initial employment to fifteen men and two girls. When fully developed it could possibly give employment to twenty men and the same number of girls. It is reckoned that the cost of this factory would be in the region of $125,000. This venture is eagerly supported by the Government. I hope to go to New York early in November. In the meantime please promote this cause. Hoping then to see you in Gaelic Park on the 24th of November.

God bless you all
Father Phil Brady[15]

Finally, the next excerpt demonstrates the abiding interest in linking Irish Americans with the events in the land of their fathers. In voicing his pleasure at the meeting between Irish Prime Minister Charles Haughey and United States President Ronald Reagan in 1982, the spokesman for the Ancient Order of Hibernians expressed the sentiments of the oldest Irish-American organization.

29 March 1982

The Honorable Charles Haughey
An Taoiseach
Government Buildings
Dublin 2, Ireland

A Thaoiseach:

Please accept the heartfelt thanks of Irish America for your forthright remarks at The White House on the 17th of March last. Yours was the clearest Irish voice heard in Washington since Harry Boland represented the Irish Republic, and the brightest Saint Patrick's Day message since Eamon de Valera cited James Fintan Lalor in 1932.

There is a significant body of Irish-American opinion which believes not only in the moral rectitude of a truly independent Irish Ireland, "not Free merely, but Gaelic as well, not Gaelic merely, but Free as well," but also that we the diaspors of the Irish race [the "spiritual Irish nation" to use your own words] do be under a moral imperative to assist in the achievement of that noble goal. Believing that your deeds shall conform to your words, we are suddenly more optimistic for Ireland's sake than we have been these many years. Irish America shall continue to work through the American political system to seek to hasten the English withdrawal and the reunification of Ireland that are the sin qua non of a just and lasting peace for all of Ireland. We are delighted that the Primate of All Ireland and An Taoiseach alike recognize both the legitimacy and the utility of the American dimension.

The Ancient Order of Hibernians in America, Inc., through our own Political Education Committee and in cooperation with Congressman Mario Biaggi and the Ad Hoc Congressional Committee for Irish Affairs, with the Irish National Caucus, and with a variety of other Irish-American organizations and prominent individuals shall continue to strive for true Irish independence on a variety of fronts. We welcome the opportunity to enter into a constructive dialogue with any government in Dublin which truly shares with us the bright dream of Padraic Pearse and the men of Easter Week 1916.

Go saoraidh Dia Eire!

Again, with sincere appreciation for your Saint Patrick's Day statement, I remain,

yours in Friendship, Unity,
and Christian Charity,
John P. Connolly[16]

THE SCANDINAVIANS

Scandinavian emigration to America can be attributed to several causes, each cause occupying different degrees of intensity at various periods. Thus religion constituted the first really dominant cause in the early part of the nineteenth century as Norwegian Quakers left their homeland for New York State in 1825. Other operative causes included a desire to avoid required military service which was contrasted with the attractivness of the freedoms of the new country which was learned from letters homeward bound from countrymen already emigrated. The strongest factor of all, however, was the economic one—a compound of financial and monetary developments such as the devaluation of Norwegian money, inflation, and the high cost of borrowing as well as dissatisfaction with the governing class—all of which proved powerful incentives to emigrate.

Although the bulk of Scandinavian immigration took place in the mid-nineteenth century, especially after the conclusion of the Civil War, there was nevertheless, a presence of Scandinavians prior to this period. Danish sailors accompanied the Dutch explorer Henry Hudson on his famous voyage in 1609 and one of the early Danish immigrants gave his name to the Bronx, a borough of New York City. The seventeenth century also saw an attempt by Swedes to establish a colony on Delaware Bay. It was the 1860-1890 period, however, which was the briskest period era of emigration for Scandinavians as over a million entered the United States helping to assure the Teutonic predominance of that phase of immigration. Altogether two and a half million Scandinavians have emigrated to this country.

Norwegians

Norwegian immigration may be divided into three periods. First is the 1825-1860 period in which the settlers are described as "more Norwegian than American" in language, ideas, ideals, worship, and

ways. The second period encompasses the 1860-1890 period in which
Norwegians could be characterized as being as much American as
Norwegian in these characteristics. The third period is the 1890-1925
period in which most spoke English even when they knew the
Norwegian tongue. This period saw the dismantling of Norwegian
language schools which had been created in the earlier period—clear
reflection of the inroads of assimilation. It was this last period which
saw the Norwegian language dying as the language of the church and
the home. And finally, the supreme test of assimilation—Norwegian
immigrants and their descendants looked down upon immigrants
from southern and eastern Europe as "foreigners."

The first selections are songs. The first, written by a Norwegian
immigrant, extols the virtues of the new country to which they expressed loyalty, while the second song was written by an American of
Norwegian heritage and expresses a sense of attachment to the land of
his ancestors.

America, My Country

1. America, my country, I come at thy call, I plight them my troth and I
   give them my all; In peace on in war I am wed to the weal—I'll carry
   thy flag thru the fire and the steel. Unsullied it floats o'er our peace-
   loving race, On sea nor on land shall it suffer disgrace; In reverence I
   kneel at sweet liberty's shrine: America, my country, command, I
   am thine.

2. America, my country, brave souls gave thee birth, They yearned for
   a haven of freedom on earth; And when thy proud flag to the winds
   was unfurled, There came to thy shores the oppressed of the world.
   Thy milk and thy honey flow freely for all—Who takes of thy bounty
   shall come at thy call; Who quaffs of thy nectar of freedom shall say:
   America, my country, command, I obey.

3. America, my country, now come is thy hour, The Lord of hosts
   counts on thy courage and pow'r; Humanity pleads for the strength
   of thy hand, Lest liberty perish on sea and on land. Thou guardian of
   freedom, thou keeper of right, When liberty bleeds we may trust in
   thy might; Divine right of kings or our freedom must fall—America,
   my country, I come at thy call.

Chorus

America, my country, I answer thy call, That freedom may live
and that tyrants may fall; I owe thee my all, and my all will I give—I do
and I die that America may live.[17]

To Norway

Thou land of our sires, where the northlight is gleaming
In frostbitten, quivering ray,
And yet where the balmiest sunshine is beaming
Its glories by night and by day,
Where mermaid and nock in the billows are dreaming
Or charmingly chanting their lay,
Old Norway, thou mother of song,
Our tenderest mother so long,
Some never have met you,
Yet cannot forget you,
And therefore they greet you in song!
In song, in song, in heartiest song,
We greet mother Norway in song!

Thou land that with continents bravely art vying
In all that is noblest and best,
Whose banner of freedom as proudly is flying
As that of the Queen of the West
Thou land where our fathers and mothers are lying
In slumbering grave-yards at rest,
Old Norway in right or in wrong
You were our dear mother so long;
Some here never met you
Yet cannot forget you
And therefore they greet you in song
In song, in song, American song
We greet mother Norway in song![18]

In the following selection, the historian Olaf Norlie describes the role of Cleng Peerson as the pioneer of Norwegian immigration. Serving as the advanced agent of Norwegian "Sloopers"—a team designating those who debarked for America on sloop ships—Peerson was regarded as the "Father of Norwegian to America," the man who provided the leadership causing Norwegians to settle in the Midwest.

Norwegian Settlements, 1825-1860

Birds of a feather flock together. So do immigrant newcomers from foreign lands, whenever possible. Thus our Slooper friends found it expedient to settle down together at Kendall, N.Y. Later, most of these moved farther west and made new settlements, similar to the one they forsook. In 1830 there was as yet only one Norwegian settlement. In 1840 there were seventeen, located in six different states. In 1850 there were fifty-three more distributed throughout a dozen states. In 1860, more than 110 countries, scattered over fifteen states, had one or more Norwegian settlements. In addition to this there were Norwegians who for valid reasons did not live in a Norwegian settlement. Thus, Lars

Larson, the leader of the Sloopers, did not go to Kendall, but preferred
to remain at Rochester, where he could ply his trade as boatbuilder. The
U.S. Census of 1850 shows that there were Norwegians in 26 states, that
is, in fourteen states besides those that had Norwegian settlements. The
U.S. Census for 1860 shows that there were Norwegians in thirty-six
states, that is, in twenty-one states besides those that had Norwegian
settlements. The Norwegian foreign-born population had increased
from about 100 in 1830, to about 1000 in 1840, to 12,678 in 1850 and
43,995 in 1860.[19]

In the succeeding selection Norlie comments on the Norwegian
predilection toward education which accounted for a high rate of
literacy among the ethnic group.

The universal passion for letters which the Norwegian inherited
from Norway was not lost in this country. In fact, in this country all immigrant groups vie with one another to give their children a good education. In the Census for 1920, for example, 2.5 per cent of the native
white are illiterate, 22.9 per cent of the native Negroes; 13.1 per cent of
the foreign born whites are illiterate, but only .8 per cent of their
children. There is no class in America more anxious to get an education
than the children of the foreign-born, and there is no class of foreign-
born more eager than the Norwegians. The average percent of illiteracy
among the people of foreign-born parentage in the states where the
Norwegians are quite numerous is a trifle over .4 per cent. The actual
average for the Norwegians is possibly not over 1 per cent. These
Norwegians have been faithful patronizers of the public schools, both
elementary and higher, from the kindergarten to the university. They
have promoted the public schools in every possible way. They have
built them and paid taxes for their support. They have sent their
children to them and urged their sons and daughters to teach in them.
They have tried to keep the non-sectarian and free from anti-Christian
doctrines and practices. The history of the public schools show that
thay have had their greatest relative strength and progress in the Northwest, where the light-haired Scandinavians have come to stay.

Parochial Schools

In America they had to adjust themselves to new conditions and
provide for new emergencies. Life was more strenuous here, and there
was less time for home instruction. Besides, it was not customary in this
land to pay so much attention to parental teaching. The public schools
were secular; they could not teach religion there if they would and they
would not if they could, on account of the many creeds represented in
this country, all on an equal footing before the law. Furthermore, the
language of the public schools was exclusively English, and the parents
could not keep pace with the children in acquiring it. In this way the
parents could not very easily assist the children in their school work,
and the religious instruction was bound to be neglected even in the best
of families.

The congregations, therefore, made provision for maintaining parochial schools, in a very few cases to supplant the public schools, in nearly all cases to supplement them. These schools were held at the most convenient times, whenever, the public schools were not in session and the farmers could most easily spare their children, for in those days all children had to work side by side with father and mother, and there was no talk about getting an amendment to the Constitution of the United States to forbid the employment of children under 18. So these schools were held, in the heat of summer or the cold of winter, as the case might be, from a month to three months at a time. The subjects were mainly religious, along doctrinal, historical, Biblical and practical lines. The Smaller Catechism by Luther and some Explanation of it—Pontop- pidan, Sverdrup, Synodens—were learned by heart. The Bible history, with a taste of church history, was carefully mastered.[20]

Preoccupation with 100 percent Americanism was widespread in the early twentieth century. Likewise it presented problems and ques- tions for Norwegians in America.

The third period of the century that we are reviewing may be called the American Period. It begins around the year 1890 and occupies 35 years of time. In this period we shall find that the Norwegians in America are far more American than Norwegian and that they are assuming positions of trust and influence in state and nation as though they were to the manor born. In 1925, at least five of the 48 governors of the United States happen to be Norwegian and a sixth governor is Norwegian in his remote ancestry. In the Norwegian Period, no Norwegian could ever have reached the governor's chair. Such things do not happen. In the Norwegian-American Period, it might have hap- pened, but it didn't. In the American Period, there is no reason why it should not happen to a man of Norwegian descent as well as to a descendant of Irish or English forebears. The Norwegians in this period are in every way native to the American soil just as their fathers before them were born and bred in America. They are Americans all, even if one-half of them still can speak Norwegian and are familiar with Norwegian culture. They are 100 per cent Americans even if they all nourish kindly thoughts of the land of the North that gave birth to their grandsires.

It can be truly said even of the immigrant, the Norwegian of the Norwegian Period, if you please, that he, too, can be 100 percent American, notwithstanding all the unjust things which have been said to the contrary during the recent War and since. Speaking on this point, Kristian Prestgard very aptly remarks: "Lately much has been spoken and written about this matter, but the amount of nonsense which has been uttered reveals an astonishing ignorance of the difficult position of the immigrant. I do not refer merely to the hysterical absurdity to which we were treated during the war. But even highly cultivated and in- telligent men and women have talked away about these things without thinking. Even former President Roosevelt, who was such a master in coining striking phrases, said once that it was just as impossible to love two countries at the same time, as to be faithful to two women. Now, I am sure that I am in no way an exception when I state that I have loved two women at the same time, and that, as far as I know, I have been faithful to both. One of them was my mother; the other, my wife. It has never occured to me that I loved my wife less because I also loved my mother, and am sure that President Roosevelt would have said the same. But without thinking he coined a phrase that has done great harm."

Now, if it can be said of an immigrant that he can be 100 percent American and still be deeply attached to the land he forsook, it surely ought to be true of the Norwegians of the third, fourth, fifth, and sixth generations. The America-born Norwegians would love America even if they had never been taught to do so. It is natural for a man to love his native land, as natural as for him to care for his kith and kin.[21]

The process of assimilation is alluded to in the selection which follows which describes the triumph of the American public schools over the Norwegian parochial school system. The consequence was that institutions responsible for Norwegian heritage began to disappear.

The fact that the Norwegian people of America have now entered the American stage so their sojourn is very forcibly brought out in the story of their schools. Never before have patriotic Norwegians and consecrated Lutheran Christians pleaded so eloquently for the support of the Norwegian schools, and never have they been maintained with so much difficulty.

The period started with practically every Norwegian believing in the whole school system as an absolute necessity—parochial schools for the children, academics for the youth, and colleges for young manhood and womanhood besides the theological seminary for the training of ministers and missionaries, normal schools for the training of parochial teachers and deaconess homes for the training of deaconesses. In the faith of the fathers they founded a number of academics and colleges in the first half of this period, and, up to 1907, the attendance at these schools was steadily on the increase year by year.

But, beginning with 1907, the attendance has gradually declined and one precious school after another has given up the ghost and is no more. The Norwegian academies are going. A wind has passed over them, and they are gone; and the place where they stood shall know them no more. Such seems to be the sad educational tale of the American Period. They prospered nicely as long as the Norwegians were Norwegian-Americans but they were starved out for want of students and other support as soon as the Norwegians became Americans. As Americans the Norwegians prefer to give their undivided support to the American school system. The American public schools are free, publicly controlled, tax-supported and non-sectarian. The system extends from kindergarten to the university. It teaches everything except the cultural heritage of the immigrant and the Christian religion. It often blots out that heritage and robs one of his Christian faith.[22]

Although the immigrant experience was an uprooting one for all, it was especially traumatic for the Norwegian woman. Isolated in a strange, new land, without the comfort of familiar landmarks and neighbors, her experience in the American Midwest was a searing, devastating one and is graphically depicted in the novel by Ole Rolvaag, *Giants in the Earth*. The excerpt which follows describes the fatal premonition of one such woman.

"There isn't much to say about such things," Per Hansa began. "She has never felt at home here in America . . . There are some people, I know now, who never should emigrate, because, you see, they can't take pleasure in that which is to come—they simply can't see it! . . . And yet, she has never reproached me. And in spite of everything, we got along fairly well up to the time when our last child was born. . . . Yes, the one you baptized today . . . . Then she took a notion that she was going to die—but I didn't understand at the time. . . . She has never had the habit of fault-finding . . . . She struggled hard when the child was born, and we all thought she wouldn't survive—or him, either. That's why we had to baptize him at once.[23]

The life story of Lars M. Larson affords another example of ethnicity among Norwegian Americans. Born in Norway in 1868, Larson was brought to the United States when his family emigrated in 1870. He was raised in the Norwegian-American social, religious, and cultural milieu of the American Middle West and went on to fame and fortune in his chosen profession as a historian, eventually becoming president of the American Historical Association. His autobiography excellently records his growth and experience against the background of an ethnic upbringing. After describing the problems revolving around the English language, the place of ethnic institutions, and the Americanizing influence, he affirms his ethnic sense while acknowledging his Americanness.

But I have not forgotten my past. The knowledge of things Norwegian, new and old, which came to me in early life is a heritage that I prize most highly and should be loath to lose even in the slightest measure. As the years have come and gone, my interest in all those mighty forces that shaped the culture and the civilization into which I was born has, if anything, become deeper and more intense, possibly because their significance has come out into clear light. Nor can I deny that it is a matter of real pride to me that my cradle stood in that stern and rugged but grandly beautiful country whence so much of human strength has gone forth into all the western world.

For more than sixty years I have shared in the citizenship of the great Republic. I owe no allegiance, political or spiritual, to any other land; but my past is a fact and a vital fact that I cannot ignore. Between an active loyalty to a land and a system into which one has been received and an honest recognition of the values that inhere in a culture out of which one has come, there need be no conflict. America herself has a European past, from the long experience of which she has drawn knowledge and wisdom and power. And the individual citizen no more than the nation itself can escape the implications of his past.[24]

The Swedes

Contemporaneous with English and Dutch colonization came Swedish settlement in the colonial period of American history. The first company of Swedish immigrants, intent upon founding a colony called Christiana along the Delaware River, arrived in 1638 and even though they failed to develop a major enterprise they numbered a thousand by the end of the seventeenth century. They were regarded as plain, solid citizens who were served for many years by Swedish-speaking clergy sent from Stockholm.

The pioneer Swedish settlement was already several generations advanced before truly massive emigration unfolded in the mid-nineteenth century. This newer immigration made its impact in the northern Midwestern states where Swedes would emerge as among the largest nationality stock in several of these states. As this stock increased to hundreds of thousands, it was evident that the people were conscious of their roots and endeavored to retain their ethnicity. The author of the following selection refers to the idea of "Swedish-America," the notion of replicating the "old country" world in a new settting. He describes the role of the Swedish press and language in the development of an ethnic consciousness in America.

Foremost of the instruments in the creation of "Swedish-America" was the press. In almost every community of Swedish settlers an organ of public opinion soon sprang up. Chicago became the center where journals suddenly appeared and as suddenly died. A few gained a foothold and by mergers attained national circulation . . . .

Wherever these papers reached they proclaimed a solidarity of the Swedish population. The music was not always harmonious. Some of the papers were in constant warfare against each other . . . .

But whatever the political or religious platform of the paper, one note was sounded throughout all: "We are a Swedish people." A good deal of space was given to news from Sweden, and the reader was given the impression that events in that country still concerned him. The weather with its consequences for crops, the labor situation, the economic and political crisis, the military program, the royal house, unusual happenings in city and countryside—such gave grist for the printing press. Swedish-Americans followed with eagerness the relations of Finland and Sweden.[25]

The story of John Nordstrom is a human account of adversity and opportunity, typical of the lives of millions of immigrants. Born in Sweden in 1871, he emigrated to America at the age of sixteen living first in San Francisco, then in the Klondike region of Alaska and finally in Seattle. At the age of seventy he wrote his autobiography in order for "my grandchildren to read after I am gone, to let them know what the average immigrant had to go through in the 1880s." The excerpts which follow describe his identification with ethnic ties as indispensable to survival and success.

From Liverpool we got steerage passage to New York, which took ten days. The food was very bad and we were all seasick most of the time. On arriving at New York we landed at Castle Garden and immediately took a train to Stambaugh, Michigan, getting there on the third day we had been in America, each with only five dollars apiece left in our pockets.

When we reached Stambaugh all we could see was the little red depot in a gulch, and, as the station master could not understand us, we didn't know what to do. We stayed around there about two hours until a young man came along. He could easily see that we were greenhorns and came over and spoke Swedish to us. This made us very happy and he asked us if we knew anyone in Stambaugh. We said we had the name and address of a cousin of mine, Samuel Berlin, and he said my that was funny, for Mr. Berlin was his room partner. They were both bartenders but not on the same shift.

He took us up the road and up a hill and when we got to the top of the hill there was the town in a valley on the other side. It was a village of five or six hundred people, three saloons, two or three stores and some boarding houses for the miners who worked in the iron mines close by.

When we got to the bar where my cousin was working, we had to have a glass of beer first thing, and as I had never tasted beer before, I had a hard time getting it down. My cousin I had only seen once as a small boy, and I had to tell him who I was. Then he took us to a Swedish boarding house and thought the food was wonderful, as the food on our trip had been so terrible, and besides our money had been low and we could not afford to buy extra food.

Now the next day my cousin took us down to the iron mine and got us all jobs. Three days later we went to work, loading iron ore into wheelbarrows, carting it about one hundred feet to a platform and dumping it into railroad cars. The weather was very hot and the iron ore heavy. Our working hours were ten hours a day at a dollar sixty cents a day. Out of this we paid fifteen dollars a month for room and board.

When evening came I was so tired I could hardly walk uptown, and my hands and feet were blistered. Perhaps my blistered feet were caused by a pair of cowhide boots that I had bought for two dollars. The third day we worked there I was just about ready to give up my job when the foreman from the mine came and spoke Swedish to us. He wanted three men to go down in the mine and work. Right away we threw away our shovels and followed the foreman down to the bottom of the mine, about four hundred and fifty feet underground. It was as cool as a cellar, and I thought heaven could not be any nearer.

I felt fine that evening and the next day the foreman came and put me to work with another gang of men. I could not understand them but listened carefully for several days, trying to pick up a few words of English. After a few days, I told a Swede in our boarding house that I didn't think I could ever learn to speak the English language as I hadn't been able to learn a thing from the men I worked with. He laughed and said naturally I couldn't learn to speak English from them as they were Polacks and couldn't speak any more English than I could.[26]

Although the population of Americans of Swedish descent is heaviest in northern Midwestern states like Minnesota, Illinois, North Dakota, Kansas and Nebraska, the resurgence of ethnicity among Swedes from other states is also interesting. Thus a Swedish consciousness was clearly discernible in New Jersey in the latter part of the nineteenth century as many Swedish Americans exhibited an ethnic sensitivity to the role of Swedes in the colonial period of American history.

The year 1874 marks a turning point in Swedish consciousness in the East, for it was then that Israel Acrelius' *History of New Sweden* was first translated into English and published in the United States. The Centennial of American Independence, celebrated two years later, helped to awaken interest in all phases of American history and served to make Swedish-Americans sensitive to their nation's part in the development of America. As historical and genealogical societies became more important gradually more and more information was revealed about the half-forgotten role of Sweden in the New World . . . .

Interest in the history of New Sweden reached a climax in 1909 with the founding of the Swedish Colonial Society at Philadelphia. On its rolls were immediately found the names of many Swedish families which recalled the original voyages up the creeks of New Jersey.

Constant intermarriage gradually obliterated the physical characteristics of the Swedes and Finns, and by the twentieth century they were virtually indistinguishable from the other nationalities in South Jersey. The Anglicization of names had continued, although often the Swedish origin was apparent. For example, Bengston changed to Banks, Kyn to Keen, Bonde to Boon, Svenson to Swanson, Whiler to Wheeler, Hopman to Hoffman, and Joneson to Jones. Given names were similarly altered, Per to Peter, Lars to Lawrence, Nils to Nicholas, and Olave to William.

Place names in Southern New Jersey, however, retained a strong Swedish cast. The old New Stockholm Township now includes the three towns of Bridgeport, Gibbstown and Nortonvile; Finnstown has changed to Pinns Point, but there survive Repaupo, Rambo Station, Dalbo's Landing, Helm's Cove, Elsinborough Township, and Swedesboro itself. As noted earlier, Eric Mullica and James Steelman left their names over a wide area of the coastal region. A few Swedish names are even of comparatively recent origin, as in the case of New Sweden Crossroad in Gloucester County and Swedes Run in both Burlington and Salem Counties.

Yet in the southern part of the State persons of Swedish descent are no longer concentrated in the historically Swedish regions. Gloucester and Salem Counties were the eighteenth century strongholds of the Swedes. According to the 1930 census, these two counties contain only one-seventh of the Swedes in southern New Jersey. Atlantic and Cape May Counties once sparsely settled with Swedes, now have more than one-third of the South Jersey total.

The descendants of the Swedes of Colonial times are still concentrated in Camden, Gloucester and Salem Counties. Town and City directories in these sections are studded with names transplanted from abroad while New Sweden was still a political entity in the Delaware Valley. Among them are Hanson, Tallman, Mecum, Steelman, Dalbow, Helms, Erickson, Sinnickson, Hendrickson, Vannaman and Lock. These Swedish-Americans, as well as later Swedes in the area, follow generally the custom of the earlier Swedes by crossing the Delaware for the continued observance of Swedish ways. They attend Swedish Lutheran Churches in and around Philadelphia and belong to the Swedish Colonial Society. Many have joined the Swedish singing societies in Philadelphia[27]

The Danes

Jacob August Riis was one of the most famous of the Danish immigrants. He came to the United States in 1870 at the age of twenty-one and gained fame as a newspaper reporter and social reformer. His many years of work in slum and immigrant neighborhoods led him to develop ideas for social improvement that spread throughout the land. Nevertheless, Riis could not forget his Danish roots and culture, and he found it possible to be both a useful United States citizen and one who was conscious of his non-American ethnic lineage.

I was back in the harness of the carpenter-shop when, in the middle of July, the news struck down in our quiet community like a bombshell that France had declared war on Prussia; also that Denmark was expected to join her forces to those of her old ally and take revenge for the great robbery of 1864. I dropped my tools the moment I heard it, and flew rather than ran to the company's office to demand my time; thence to our boarding-house to pack. Adler (a German worker) reasoned and entreated, called it an insane notion, but when he saw that nothing would stop me, lent me a hand in stuffing my trunk, praying pathetically between pulls that his countrymen would make short work of me as they certainly would of France. I heeded nothing. All the hot blood of youth was surging through me. I remembered the defeat, the humiliation of the flag I loved,—aye! and love yet, for there is no flag like the flag of my fathers, save only that of my children and of my manhood. . . .

In the midnight hour we walked into the Church Street police station and asked for lodging. The rain was still pouring in torrents. The sergeant spied the dog under my tattered coat and gruffly told me to put it out, if I wanted to sleep there. I pleaded for it in vain. There was no choice. To stay in the street was to perish. So I left my dog out on the stoop, where it curled up to wait for me. Poor little friend! It was its last watch. The lodging-room was jammed with a foul and stewing crowd of tramps. A loud-mouthed German was holding forth about the war in Europe, and crowding me on my plank. Cold and hunger had not sufficed to put out the patriotic spark within me. It was promptly fanned into flame, and I told him what I thought of him and his crew. Some Irishmen cheered and fomented trouble, and the doorman came in threatening to lock us all up. I smothered my disgust at the place as well as I could, and slept, wearied nearly to death. . . .

With angry tears I went up and complained to the sergeant that I had been robbed. He scowled at me over the blotter, called me a thief, and said that he had a good mind to lock me up. How should I, a tramp boy, have come by a gold locket? He had heard, he added, that I had said in the lodging-room that I wished the French would win, and he would only be giving me what I deserved if he sent me to the Island. I heard and understood. He was himself a German. All the suffering rose up before me, all the bitterness of my soul poured itself out upon him. I do not know what I said. I remember that he told the doorman to put me out. I remember that he told me and threw me out of the door, coming after to kick me down the stoop. . . .

It was when I went home to mother that I met King Christian last. They had told me the right way to approach the King, the proper number of bows and all that, and I meant to faithfully observe it all. I saw a tired and lonely old man, to whom my heart went out on the instant, and I went right up and shook hands, and told him how much I thought of him and how sorry I was for his losing his wife, the Queen Louise, whom everybody loved. He looked surprised a moment; then such a friendly look came into his face, and I thought him the handsomest King that ever was. He asked about the Danes in America, and I told him they were good citizens, better for not forgetting their motherland and him in his age and loss. He patted my hand with a glad little laugh, and bade me tell them how much he appreciated it, and how kindly his thoughts were of them all. As I made to go, after a long talk, he stopped me and, touching the little silver cross on my coat lapel asked what it was.[28]

The Finns

Though the Finns brought the sauna to American civilization, their greatest contribution was the consumers' cooperative. "One of the most legible stamps of Finnish-American influence has been in the development of consumers' cooperatives," concluded Professor Arnold Alanen. The Finns believed that since everyone is a consumer, therefore every one is a potential cooperator, and the retail store was the most effective type of consumer's cooperatives. In a detailed study of the subject in the twentieth century, Professor Alanen sums up the significant part played by the Finnish Americans.

> The consumers' cooperative, which eventually would become an important facet of social and political life in many Finnish-American communities, was initially fostered as a counterpoint to the severe economic difficulties faced by recent immigrants. Leaving a familiar but troubled-plagued Finland behind, only to find a strange and often harsh environment in America, the consumers' cooperative movement represents an amalgam of forces and events occurring on both sides of the Atlantic. Kolehmainen and Hill have stated:
>
> The cooperative David had sprung from honorable parentage. Its grandparents were the Old Country, which had schooled the immigrants the hard way—in the virtues of thrift, tenacity and united effort, and had inculcated in them a critical attitude toward the unrestrained acquisition of individual wealth. Its American mother was need. The immigrants quickly came to feel their common insecurity as unskilled wage earners and backwoods farmers.
>
> From these beginnings, the Finnish cooperative movement passed through many, often traumatic stages of activity which ranged from expansion to retreat, ideological advocacy to quiet neutrality, and Finnish domination to Americanization.
>
> There is little doubt that contemporary consumers' cooperative activities, whether conducted in the Western Great Lakes Region or anywhere in the U.S., do not possess the same fervor and intensity of Finnish pioneer efforts. The loyalty and support given by these Finns to local stores and general cooperative efforts find few parallels in the annals of American economic endeavor. K. A. Nurmi's statement. . . . the Finns have learned that the cooperative store is equally as important to each and every member as, if not more important than, their homes and farms, certainly could not be applied to all Finnish cooperators; but the willingness of some individuals to mortgage even their hard-won property to save the local cooperative.[29]

1. Reprinted from Albert B. Faust, *The German Element in the United States*, vol. 1 (New York: Arno Press, Inc. 1969), pp. 66-67, 72.

2. Ibid., pp. 146-47.

3. Ibid., pp. 150-51.

4. Reprinted from Carl Schurz, *The Reminiscences of Carl Schurz*, vol. 3 (New York: The McClure Co., 1908), pp. 258-62, 298-99.

5. Reprinted from Richard Bartholdt, *From Steerage to Congress, Reminiscences and Reflections* (Philadelphia: Dorrance, 1930), pp. 82, 84, 86, 88, 89, 90.

6. Richard O'Connor, *The German Americans*, (Boston: Little, Brown & Co., 1968), p. 453.

7. Ibid., 458.

8. Reprinted from Tyrone Power, "Irish Workmen Build a Canal near New Orleans," in Rhoda Hoff, *America's Immigrants* (New York: Henry Z. Walck, 1967). p. 22.

9. From Abbott, *Historical Aspects of Immigration Problem*, pp. 438-39. Copyright 1926 by University of Chicago Press. By permission of Arno Press.

10. Reverend John O'Hanlon, *The Irish Emigrant's Guide for the United States* (Boston: Patrick Donahoe, 1851), pp. 78, 119, 165.

11. From Abbott, *Historical Aspects of Immigration Problem*, pp. 817-19. Copyright 1926 by University of Chicago Press. By permission of Arno Press.

12. Reprinted from John Francis Maguire, *The Irish in America* (reprint ed., New York: Arno Press, 1969), pp. 236, 270, 271, 277, 280, 281, 283, 286.

13. Reprinted from Edith Abbott, *Historical Aspects of the Immigration Problem*, pp.530-31. Copyright 1926 by University of Chicago Press. By permission of Arno Press.

14. Ibid., pp. 532-33, 535.

15. *The Irish People*, (Weekly Newspaper), Bronx, N.Y., Nov. 18, 1972.

16. *The National Hibernian Digest*, March-April, 1982.

17. Norlie, Olaf Morgan, *History of The Norwegian People in America*, 1925. Reprinted by Haskell House Publishers, Ltd. (New York: 1973).

18. Ibid.

19. Ibid.

20. Ibid., pp. 214-15.

21. Ibid., pp. 302-03.

22. Ibid., p. 375.

23. Abridged from pp. 127, 129, 159, 385 in *Giants in the Earth* by O.E. Rolvaag. Copyright 1927 by Harper & Row, Publishers, Inc.; renewed, 1955, by Jennie Marie Berdahl Rolvaag.

24. Reprinted from Lawrence Marcellus Larson, *The Log Book of a Young Immigrant* (Northfield, Minnesota: Norwegian-American Historical Association, 1939), pp. 301-02.

25. Conrad Bergendoff, "The Role of Augustana in the Transplanting of a Culture Across the Atlantic," *The Immigration of Ideas*, ed. by J. Iverne Dowie and J. Thomas Treadway, (Rock Island, Illinois: Augustana Historical Society, 1968), pp. 68-71.

26. John W. Nordstrom. *The Immigrant in 1887*, (Dogwood Press, n.p. 1950), pp. 11-13.

27. Reprinted from the Federal Writers' Project, *The Swedes and Finns in New Jersey* (Bayonne, N.J.: Works Projects Administration (WPA), 1938), pp. 105-07.

28. Reprinted from Jacob A. Riis, *The Making of an American* (New York: Mac-Millan, 1901), pp. 46, 47, 71, 72, 428, 429.

29. Arnold Alanen, "The Development and Distribution of Finnish Consumers' Cooperatives in Michigan, Minnesota and Wisconsin, 1903-1973," *The Finnish Experience in the Western Great Lakes Region: New Perspectives,* (ed. by Michael Karni, Mattie E. Kaups, and Douglas J. Ollila), (Turku, Finland: Institute for Migration, 1975), pp. 128-30.

KEY QUESTIONS

1. Describe the three periods of Norwegian immigration.
2. Compare and contrast the role of language in the retention of ethnicity among Scandinavians.
3. According to the experience of the Scandinavian population, was it possible to remain isolated in an ethnic community beyond the first generation?
4. In its attempt to unite its people into groups, was the German-American experience different from that of the Irish?
5. Comment on the phenomenon of Catholic immigrant groups entering into ethnic discord although possessing the same religious creed.
6. What was the view of nineteenth century observers regarding the Irish tendency towards clannishness?
7. What was the reaction of the Irish Americans toward Know-Nothingism?
8. Discuss the position of the Ancient Order of Hibernians with respect to the current troubles in Ireland.

THREE

Eastern and Central European Immigrants: The Poles, Hungarians, Russians, Jews, Ukrainians, and Ruthenians

Emigration from Eastern and Central Europe can be traced to the earliest period of English colonization. For example, there were some Polish craftsmen and artisans in Jamestown at the beginning of the seventeenth century as well as Czech and Moravian and Slavic Protestant refugees in New Sweden and New Amsterdam in 1654.

Indeed, by the time of the American Revolution a number of individuals from this part of Europe were prepared to play more important roles in that conflict, such as Count Casimir Pulaski and Thaddeus Kosciusko of Poland and the Polish Jew Haym Salamon who helped finance the Revolution.

In the decade following the birth of the American republic, Eastern and Central Europeans made up a mere trickle in the stream of transatlantic migration, including in their company occasional clergymen, veterans of Napoleon's army, and others of varying backgrounds. Some considered themselves temporary exiles, not immigrants, while others dreamed of establishing ethnic enclaves on the American frontier—New Polands, New Bohemias, New Hungaries, and so forth—where their ethnic integrity would be maintained and secured for the inheritance of future generations. As with other groups of similar mind, efforts to establish "foreign colonies" in the United States failed, as immigrants turned to more practical pursuits such as the founding of fraternal organizations and ethnic newspapers. The Czechs, for example, had organizations and journals in the 1850s, while the Polish success in these endeavors can be traced to the 1880s. The First Polish-language newspaper in America began in 1863.

Some of these immigrants found careers in medicine, engineering, surveying, cartography, and other fields which required technical skills. Others entered teaching (especially of languages), the arts, and government service. They maintained their individual ethnicity and kept in touch with each other and exrevolutionaries from other nationalities in America and Europe. Yet they married American women and raised their offspring in the American liberal Protestant milieu. Several, such as Turchin (a Russian), Krzyzanowski and Karge (Poles), Schoepf (part Hungarian, part Pole), and E'Utassy (a Hungarian), attained at least field grade rank during the Civil War.

Agricultural-populational crises in the homelands and industrialization in the United States accelerated as Eastern and East Central Europeans flowed into the tide of the post-Civil War immigration. Those who made it up, with the significant exception of the Jews, were mainly peasants repelled by poverty and attracted by economic promise. They arrived with their own linguistic and cultural-religious identities, but not with the political awareness and sophistication of nationalism. They were mainly semiliterate, from submerged nationalities under the rule of the Russian, Austrian, or Prussian Empire.

Austria claimed the lion's share of them: Hungarians, Czechs, Slovaks (who were distinct as a nationality from the Czechs), Poles, Ukrainians, Ruthenians, Slovenians, and other South Slavic people. Together they constituted a complex folk patchwork. The unfortunate Jews, with their own religion and Yiddish culture, were interspersed throughout the patchwork; deliberate overcrowding and anti-Semitism, often fostered by the imperial regimes, had been their lot and made them candidates for emigration along with the others.

A pithy summarization of the motives behind the "new immigration" is contained in the expression "after bread," common to almost all Eastern and East Central European vocabularies. As a rule, freedom took second place, and it was usually freedom from something, such as military conscription and immobility imposed by social discrimination, rather than freedom of such things as religion and expression. They did not feel themselves to be exiles as did their predecessors, but a foremost thought in the minds of many (excluding the Jews) was that of saving enough money to return to their homeland and buy a piece of land on which to settle permanently. The overwhelming majority of the hundreds of thousands of them never did return. Most of them were destined to spend the rest of their lives in ethnic communities around mills, factories, or mines. Many got their wish of land ownership when they paid off their mortgages on homes in such communities. Some began or returned to farming. A small fraction went into business, mainly as tavern owners, undertakers, or proprietors of small grocery stores. Rarely did they venture into anything larger.

A classic among firsthand accounts of the beginnings of the "new immigration" is contained among the journalistic writings of the Polish author and eventual Nobel laureate, Henryk Sienkiewicz. In 1876, Sienkiewicz, who was then thirty years old, came to the United States on a two-year visit. In addition to becoming involved in an experiment in utopian colonization in California, he traveled widely and recorded his impression in the form of letters which he sent to Polish journals. In them he frequently dealt with the phenomenon of ethnicity in America and expressed pleasant amazement at its seemingly successful existence in American society. For many years, the letters were known only among those who read Polish. In 1959 they were translated, edited, and published. Of particular interest is the thirteenth letter. It begins with Sienkiewicz's valid description of typical ocean crossings in steerage. It follows the immigrant's first steps on American soil, notes his puzzlement at his new environment, and decries his exploitation by greedy boardinghouse owners. Sienkiewicz summarized the plight of his newly arrived compatriots.

> Their lot is a severe and terrifying one and whoever would depict it accurately would create an epic of human misery. . . . Their early history is a tale of misery, loneliness, painful despair and humiliation. . . . Almost a hundred thousand peasants sent by our land across the ocean have gone through such a Dantean inferno—in search of a better life.[1]

After digressing on the value to America of European immigration and describing "immigrant homes" where newcomers could stay but which the unduly frightened Polish peasants avoided because of their institutional appearance, Sienkiewicz resumed:

> And yet, is there nothing that our peasants bring to the New World that might guarantee them a peaceful life and a secure livelihood? Of course there is. They bring with them the habit of being content with little, true peasant endurance, patience and an iron constitution. . . . He does not even comprehend the need for various comforts that the German and French immigrant regard as necessities of life. Sun does not burn him; snow and wind do not chill him. In cold Wisconsin and Minnesota he is not perturbed by the snow drifts; in semitropical Texas, once he throws off the fever, he works in the scorching heat like a Negro. Perhaps he may be less skillful than others, but he has greater endurance and he is a humble and quiet worker. . . .
> There is a saying in the United States that he who comes here is critical during the first year, begins to understand the country in the second year, and falls in love with it the third year. I have myself experienced the truth of this saying. As for the Poles who have long resided in the United States, I have only this comment:. . . it would be dangerous to speak disparingly of the United States to any Pole residing here. He does not cease to love his former fatherland, but after Poland he loves most the United States.[2]

Sienkiewicz concluded that the Polish "emigration fever" would be transitory and that assimilation of the earlier Polish arrivals would be rapid. He predicted a quick change on the part of succeeding generations including intermarriage with other groups and name changes.

Circumstances were to delay fulfillment of Sienkiewicz's prophecy. For almost four decades following his visit, the supply of first-generation Polish Americans was constantly replenished. Polish neighborhoods remained, solidified, and grew. Attempts were made to unify the entire "emigration" under the umbrella of a national organization. In 1880, mainly at the behest of political exiles, the Polish National Alliance was organized. It was secularly controlled and committed to activism on behalf of Polish independence. Its main attraction for membership lay in the burial insurance which it provided. The Alliance's combination of nationalism and progressivism may be seen in the editorial which appeared in the first issue of its official journal *Zgoda (Harmony)*:

> Posing this question, we have in mind the many thousands of the Polish people scattered throughout the area of the New World without a link among themselves.
>
> One fact strikes the eye: From amid such a numerous Polish emigration, not only has not a single strong personality emerged to shine forth but also its level has not even reached that of the most oppressed of European people, of the Irish nation.
>
> Thus it is a matter of concern as to the dignity with which the Poles will wear on their temple the crown of American citizenship. Whether they will remain behind the Irish and become mere "voting cattle," whether they will forever crush rocks, dig in the mines, fell timber, drive mules, etc., or whether they will stand on a par with the Germans, Frenchmen and Englishmen in higher callings, in journalism, commerce, politics and the crafts.
>
> The field here is open to all, the most talented will triumph, whatever is incapable, unenlightened and infirm, remains at the bottom, behind. This cannot be helped, it is the necessary result of republican freedom.
>
> Therefore, the answer to the above questions will depend upon the influence which the varied and many Polish organizations in this country will have on the totality of the emigration, for, so long as the emigration does not have command of the English language, they will be the only school in which the Poles arriving here will be able to educate themselves.
>
> But then, we can say that if our emigration will fall under the influence of obscurantism as up to now, under the influence of those who for ages kept our people in blindness, it will never rise above the level of the Irish, and the Polish name will shine with no gleam on this land.

It is necessary first of all that associations of Poles which already exist, bind themselves together into one national whole. Secondly, that the Polish National Alliance use the strength of its great organization to support an organ, a progressive journal, which would enlighten and educate the emigration. It is necessary that every group set up a Polish reading room where more enlightened compatriots would conduct lectures for their brethren. Let past and current Polish affairs be discussed at national commemorations; through such means not only will our emigration uplift its spirit and rise above the unenlightened masses, but it will also fulfill its mission towards Poland to which our free voice will reach, with which our thoughts will meet and join. Through oceans, through thousands of miles, we will send our brothers in the homeland the ideals of freedom and equality of the New World, that will awaken new life within them. They, in turn, will send us the sparks of the holy fire of patriotism, which does not burn out in their hearts but merely smoulders covered with ashes.[3]

The Alliance was challenged soon after its creation by a revived clerically dominated organization, the Polish Roman Catholic Union.

Instead of being "unified," the American Polish community became polarized. Leaders of the Alliance were given such labels as "nonbelievers," "Masons," and "socialists." In return, politically conservative priests who ran the Union were called "sellouts" or "collaborators" by Alliance spokesmen. In some parishes, readers of pro-Alliance newspapers were threatened with excommunication or denial of sacraments. In one instance, in the Green Bay, Wisconsin, diocese, the excommunicating clergy had the backing of the bishop, who happened to be of German birth. Alliance supporters capitalized on this, likening him to the German chancellor Bismarck and his action to Bismarck's policy of oppression of Poles under German rule.

In some Polish-American quarters the analogy was to be extended to the entire American hierarchy of the Roman Catholic Church. The decree of the 1884 Baltimore Council, which gave bishops title to all property in their dioceses, coupled with the policy of "Americanization" of the church at a time when one out of every eight of the faithful was likely to be either a Polish immigrant or the child of Polish immigrants and when many hundreds of churches and parochial schools had been built by Polish immigrants, provided the fuel for a number of flareups.[4] There were fears of "denationalization" (wynarodowienie) and of forced elimination of ethnoreligious customs and traditions brought over from the old country. Sometimes—especially when there was the added disillusionment of an unpopular, heavyhanded pastor—parts of congregations would even secede from episcopal jurisdiction and become "independent."

By the 1890s, some of the "independent" parishes that managed to survive began to form movements. On the appeal of truly owning their churches, allowing a democratic lay voice in governance, and, last but not least, having the only Polish bishops in the United States, the movements made some headway. While condemning the "independents" in the strongest language, the Catholic clergy of the American Polish community were in a tight predicament. The policy of patience urged by the most moderate among them seemed to go unrewarded. Finally they met in their own congresses and delegated representatives to go directly to Rome with petitions for a Polish bishop. Their leading spokesman was the young Father Waclaw Kruszka. Father Kruszka made his debut as an activist with an article which to him seemed to embody a most logical principle. In the New York Catholic *Freeman's Journal* of August 3, 1901, he called for "polyglot bishops for polyglot dioceses," advocating the creation of vicars-general to serve particular ethnic groups in dioceses where the proportion of such groups warranted it. His article immediately stirred up severe criticism. Perhaps the epitome of it was expressed in the weekly *Michigan Catholic* of January 16, 1902: "When the time comes that there are Polish-American bishops they will be chosen, not because they represent a single race extraction, but because of their learning, their piety and their true Americanism."

Embittered at this, Father Kruszka became more fiery. In comments to Polish-speaking audiences he spoke of a vicious alliance between chauvinist Masons (the Protestant-owned *Chicago Tribune* had advised the Poles to learn English so that they would not be able to say that "their bishops cannot talk with them") and the Irish, who were able to cloak the church in "Americanism" while running it as their own monopoly. In the comments that he made in English there was less sting but, nevertheless, a frankness which made him a controversial figure. A sample of this is contained in a letter written September 8, 1905, to the editor of the *Milwaukee Sentinel:*

> It is an undeniable fact that although the Irish form only about one-third of the Catholic population, of the hundred Catholic bishops in the United States, almost all are of Irish nationality, a few German bishops being only a drop in the sea.[5] This is a fact, and against a fact there is no argument. From this fact one can easily deduct the conclusion that the Irish want a certain priest for a bishop, just because he is Irish; but how in the world can you show me a single fact that the Poles want the same.
>
> What the Poles in their movement for a Polish bishop want is this: To have bishops from any nationality, and not only from one exclusively as it is practiced at this time. The Irish, as facts prove, presented always and still present candidates of Irish extraction, to the

exclusion of other nationalities, as if they alone had the monopoly of wisdom and sanctity and episcopal dignity. Now it is wrong to want a certain Polish, Bohemian, etc., priest for a bishop, just because he is a Pole, Bohemian, etc. It is not even wrong to exclude him from the list of candidates just because he is a Pole, Bohemian. But why do the Irish mostly succeed in Rome? Simply by persuading the Roman authorities that the Irish nationality is the only American nationality—all others are "foreign" nationalities. Of course, one must be narrow-minded to call Americans only those who speak exclusively English, and consider others as "foreigners" just because they, besides English, know how to express their thoughts also in other human languages. The Poles, Bohemians, etc., adopted the language and customs of this country. . . . The Poles, Bohemians, etc., are not worse Americans, therefore, than the Irish. . . .

Starting to immigrate in 1831, already since 1854 the Poles built every year churches, schools, asylums, colleges, etc., paid always faithfully their church taxes . . . in a word, they did their duty as Catholics . . . and during this long period never enjoyed any rights and privileges in the church, never had any representation in the hierarchy. This is evidently unjust and un-American! And now, when we make a just complaint, they say to us that there was not as yet any Bohemian, Polish, etc., priest worthy to become a bishop but as soon as they will find one they will make one. I need not say that this is a poor excuse, and an uncharitable one, not worthy of a true Christian. It is an open insult to the whole Polish, Bohemian, etc., clergy. Were so long the Irish and the few Germans the only worthy [ones] upon whom the Holy Ghost deigned to descend? One must be arrogant to assert this. Indeed, to this privileging of one and the disregarding of other nationalities, we safely ascribe the fact, that there was in the United States no gain but a loss of millions of Catholics. The Independent Polish sect says: "If the Pope allows the organization in the United States of an Irish national hierarchy, why does he not allow the formation of a Polish national hierarchy?" And even pure Americans, I mean those of no denomination, either religious or national, I have heard asking: "Where is the mark of catholicity in your church? Is it not predominantly Irish Catholic?" . . . [5]

The petitions which the Polish-American delegates brought before the papal throne were sidetracked.

Developments in Poland, such as the efforts toward achievement of Polish independence in World War I, remained sources of concern to Polish Americans throughout the first generation of the twentieth century. Immigrants from Poland felt that their financial aid and human contributions entitled them to some voice in that country's postwar destinies. Conversely the political and ideological currents and controversies developing in the homeland were in turn exported to these shores. The result was disillusionment and disunity among Poles in America.

Among the factions were Polish-American socialists represented by several left-wing Polish-American newspapers like *Ameryka Echo*, while on the other end there was a right-wing clerical faction represented by newspapers like *The Catholic Leader*. The latter, published by the extremely energetic priest Father Bojnowski of New Britain, Connecticut, declared open warfare against all the enemies of Polish Catholics. In 1921, Father Bojnowski set down some guiding principles for Polish Americans to embrace which clearly reflected his orientation and had deep influence on this ethnic people.

> "Whoever is not with the Church is
> against the Church and the Fatherland."
> "Since you are a Pole, speak Polish."
> "Love your Fatherland, drenched with
> the blood of your forebears who fought
> incessantly for her."
> "Great is the power of organization."
> "Unite. Enroll in national
> and religious associations. At the
> polls vote only for Catholic Poles."
> "Marriages should be only between
> Polish men and Polish women."
> "Even if no one around you observes
> these principles, be strong as steel:
> persevere in the Church and in Poland.
> You must be a propagator of these Catholic
> and national principles."[6]

Throughout the 1920s and 1930s Polish Americans were confronted with Americanization—the effort to quickly assimilate all foreigners by requiring them to eschew the language and the culture of their origins. This movement was making a large impact among the younger generation. However, it was resisted strongly by Father Bojnowski who acknowledged that the theory of cultural pluralism was much more preferable to total assimilation. Thus even as many succumbed to the "melting pot" theory, he inveighed against it. "A truly tolerant American, in the full meaning of the term, must be sought with a candle and he will be found most frequently . . . among descendants of newer arrivals from Europe who have not lost their tradition and ideals from their European fathers."

Both the bishops and the Polish-American clergy used the "Independents" in their arguments. The bishops could claim that the Poles were by nature troublesome and rebellious, while the clergy could claim that the consecration of bishops from the ranks of the Independents would stir up trouble and rebellion. As the arguing continued, there was a consolidation in the rebel ranks. It occurred under the leadership of Father Francis Hodur, a young priest in the Scranton, Pennsylvania, area. Hodur, unlike Kruszka, defied the authority of a bishop to a point where he and his rebellious parishioners suffered excommunication. Peasant-born himself, Hodur developed a movement with strong appeal for the laboring immigrant who felt especially sensitive to exploitation and injustice. His message was often social and nationalistic as well as religious. It was invariably simple. In his hierarchy of figures to be emulated he included, along with canonized Catholic saints, such pre-Reformation heroes as Hus, Wycliffe, and Savonarola and added Polish patriots and "Messianic" poets who had prophesied Poland's resurrection, among them Adam Mickiewicz and Juliusz Slowacki. He also included George Washington and Abraham Lincoln.

The framework of the new movement was essentially Catholic, but modifications were to be made. Besides abolishing auricular confession for adults and making "the word of God as preached by the Church" a sacrament, the movement accepted the use of Polish rather than Latin in the Mass. The translation was done by Father Hodur himself. Added to the movement's hymnology were several well-known Polish patriotic melodies with new emotion-stirring words written by Hodur.

In 1904, representatives from various "independent" parishes met in Scranton and elected Father Hodur bishop of what was called the Polish National Catholic Church. In 1907, he traveled to Holland, where he was consecrated by bishops of the Old Catholic Church. By virtue of the consecration he could claim apostolic succession in a line going back to the first days of Christianity. One year later, Father Paul Rhode was consecrated the Roman Catholic auxiliary bishop of Chicago. At last, and probably not by mere coincidence in the wake of Bishop Hodur's consecration, a priest from the Polish ethnic group attained a place in the American clerical hierarchy. Others were to follow, but never did their number approach a proportional representation.

Other Eastern and East Central European immigrants also had their share of religious troubles on American soil. Much of it was caused by internecine quarrels over administration (this was especially so in the case of members of various Orthodox denominations). The Ukrainians, Ruthenians, and others who belonged to the Uniate or Greek Catholic rite of Roman Catholicism had some initial struggles with the American bishops to maintain the same autonomy which their rite enjoyed in Europe. The bishops were sometimes averse to their unique practices, especially to their having a married priesthood.

Lithuanian Catholics sometimes had three fronts for friction: within their own ranks, with the Roman Catholic hierarchy, and with Polish pastors who were grudging about recognizing their ethnic uniqueness. Eventually, most split off into separate parishes. Where this was made impossible or where internecine quarreling went unresolved, they, too, went "independent," and there was also a separate Lithuanian National Catholic movement.

Just as the Slavs and Lithuanians faced turmoil on American soil on other issues, they were to become involved in some of the most violent labor strifes that broke out in the United States in the late nineteenth and early twentieth centuries. The labor region which saw some of the bloodiest combat was anthracite coal mining. Already by the 1880s their number in the anthracite region of Pennsylvania was significant enough for them not only to be noticed but also to have become simultaneously objects of prejudice and potential recruits for union organizers.

The story of the Slavs in anthracite mining, set in the small Pennsylvania "patch," has been reconstructed from a number of sources by Victor R. Greene and incorporated into the opening chapters of his work *The Slavic Community on Strike*. Green begins:

> The typical greenhorn would have alighted from the immigrant train in the Pennsylvania hard-coal region undoubtedly apprehensive if he had not yet met his correspondent. With luck, one or both had a photograph to aid in recognizing the other. Otherwise the weary traveler at the depot asked or shouted the name of his sponsor. One can imagine the tears of joy on both sides when to the immigrant's call his countryman responded, and their relief was expressed in a demonstrative embrace.
>
> The sponsor then led his charge to a group of shacks usually at the edge of town. This ghetto was separated from the rest of the populace just as in other places in America where the East Europeans lived. . . .
>
> And the newcomer felt even more at home when he discovered that this nucleus of the Slavic-American community even represented specific geographic sectors of the old country. In fact, a similar housing arrangement flourished among all the Slavs everywhere, Poles, Lithuanians, and other, who wanted an economical place to live—"trzymanie bortmikow," the boarding-house system. . . .[7]

The transformation of the immigrant within one lifetime was a phenomenon to behold. In *Americans from Hungary* Emil Lengyel describes the process of transformation. From peasant backgrounds, lovers of the soil, they came to be strong mineworkers who with frugality managed to save some money and achieve a degree of economic independence. Simultaneously with their efforts to improve their lot in America, Hungarians attempted to develop "Little

Hungaries" and, with more success, ethnic-oriented fraternal and social organizations.

Once the Hungarian immigrant left home he underwent a remarkable sea change. At home he had been a peasant, hopelessly in love with the soil which refused to yield herself to him. He was a peasant not merely as an occupation but also as a profession of faith. He was a Catholic or Protestant, but in his heart of hearts he was a nature-worshiper, faithful to only one soil, his own, that of his own village, his own very limited horizon. But when he reached America he never thought of going to work on a farm. He, the thoroughbred peasant, turned his back on the soil and turned toward the mine and the blast furnace. . . .

The Hungarian immigrants settled in the neighborhood of mines and steel furnaces. They settled everywhere the industrial molochs needed unskilled workers, ready to perform the least desirable types of chores. The hardest industrial job was easy in comparison with peasants' work; the working day was short, not more than ten to twelve hours a day. Most of the Hungarians settled in four States: Ohio, New York, New Jersey, and Pennsylvania. Large groups settled also in Illinois, Indiana and West Virginia.[8]

THE RUSSIAN IMMIGRATION

With tumultuous events in Russia serving as catalysts, over four million immigrants came to the New World from Czarist Russia between 1883 and the beginning of the First World War in 1914. The vast majority came from the failed Revolution of 1905. This fantastic emigration included the so-called Great Russians (out of the region expanded from the medieval duchy of Moscovy), White Russians from the western regions bordering on Poland, Little Russians from the Ukraine, and Russian Jews from the famous Pale of Russia. Other national minority groups and ethnic peoples, Poles, Lithuanians, Estonians, Letts, and Finns, all assembled together in the "prison house of the peoples" known as the Russian Empire—formed part of this exodus, but in considerably smaller numbers. The gates of the Czarist regime were wide open at all times, and the inhabitants of its vast world were encouraged to take the road to exile, never to return.

In the mid 1870s, when the Czar began his campaign to "Russianize" the Mennonites by imposing the Russian language and culture upon them and inducting their men into the army, the exodus of the persecuted began. These people, along with other non-Mennonite German groups located along the Volga and the Don, set themselves up against the Imperial Government and set out for the United States in organized groups. Between 1874 and 1894 they formed a trickle of approximately two to three hundred families per year; between 1898 and 1914 this grew to approximately one thousand families annually. Farmers and artisans, quite similar to the German peasantry from Westphalia, Baden, and other parts of Rhineland Germany, their destination was the great open spaces of the New World: Nebraska, Oklahoma, Kansas, Wisconsin, the Dakotas, and Minnesota. Russian Mennonite migration did not last for long, but their contribution to American agriculture, as the following document indicates, was inestimable.

Among the many interesting features of the Mennonite economic development which might be discussed, most noteworthy is that of their introduction of the Turkey wheat into America. Thoughtful as they were of what might grow in the new country, these German colonists took with them various seeds, among others also hard winter wheat, the so-called Turkey wheat, a fact which was to become of high significance not only for their own farming, but for the whole wheat production in the United States. . . .

Reference need only be made to the statement of the United States government authorities in order to see the relation between the development of the Turkey wheat in the United States, and the German immigration from Russia.

"The history of hard winter wheat in the United States is closely associated with the movement of the Russian Mennonite immigrants to the middle Great Plains. These people originally went from West Prussia to Southern Russia about 1770 because of certain land grants and civil privileges offered by the government under Empress Catherine. Over one hundred years later their descendants, desiring further advantages to be obtained in America, emigrated to the middle Great Plains and settled principally in Kansas. . . .

"The good qualities of the Turkey wheat were not generally appreciated much before the close of the last century, twenty-five years after its introduction by the Mennonites. At the Kansas experiment station its superiority came to light about 1897, though it had been under experiment for some time. . . . As early as 1901 hard winter wheat at New York was quoted at a fairly good price. All recent prices (1914) at the important markets show a decided but gradual change in attitude toward hard winter wheat, so that it is now ranked, where it should be, among the first class wheats. It has 'won its way' through difficulties in accordance with the motto of the state where its production is greatest . . . and is now more generally in favor in this country than any other winter wheat. In California, where it is not adopted, a third to a half of all wheat annually used by the mills is imported from the middle Great Plains. It has encroached upon the hard spring wheat area to the northward in Iowa and Nebraska and upon the area of softer wheats to the westward in the Rocky Mountain States, and has made Montana a wheat state . . . making in all 350,000,000 bushels as the approximate average annual hard wheat production in this country. This is about a half of the average total wheat production in this country."[9]

Russian immigration reached its peak strength in the years 1910-1914. First came individual Russian males, followed within a few years by their large families. A few were educated, some were political refugees from one or another of the numerous radical opposition organizations within Czarist Russia (all illegal and underground), but the vast majority were ordinary Russians, lacking in the most rudimentary education and illiterate in the full sense of the word. Workers and peasants, they possessed a high degree of physical stamina and an even higher degree of personal courage and determination. Once in the United States, they joined and swelled the ranks of the unskilled, toiling away at hard labor. Coal miners, steelworkers, factory hands, farm laborers—they concentrated in the eastern and midwestern industrialized states of America.

That the Russian immigrant factory and mine worker was at the bottom of the ladder in terms of human exploitation seems beyond question. There is a considerable body of evidence indicating that the Russians did not hesitate to complain or to express their feelings, often indicating great bitterness with respect to their adopted land. Below are excerpts from a document circulated by the Russian Orthodox Church in America.

> All the factories are the selfsame ichor which poisons the worker's soul and body. Capital is a cruel master; workers are his slaves foredoomed to death. Each working day shortens the worker's life for a few months, saps the living juice out of him, dries out the heart, dampens the noblest aspirations of the soul; transforms a living man into a sort of machine, embitters the whole life. The ragged soul and body of the worker bring forth to the world half sick children, paralytic, idiotic—therefore the factory's poison kills not merely the unfortunate workers, but also whole generations. It kills invisibly, imperceptibly, in such a manner that the workers themselves—the voluntary slaves of capital—fail to see the whole frightfulness of their own situation. . . .
>
> In Russia, more attention is paid to the man. There, they say: "Men are not cattle"; "Men are not made of iron"; "Work and rest." The mining of gold and silver and iron is called in our land "sing-sing work" (hard labor) which is done by the most hopeless of criminals, not by thieves but by cut-throats—soul-killers or traitors to the State; whereas in America any work is sing-sing (hard labor), and the workers are galley slaves although they call themselves free citizens.[10]

Until either the Russian worker or his children (a native-born second generation) rose out of the factory working class and thus managed to shift to easier lines of work, harsh exploitation would be his lot. In the end, relief came primarily in the 1930s, when the Committee for Industrial Organization (CIO) under the leadership of the miners' union chief, flamboyant John L. Lewis, began the formidable task of organizing the millions of unskilled in the country's basic industries. Until then, the descriptive excerpt that follows tells the story of a life in the mill.

It is true that some of the Russians draw a distinction between the squad foreman who works with them and the boss foreman. The former shares in their labor and is often friendly, but they consider the latter as almost invariably bad, feeling that he deliberately makes them do work that is too difficult. For example, a Russian in Philadelphia said, "The boss makes two of us carry steel which should require four. If I refuse, I lose my job. Lots of weeks the work is so heavy I get pains in my back and have to lay off three days out of seven." Or again, in a mill in Pittsburgh, the boss, Pete, according to the testimony of a Russian, is a giant who can do the work of two ordinary men. In somewhat exaggerated language more clearly to convey his meaning, he said: "The boss can lift two tons himself. He will watch us straining to lift a two-ton iron and will laugh at us and yell, 'You — — Polack, push.' We will break our backs trying and he will not lift a finger to help us." . . .[11]

Likewise, in the same excerpt, a Chicago Russian evaluated his situation after World War I.

"Before war, very good; but now all, no matter what nationality, laid off on least excuse. If horse no can pull wagon, put on another horse. If man no can pull truck, lay him off."

"Foreman very severe; sometimes lay off day for being minute late. Rush so at work that you almost faint. Treatment worse now since it is very easy to replace men."

"Boss very hard. Fired one man, he was in his place two minutes before whistle blew to enter shop."

"Bosses very unreasonable. One man left truck to get drink and boss fired him. Have to bribe boss to keep job."

"Too strict about time; if one minute late, dock one-half hour. Getting worse all the time. Often work so hard get weak and when tell foreman he say we are drunk."

"Treat Russian like dog."

THE JEWS OF RUSSIA

It is generally agreed that Jewish immigration to the United States from Czarist Russia in the early part of the twentieth century forms one of the most complex and significant episodes in our entire immigration history. This is true both from the standpoint of the numbers of immigrants involved (within a twelve-year period from 1899 to 1910, a total of 1,074,442 Jews were admitted to America from all over Eastern Europe, or an average of 90,000 per year) and from that of the importance of the contribution of these people to American life.

The Jews of Russia lived in a region known officially as the "Pale of Settlement" and popularly and simply as the Pale. The Pale at its largest consisted of some fifteen provinces extending 1,500 miles along the border of Germany and the Austro-Hungarian Empire at an approximate average width of 240 miles; even lands wrested at one time from the Turks were included in this region. It included areas in the Ukraine, parts of ancient Slavic Poland, and regions, tributaries, and stretches of Russia, such as Lithuania, Volkynia, Bessarabia, Galicia, and Roumania.

A Jewish population was already present in the United States. Forced to flee Spain and Portugal, Sephardic Jews had emigrated to the New World in the seventeenth century. The majority were either small tradesmen or workers, and a few became wealthy businessmen. The first synagogue built by these earlier comers was about a century old when another migration of Jews found its way here. The latter, comprised of ten thousand people from the Bavaria region of Germany, were prompted by a desire to escape from anti-Semitism. Because they were an exodus of tradespeople and professional classes, they did not congregate in one concentrated area of the country, but on the contrary tended to move widely into all sections of the nation. Those with enough funds established themselves as merchants in the cities, while the majority trudged as peddlers throughout the land before making permanent homes for themselves in a given locale. This Jewish population—many German-Jewish—was completely unprepared either to help or to assimilate the great surge of Russian Jews about to flood the New World. The extract below summarizes the problems that faced the Jewish immigrant upon his arrival.

> In the ten years covered by our record of the arrival of Jewish immigrants, there has been added to the Jewish population of America, through the port of New York alone, the enormous number of 313,035 foreign Jews, of whom 242,199 were Russians and Roumanians, and 57,818 were Austrians. To this number must be added the Russians who came to America between 1880 and 1884, who certainly numbered 80,000. In viewing our problem, it has not been the practice heretofore to consider Austrian immigration as material. But it should be remembered that the bulk of it is received from the province of Galicia, and that most of the inhabitants of this province are strongly akin to the Russians in all the respects that make the Russians difficult to deal with.
> Of the foreign arrivals, by far the larger percentage, safely estimated at seventy-five, remained in New York. In the beginning of the movement to America, the percentage requiring assistance was small, but it has grown constantly until the large expenditure of the year 1891-92 was called for. That the heavy immigration has greatly added to our burden may be understood from the fact that of the $1,850,000 ex-

pended by the United Hebrew Charities since its organization, twenty years ago, upwards of $1,000,000 has been expended in the past five years.

Were no other influence than immigration to be taken into account an appalling problem would still confront us when considering how to deal adequately with our poor. But there were evils awaiting the foreigner in New York which, in the nature of things, he himself intensified, and which have rendered efforts to make an impression upon the whole seem well-nigh fruitless. First, and perhaps as important as any of these evils, are the tenement houses. For years the public [officials] of New York have inveighed against the tenement house, yet it exists today in all its virulence, despite public disapproval, rigid sanitary laws and inspection, and the attempts of noble men and women to remove the poor from their vile surroundings. The assertion has been made repeatedly that the amount of illness, especially of a zymotic nature, is hardly greater in the tenement houses than in the better portions of the city. This is probably true, but it should not delude us into believing that therefore the tenement does not complicate our problem. The worst result of tenement-house life is an under-vitalization of tenement dwellers both mentally and physically, and they who have searched carefully into the homes of the poor have found also a moral degradation as serious as the mental or physical deterioration. Without a sound body, a sound mind, and sound morals as a base, how shall we be able to raise the standard of the submerged tenth?

The second evil lies in the wage question. It will be remembered that the bulk of the immigrants especially those from Russia and Galicia are unable to perform outdoor work. This caused the larger percentage to secure in-door employment which they found almost entirely in the garment manufacturing trades. Unscrupulous sweaters and middle-men seized upon the poverty of these unfortunates and, finding an opportunity to hire men and women at prices reduced to the starvation point by unwholesome competition, forced thousands into a method of living literally from hand to mouth. The major part of their wages is absorbed by rent for dwellings that are inadequate and unsanitary, their clothing is insufficient, their food the most meagre, and savings are absolutely impossible. The last year has brought home to us in all its horror the result of this form of what might almost be called slavery.[12]

It is estimated that in the thirty-year period between 1881 and 1910 over a million Jewish refugees arrived in the United States; then, between 1910 and 1914 another 200,000 to 300,000 came, making this group one of the largest of the "new immigrant" peoples. In the peak year of Jewish immigration, 1906, they constituted 13.5 percent of the total individuals entering the country.

Nearly all of the immigrant Jews settled in the cities of the American east coastal region; some families, not considerable in number, went to the West. The percentage of skilled artisans was considerable: tailors, furriers, and jewelers, for example, quickly constituted a major element of the skilled labor force required in such industries as the manufacture of garments, millinery, the fur industry, and so forth. Manufacturing, wholesale and retail businesses, peddlers whose successful activities led to the opening of retail stores in many regions of the United States, all of these became familiar byproducts of the great Jewish migration. Finally, as the good word spread to Slavic Russia, the wave of non-Jewish Russians previously described began to build up from the 1890s onward as the pull to cross the Atlantic became irresistible.

What, if anything, distinguished the Jewish immigration from other immigrant groups? According to L. Hersch, who closely studied statistical material of the U.S. Immigration Service, the outstanding feature of migrant Russian Jewry was its high proportion of active professionals and skilled people.[13] A significant number of Jews who came to America were skilled workers, with almost 400,000 skilled Jewish workers entering the United States in the years 1899-1910. This was an almost unprecedented contribution to the skilled manpower pool of the United States, and its significance cannot be measured. Out of forty-nine professions and skills listed in American immigration statistics for these years, the Jews had an absolute or relative majority in twenty-five, including hatmakers, furriers, tailors, clockmakers, and jewelers, among others.

Migration was, of course, a familiar part of the history and tradition of the Jews. But this time there was a significant factor in their favor. Word of their persecution in Czarist Russia had reached America and was known to the general population. Hence, public opinion was not favorable to traditional forms of Jew-baiting and anti-Semitism when Jews began to arrive in large numbers. It is not difficult to grasp the grateful excitement and the sense of exalted liberation of these hundreds of thousands in the excerpts that follow from a novel by the popular Jewish authoress, Anzia Yezierska.

Mostly About Myself

I feel like a starved man who is so bewildered by the first sight of food that he wants to grab and devour the ice-cream, the roast, and the entree all in one gulp. For ages and ages, my people in Russia had no more voice than the broomstick in the corner. The poor had no more chance to say what they thought or felt than the dirt under their feet.

And here, in America, a miracle has happened to them. They can lift up their heads like real people. After centuries of suppression, they are allowed to speak. Is it a wonder that I am too excited to know where to begin?

I'm too much on fire to wait till I understand what I see and feel. My hands rush out to seize a word from the end, a phrase from the middle, or a sentence from the beginning. I jot down any fragment of a thought that I can get hold of. And then I gather these fragments, words, phrases, sentences, and I paste them together with my own blood.

Think of the toil it takes to wade through a dozen pages that you must cut down into one paragraph. Sometimes, the vivisection I must commit on myself to create one little living sentence leaves me spent for days.

Now I no longer live in a lonely hall-room in a tenement. I have won many friends. I am invited out to teas and dinners and social affairs. And, I wonder, is my insatiable hunger for people so great because for so many centuries my race has been isolated in Ghettos, shut out of contact with others? Here in America races, classes, and creeds are free to meet and mingle on planes as high and wide as all humanity and its problems. And I am aching to touch all the different races, classes, and creeds at all possible points of contact, and I never seem to have enough of people.[14]

By the year 1900 America had the largest community of free Jews in the world. The growth in the capacity of the Jewish community to take care of its own newcomers had reached the point where the case of the helpless Jewish immigrant was practically unknown. However, a so-called Jewish Problem had reentered the picture in the sense that the influx of Russian Jews destroyed all possibility of completion of the assimilation process which the older Jewish groups (Portuguese, Spanish—also known as Sephardic; German—also known as Ashkenazi) were on the brink of achieving. A counterpart to the revival of insistence upon a Jewish identity was the rise of an active Zionist movement (opposed by Jews of Western European origin) and the birth of a strong Jewish working class and trade union movement of socialist persuasion.

According to the *American Jewish Yearbook*, the number of Jews in the city of Chicago had grown to 75,000 by 1904. This is under 5 percent of Chicago's then population of 1,600,000 but more interesting is the division of Jews into the following national categories: 50,000 Russian Jews, 20,000 German Jews, and a balance of 5,000 of those of other national origins. This proportion would be repeated elsewhere, indicating that the older Jewish groups had already been swamped by the influx of arrivals from the Pale. With their strong sense of organization and association, the 75,000 Jews of Chicago were already divided into 50 religious congregations, 39 charitable societies, 60 lodges, 13 loan associations, 11 social clubs, and 4 active Zionist societies!

In the life of the ghetto Jew, religion played a particularly important role. In Judiasm, learning and education are of vital concern to the religious practitioner in the sense that education is, for him, an essentially religious activity. Both the spirit and practice of the great, orthodox centers of learning in eastern Poland and the Russian Pale were tranferred successfully to the New World, thanks to the scholarly rabbis who made the trip. Under their leadership, the synagogue was all-powerful in the Jewish community, its influence going far beyond the usual boundaries of religion. One may grasp the reality of life in the ghetto and its culture by putting together three basic elements: *Yiddish*, the spoken language common to all; the *Landsmannschaft*,or association, which brought together in the same place and organization all those emanating from the same village back in the "old country"; and the *chevra*, or the entire religious community and entity. A strict and orthodox brand of Hebraicism, built upon the traditions of thousands of years, prevailed over the challenging conservative and liberal-reform versions. Centers of religious orthodoxy, built upon particular synagogues and located within the Jewish ghettos, could match in wealth, prestige, and influence the great orthodox centers of learning left in the Old World. Little wonder that the first serious controversy in which the American Jewish community became embroiled was the issue of permitting Jewish stores to be open on Sundays, since the Hebrew Sabbath was, of course, on a Saturday.

The specific role of the Russian Jewish synagogue is partly described in the passage that follows.

> The Russian Jew brings with him the quaint customs of a religion full of poetry and of the sources of good citizenship. The orthodox synagogue is not merely a house of prayer; it is an intellectual centre, a mutual aid society, a fountain of self-denying altruism, and a literary club, no less than a place of worship. The study-rooms of the hundreds of synagogues, where the good old people of the Ghetto come to read and discuss "words of law" as well as the events of the day, are crowded every evening in the week with poor street peddlers and with those gray-haired misunderstood sweat-shop hands of whom the public hears every time a tailor strike is declared. So few are the joys which this world has to spare for these overworked, enfeebled victims of "the inferno of modern times" that their religion is to many of them the only thing which makes life worth living. In the fervor of prayer or the abandon of religious study they forget the grinding poverty of their homes. Between the walls of the synagogue, on the top floor of some ramshackle tenement house, they sing beautiful melodies, some of them composed in the caves and forests of Spain, where the wandering people worshiped the God of their fathers at the risk of their lives; and these and the sighs and sobs of the Days of Awe, the thrill that passes through the heartbroken talith-covered congregation when the shofar blows, the mirth which fills the house of God and the tenement homes upon the Rejoicing of the Law, the tearful greetings and humbled peace-making on Atonement

Eve, the mysterious light of the Chanuccah (a festival in memory of the Restoration of the Temple in the time of Maccabeans), candle, the gifts and charities of Purim, a festival commemorating the events in the time of Esther, the joys and kingly solemnities of Passover—all these pervade the atmosphere of the Ghetto with a beauty and a charm without which the life of its older residents would often be one of unrelieved misery.[15]

Jews entered American professions on a large scale, soon becoming physicians, druggists, dentists, lawyers, and educators. Energetic and creative, they left their mark everywhere. Irving Howe, the literary critic, has written about Abraham Cahan—long editor of the *Forward*, author of the famous novel, *The Rise of David Levinsky*, Yiddish critic and publicist, and political leader of socialist persuasion—as characteristic of the successful Jewish professional. Cahan came to America in 1882, after the pogroms and the assassination of Alexander II. He rose rapidly and with astonishing success. But his most important function was to articulate the aspirations of the New York East Side Jewish masses. In the words of Howe:

Cahan was the kind of publicist who stands uneasily between intellectuals and masses, transmitting the sentiments of one to the other, yet soon making his position into a sort of fulcrum-point for a Bonapartist exercise of his will.[16]

In the life and activity of hundreds of men like Cahan, the Lower East Side created a distinct Jewish subculture which, years later and not until the Thirties, finally took a gigantic leap forward into the cultural and historic stream that is America.

The ghetto of the Jew is now a closed eqisode in the long history of these people. Dispersed and scattered in various parts of our great cities, but mainly removed to suburbia, the offspring of the Jewish immigrants holds but a rapidly fading memory, nostalgic and idyllic, of what life in the ghetto once was. Our present notion of the ghetto is, of course, built on our vision of the black ghetto: Harlem, Bedford-Stuyvesant, Chicago East Side. This is a far cry from the home of the newly arrived ethnic immigrant of the "new" immigration. Even in terms of health and living conditions, the old ghetto was preferable.

Politically, with the exception of the active and substantial minority of Jewish workers and intellectuals (professionals) who embraced the socialist and radical movement of their day while still retaining the kernel and flavor of their Jewishness, most Jews of the ghetto followed the traditional immigrant and American path. The Jewish wards were dominated by ward machines of the respective parties—generally the Democratic Party—votes were widely purchased as elsewhere, and the Jewish voter tended to live and let live. The Jew was as patriotic as the next, serving in the army and in the various wars of the twentieth century.

To summarize, if the ghetto may properly be considered an organized cultural community, the New York City Lower East Side ghetto, the patriarch of them all, was the undisputed center of American Jewry and Jewish cultural life. The synagogue, dominated by the rabbinate and the Jewish elders, was the key institution of the culture. The ghetto was a physical fact, a geographic fact, and, perhaps most importantly, a state of mind. If we read the following excerpt taken from Michael Gold's famous novel written in the social-realist style, we may obtain a more balanced picture of the ghetto—that is, how it appeared in the eyes of the children of these Jewish immigrants.

> I can never forget the East Side street where I lived as a boy.
> It was a block from the notorious Bowery, a tenement canyon hung with fire-escapes, bed-clothing, and faces.
> Always these faces at the tenement windows. The street never failed them. It was an immense excitement. It never slept. It roared like a sea. It exploded like fireworks.
> People pushed and wrangled in the street. There were armies of howling pushcart peddlers. Women screamed, dogs barked and copulated. Babies cried. . .
> The East Side of New York was then the city's red light district, a vast 606 playground under the business management of Tammany Hall.
> The Jews had fled from the European pogroms; with prayer, thanksgiving and solemn faith from a new Egypt into a new Promised Land.
> They found awaiting them the sweatshops, the bawdy houses and Tammany Hall.
> There were hundreds of prostitutes on my street. They occupied vacant stores, they crowded into flats and apartments in all the tenements. The pious Jews hated the traffic. But they were pauper strangers here; they could do nothing. They shrugged their shoulders, and murmured "This is America." They tried to live.
> They tried to shut their eyes. We children did not shut our eyes. We saw and knew. . . .[17]

THE UKRAINIANS

Ukrainians have been known historically under a number of names, often used interchangeably or confused. At one time or another parts of the Greater Ukraine—called Ukrainia by the nationalists—have been overrun or subjugated by either the Russians, the Poles, the Austrians, or the Hungarians. Ukrainians today constitute parts of at least three countries: Soviet Russia, Poland, and Czechoslovakia; hence, in one form or another these people live under communist rule. The issue of national independence and Ukrainian sovereignty is therefore very much alive for the typical Ukrainian. Under the Russian Czar, these people were known as "Little Russians," indicative of their lowly status in the eyes of their Great Russian lords and masters. Historians have referred to subdivisions of the Ukrainians variously as "Carpatho-Russians" and even "Russians," much to the indignation of this proud people. Ethnically, whether living in that part of Russia known as the Ukraine (now the Soviet Ukrainian Republic) or in parts of Poland and Czechoslovakia, Ukrainians possess the same national language and the same general cultural background. It is this that has kept alive the spirit of Ukrainian nationalism, which foresees the day when all Ukrainians will be united in a nation of their own. It has also, however, encouraged sharp and bitter disagreements within the Ukrainian people between those who support Russia, including the present Soviet government, and those who advocate some form of independent Ukrainian nationalism.

Immigration began on a noticeable scale only in the 1870s, largely as a result of intensive political and religious persecution at the hands of the Russian Czar. The centers of resistance to both the Russian imperial authorities and the Russian Orthodox Church were the diocese of the Ukrainian and Ruthenian Catholic Church. The church also regulated the migratory movement and, in fact, has always exercised a powerful influence over a deeply religious people. While there was never any major exodus of Ukrainians, it is estimated that by 1914 perhaps as many as 700,000 Ukrainians had entered the United States. Since ethnic differences between Russians, Ruthenians, and Ukrainians were not taken into account by the immigration authorities until 1896, this is at best a shaky estimate. Eastern Galicia, a part of Poland and, hence, a part of the Russian Empire, was the center from which most Ukrainians migrated.

Once settled in the New World, a tiny percentage of the Ukrainian immigration became wheat farmers in the West. But the bulk of these people helped to fulfill the seemingly inexhaustible need of the country for factory and industrial workers. The largest group of Ukrainians settled in southwestern Pennsylvania, in and around the city of Pittsburgh. They were employed in the soft coal mining areas of Pennsylvania and were often found in the iron foundries of the region. Others settled in Chicago, New York City, and the industrial centers of New Jersey. Some accumulated sufficient money to buy homesteads in the Dakotas, Montana, and western Canada. Still others went into small businesses (such as grocery stores) or, after obtaining the necessary education, became professional people. All, almost with exception, however, took their first job doing anything in order to pay off their debt (usually $100) for the initial trip to the New World. One notorious activity generally associated with Ukrainians was enlistment in strike-breaking activities and organizations, usually in connection with strikes initiated by the Irish in the western Pennsylvania coal fields. Other groups of Ukrainians moved into the coal mining districts of Ohio, West Virginia, Illinois, as well as the iron mines of Minnesota and Michigan. Wherever factory hands were needed in the urban and industrial centers, these powerful and long-enduring people could be found. Strongly imbued with the desire to hold onto their language and culture, they formed tightly knit groups and islands in the great sea of American life. Against heavy odds, they tried to distinguish themselves through their language and cultural associations from the Russians, with whom they were most frequently confused. It was largely a losing battle.

Wasyl Halich, author of *Ukrainians in the United States*, describes the process by which Ukrainians found a place for themselves within the American industrial order, and he relates the hardships endured by this particularly burdened ethnic group.

At Work in the Pennsylvania Mines

A very large percentage of the newcomers settled in the mining communities, beginning with Pennsylvania. The first appearance of Ukrainians in the Pennsylvania anthracite-coal mines was in the seventies (1877) in the regions of Shenandoah, Shamokin, Mt. Carmel, Olyphant, and Scranton. They were induced to come to America by an agent of coal-mining companies whose workers were then on strike. The experience of the first Ukrainian group in America contains some of the basic elements of that of other pioneers on this continent. When they landed in New York, they did not understand a word of English; their colorful attire attracted much attention, and they were regarded as a curiosity. Being unable to get lodgings, they had to leave the city. They walked to Philadelphia, being forced to sleep outdoors because people were afraid to give shelter to such curious strangers. By the time they reached Harrisburg their energy was exhausted, but a kind-hearted American, seeing their condition, had pity on them and gave them food. Other people, however, fearful of such strangers, urged them out of town. One farmer gave them lodging, but the following night they had to sleep under a bridge. Finally they reached Shenandoah, Pennsylvania, where a Lithuanian immigrant, a business man, Carl Rice by name (in Lithuanian "Ruchus"), took care of them. Rice was a great friend of the Ukrainian immigrants to the end of his life.

This group of immigrants arrived in the mining communities during a labor strike. Not understanding the conditions, or probably because of necessity, they went to work as strike-breakers; consequently they brought upon themselves the hatred of old miners, mostly Irishmen. There were frequent assaults on the strike-breakers which ended in riots. The influx of fresh immigrants tended to keep the wages low, and this prolonged the racial and labor antagonism between the Ukrainian and Irish groups. In connection with this racial animosity not infrequently the newcomer became a victim of "accidental" injury in the mine, or even death. Such were the prevailing conditions in 1884. . . .[18]

THE RUTHENIANS

Never a significant group in the history of American immigration, the Ruthenians—also known on occasion, particularly in the immigration records, as the Russniaks—had their biggest moment of migration in the year 1906 when approximately 16,000 left the northern part of what was then the Austro-Hungarian Empire and undertook the voyage to the New World.

A Slavic people, the Ruthenians had the misfortune of being oppressed by a succession of masters: first by Polish landlords under whom they were serfs when they occupied sections of eastern Poland; then by the Austro-Hungarian Empire; finally, by the Czarist Empire.

The word *Ruthenia* is the Latinized form of *Russia*. The term was originally applied to the Ukraine in the Middle Ages, when that area was ruled by the kings of Ruthenia. Later, under the Austro-Hungarian Empire, the term Ruthenians was used to designate the Ukrainian population of the western Ukraine, which included the Russian provinces of Galicia, Bukovina, and Carpathian Ukraine.

There is no ethnic or linguistic distinction between Ukrainians and Ruthenians. Culturally, however, there is a religious difference, since Ruthenians are or were affiliated with the Roman Catholic Church in distinction from the Ukrainians, who form part of the Greek Orthodox Church, which was fully restored in the seventeenth century in the Russian part of the Ukraine.

The Ruthenian immigration to America closely parallels that of the Ukrainian. Several hundred thousand came over in the years preceding World War I, entered industry along with similar Russian groups, and retained their identity for a considerable number of years through the formation of strong local clubs and language societies. Church was particularly important to these people and probably their strongest cultural bond. They settled in Pennsylvania, New York and New Jersey, with a substantial distribution in our larger cities in the Twenties: Chicago, 45,000; Pittsburgh, 35,000; Cleveland, 30,000; Detroit, 30,000; Jersey City, 25,000; and New York City, 20,000.

Playing no special or unusual role in the story of American immigration, they are by and large indistinguishable from their closely related ethnic and linguistic brethren, the Ukrainians.

Nevertheless, they had their full share of experiences as an ethnic group in America. This dimension of their lives is described in the following extracts taken from Jerome Davis, *Russians and Ruthenians in America*. Below, he records the impressions of the Ruthenians as a subculture within a culture, completely isolated from the American people.

> *First impressions.* The majority of Russians and Ruthenians are almost as completely isolated from the American people as if they were in the heart of giant Russia. They have no points of contact with the sound elements of American life. The dream of the Russian as he leaves his native shore is that everything is beautiful in America. It is the land of liberty and equality but he begins to feel that perhaps he has been hoodwinked almost as soon as he reaches Ellis Island. The Russians claim that the coarse and brutal treatment they receive at the immigrant stations is far worse than that in the Russia of the Tsars. Certainly the wholesale tagging of the immigrant, the physical inspection, the turning back of the eyelids, rushed through with machine-like regularity resembles more the inspection of cattle than of thousands of human souls. Only this year Commissioner Wallis, head of the immigrant station at Ellis Island, has complained of the methods of his subordinates who seem to think that an immigrant's time is worth nothing at all. It is small wonder that their first taste of liberty does not appeal. Then as they push on to their destination at Gary, or Pittsburgh, or Chicago, there is no one who tries to help them. I remember meeting two Russians at the Grand Central Station in New York. They were wandering about trying to find out when their train would go. Their inquiries in broken English met no response from the busy ticket agent. They stood beside their bags and baggage, a little picture of Russia in New York. They would ask passers-by about the train but at no time did anyone stop more than to say, "We don't know." One richly dressed woman replied as she would to a dog, "Get away from me." The look on their faces when I helped them showed how deep their perplexity and apprehension had been.
>
> Indeed, the treatment at Ellis Island and in the railroad trains frequently awakens other sentiments than love for the new home. The immigrant has to learn at once the dangers of exploitation which await him. If he goes into the railroad dining room he is usually hustled out. If he follows the advice of a seemingly kind friend as to where to eat he is often robbed of his money. Sometimes his baggage is stolen, and there have even been cases of the abduction of his daughter or wife before he has been on American soil twelve hours. At best, the first impressions of America are discouraging because the treatment of a vast throng of incoming strangers has not yet been put on a friendly enough basis. We still are doing largely only the things that will safeguard America from undesirables and not enough genuinely to help the foreigner.[19]

He describes the hardship of bearing a Russian or Ruthenian name during the time of American animosity toward Russia.

> *Real Americanization.* Real Americanization is a spiritual thing. It means that the Russian or Ruthenian loves our country and is willing to sacrifice in its behalf. This love can be created only by his experiencing that which is worthy of loyalty and sacrifice. If you are traveling to England your opinion of that country is determined by your experience with the English. It rests with them more than it does with you. In the same, only in a more intensified way, because the Russian does not speak our language and knows little of our history or traditions, he must judge America on his own contacts with our people.
>
> Furthermore, after the scare about Russian Bolsheviks had been widely flaunted by our press, the Russians began to be laid off right and left simply on account of their nationality. The inevitable result was that whereas these men had been good honest workers they became embittered and radical. This is expressed in a letter of an educated Russian from Worcester, Mass.: "Many thousands of Russians in this country while they work have hardly enough to live on, and now that the war is ended, they are discharged from factories, and told, 'you are a Bolshevik.' Many of them do not know what Bolshevism and what capitalism mean but they make real Bolsheviks out of them." Several large firms frankly told me that they refused employment to Russians. "We can get plenty of other nationalities," said one employer, "why take Bolsheviks?" Unfortunately from the standpoint of the Russian worker, it does not seem quite so fair. He comes to our country, works seven years in the steel plant, loses his best strength in the work and then is laid off because the Bolsheviks seize control in Russia. Can one wonder if some give up the struggle? On the bodies of two such Russians who were found dead on the railroad track, this explanation was found, "We prefer death to starvation. Have worked in the hell of a steel plant for seven years. Now they discharge us and we can't find a job."[20]

1. Henryk Sienkiewicz, *Portrait of America, Letters of Henry Sienkiewicz*, ed. and trans. by Charles Morley (New York: Columbia University Press, 1959), pp. 272-73.

2. Ibid, pp. 274-79.

3. *Zgoda*, 21 November 1881.

4. They hoped to bring all of their faithful into the same mold, especially as far as language was concerned, so that all would end up using English throughout. Some wanted to go further and eliminate religious customs and traditions brought over from the old country. The bishops advocating "Americanism" were usually trying to erase the stigma of foreignness that American Protestants often leveled against the Catholic Church.

5. *Milwaukee Sentinel*, 8 September 1905.

6. Daniel S. Buczek, *Immigrant Pastor*, Waterbury, 1974, pp. 55-56.

7. Reprinted from Victor R. Greene, *The Slavic Community on Strike*, (Notre Dame, 1968), p. 40.

8. From the book *American from Hungary* by Emil Lengyel, pp. 127, 128. Copyright © 1948 by Emil Lengyel. Reprinted by permission of J.B. Lippincott Company.

9. Reprinted from George Leibbrandt, "The Emigration of the German Mennonites from Russia to the United States and Canada, 1873-1880", Part II, *The Mennonite Quarterly Review* 7 (January 1933): 36-37; with an extract from U.S., Department of Agriculture, *Classification of American Wheat Varieties*, Bulletin No. 1074, 1922.

10. Reprinted from Jerome Davis, *The Russian Immigrant* (New York; Macmillan, 1922), pp. 98, 99.

11. Reprinted from Edward T. Devine, "Family and Social Work" in Jerome Davis, *The Russians and Ruthenians in America* (New York: Doran, 1922), p. 33-35.

12. Reprinted from United Hebrew Charities, *Twentieth Annual Report* (1886), pp. 16-17.

13. L. Hersch, Le Juit Errant d'Aujourd'hui (Paris: M. Giard and E. Briese, 1913), p. 130 *et seq.*

14. Reprinted from Anzia Yezierska, *Children of Loneliness* (New York: Funk & Wagnalls 1923) pp. 17-18.

15. Reprinted from Edmund Jane James (ed.), *The Immigrant Jew in America* (New York. 1907), p. 40.

16. Reprinted from Irving Howe, "Abe Cahan," *Commentary*, March 1970, p. 88.

17. Reprinted from Michael Gold, *Jews without Money* (New York: Liveright, 1930), pp. 13.

18. Reprinted from Wasyl Halich: *Ukrainians in the United States* (Chicago: University of Chicago Press, 1937), pp. 28-29.

19. From Davis, *Russians and Ruthenians in America*, pp. 104-106.

20. Ibid., p. 109.

KEY QUESTIONS

1. Explain the distinction between "old" and "new" immigration. Were there any connotations implicit in the use of such terms? Discuss.

2. Describe the mass of Russian immigration in terms of the following: when they came to the United States; why they came; where they located in the United States.

3. To what extent were the East European Jewish immigrants exploited in America upon their arrival at the turn of the twentieth century?

4. Compare the ethnic experiences of the Ukrainians and the Ruthenians in the United States.

5. In light of the readings, how would you evaluate the new immigrants from Eastern and East Central Europe in regard to their alleged foreign "nationalism" and their attitudes toward their new country?

6. Discuss the social institutions which seemed most significant to the new immigrants after their arrival in the United States.

7. In what respects was there discrimination against the new immigrants from Eastern and East Central Europe in the United States? Discuss fully.

8. What role did religion play in the lives of the immigrants from Eastern and East Central Europe?

FOUR

The Mediterranean Peoples:
The Italians, Greeks and Portuguese

(The "new immigration" label was placed on the bulk of newcomers to the United States in the late nineteenth century. Encompassing a pejorative connotation, the term reflected a view among native Americans that the kinds of new immigrants entering the country were strange, different, and difficult to assimilate—perceptions that perdured well into the twentieth century, indeed even to the present. Of a certainty, immigrants originating from countries bordering the Mediterranean Sea represented increased diversity. Arriving in an unfamiliar society with little or no knowledge of its languages and customs, they were expected to find their own place in society without benefit of special services from either federal or state governments.*)*

Most of the foreigners were fed into the country from the federal government's hopper at Ellis Island, with many of them intending to remain in New York City. When Americans thought about these people at all, they thought of them as "problems." As members of the new immigration they became stereotypes for the "undesirable citizens." Yet they were vital to the development of the nation's burgeoning industries, supplying physical strength and bodily labor for digging ditches for the great waterways, for working the mines, and for manning the blast furnaces. Many of these foreign workers came through the funnel of the padrone system, a method of immigrant recruitment first developed in southern Italy but used effectively among Greeks and Syrians as well. Under this system, labor bosses rounded up young Italians and transported them to America in near-servile conditions, for employment. The practice soon was outlawed and practically ceased to exist by the 1880s.

Many other agencies, such as steamship lines, railroad companies, and state-sponsored drives for emigrants operated as influences in the migration; yet the underlying forces were the same that had brought over the first great wave of immigration in the period prior to 1815, that is, religious and political discontent and especially desire for economic opportunities.

One must not overlook the official temper of the nations from which these Mediterranean immigrants came. For the first two-thirds of the nineteenth century, their governments opposed emigration if they did not prohibit it. But after Italy achieved unification in the 1860s and as large parts of the ancient Ottoman Empire freed themselves from Moslem rule, official restraint eroded. The pressures of a vastly changing agrarian economy and the ending of feudalistic practices served as expulsive forces that compelled governments now to eye emigration as a solution to situations of chronic poverty and overpopulation. What is to be remembered as well is that not only were the lands of emigration changing but so was America herself. For the Italian, the Greek, and the Portuguese, this presented additional problems of adjustment.

THE ITALIANS

Italy is one of modern history's classic examples of an emigrating country. Compared to most of the other major countries of Western Europe—Great Britian, Ireland, Norway, and Germany—Italy entered the field of emigration at a relatively late date in history. What it lacked in terms of longevity, however, it made up for in numbers. By 1900, six million Italians had emigrated to various countries. This figure would be eclipsed by an even greater number in the twentieth century. While many of these people became return immigrants to their homeland, several million found new homes in new countries, with the largest number (over five million) entering the United States.

In the early period of Italian immigration most of the emigrants came from regions such as Venezia and Liguria, in Northern Italy. Later, during the accelerated period of immigration, the Southern portion of the peninsula (La Campagna and Sicily) provided the bulk. The very size of Italian immigration posed a threat to native Americans, and thus the Italians quickly became the stereotype of the undesirable element. Indeed, much of the force behind restrictive immigration laws, such as literacy tests and the quota system, was aimed at them. While some of these immigrants came from the artisan and factory-trained class, most were versed in agriculture as farmers, foresters, workmen, and shepherds, a type of work for which they would find few outlets in the United States.

The causes of their departure from their homeland were primarily economic. They inhabited one of the most densely populated nations in Europe; industrial development was retarded; and the overworked soil continually presented the country with health crises such as malaria. While Italians emigrated to escape from hunger, they also fled from the rural padroni to whose privileged position they owed ancient social deference. Thus, egalitarian principles intermingled with economic. It is also notable that numerous Italian public officials regarded emigration as a favorable solution to various Italian economic, social, and political problems.

The experience of the early immigrants was one of shock. They were confronted with a different and higher standard of living and with unfamiliar customs in lands vastly dissimilar to the provinces from which they came. Life in the alien lands was very trying at best. This caused one astute observer to remark:

> The Italian immigrant who does not become a delinquent or crazy—is a saint. No immigrant is normal; and America is a land of immigrants who do not speak the original tongue, nor follow its religion and its political habits and its social diversions, is in fact full of the abnormal. . . .[1]

Thus Italians found themselves marginal men in an unfriendly land, or if included in the new society, it was in the most elemental way, as in the underworld. But the majority of Italians had little to do with criminality, even if they did not oppose it strenuously. The majority worked long hours in humble occupations.

The Italian immigrant experienced tribulation at every step along the way. The emigrant ship in which he was borne was buffeted by rough seas, his courage was smothered by the crowds of immigrants, and he found no surcease of his difficulties upon reaching the American shore. He was now compelled to look for work, seek living quarters in towns and cities totally foreign to him, confront people with strange and even antithetical modes of dress, and communicate in an unfamiliar language, difficult at best to learn, especially for housewives. In order to cope with these handicaps, most Italians banded together in colonies which came to be known as "Little Italies," e.g., East Harlem, the Lower East Side of New York City, or the North End of Boston. Infrequently did the immigrant leave the place of debarkation. This meant taking up residence in the industrial towns and cities along the eastern seaboard. It meant also that he would have little opportunity to practice his agricultural expertise, although he would have the opportunity to change his trade, and the comforting advantage of living next to his compatriots.

A smaller but significant number did, however, seek their fortunes in the regions west of the Mississippi River, and they seemed to experience important improvement in their living circumstances, despite encountering prejudice and adversity. It is to be remembered that in 1891 eleven Italians were hanged by a lynch mob in New Orleans and the same fate visited other Italians in the mining sections of Colorado.[2]

Not all Italians in the East remained in the "Little Italies." A minority energetically sought complete transformation of their lives rather than transplantation. They quickly learned the English language, intermarried with Anglo-Saxons, moved into non-Italian neighborhoods, scrupulously avoided contact with the old Italian compatriots, and changed their names and even their religion in their desire to be accepted. Most, however, had a conscious desire to transplant their old way of life to the New World. The first generation carried on their lives in the Italian language, shopped in Italian stores, read Italian newspapers, cooked Italian meals, went to Italian plays and movies, and continued Italian religious practices (this usually meant practices and devotions germane to a particular region of Italy). The second generation took greater strides into Americanization. They adopted American customs more readily at the expense of Italian culture and language. This often caused deep linguistic and cultural strains between first and second generation Italian-Americans. The second generation also produced individuals of some influence in American life: prominent political figures on state and local levels such as F. H. LaGuardia and Vito Marcantonio, union and industrial leaders such as Luigi Antonini of the ILGWU and the DiNapoli brothers in the construction industry, and various practitioners in the medical and legal professions.

The tenacity with which Italians held onto their culture was only one side of the picture, however. Thus, the Italo-American came to speak a language that was neither pure Italian nor pure English, but rather a combination. "Grosseria" became a new word for the grocery, "fruttistanne" for fruit stand, "ghella" for girl, and so forth. In a similar manner Italian culture has undergone great dissolution among Italian Americans. A true fusion of Italian and American has not yet taken place. Somehow the Italian Americans have not become fully assimilated but neither have they retained Italian culture. Language, the key to the maintenance of ties with the mother country, has not been extensively learned or cultivated by the newer generation of Italians in America. Nevertheless, ethnicity is still a force among many Italian Americans; they continue to socialize (not exclusively) with Italian Americans, and they take a certain pride in their ancient heritage in a kind of mystical way. At the very least they take serious umbrage at the popular notion that somehow Italians are more connected with or susceptible to criminal activities than other national groups by the mere fact of their Italian background. Thus, although greatly diluted, the persistence of ethnicity among Italians in America is an ongoing phenomenon.

One of the earliest and most complete historians of Italian emigration was Robert F. Foerster. His study runs the gamut of topics under which emigration can be studied. It also gives substance to the central theme of ethnicity that accompanied and developed among the Italians in America. In the first selection, Foerster relates the role of the Italians in industry. He demonstrates the way one ethnic group succeeds another—in this case the Italians replaced the Irish as longshoremen and railroad workers. This selection also includes evaluations of the Italians as workers (often unfavorably) and the impairment they suffered as a result of industrial accidents.

South Italians almost entirely, they first found employment on the New York waterfront about 1887. Between 1890 and 1892 they increased, and by 1896 promised to threaten the supremacy of Irish and Irish-Americans. By 1912 they had become a close second to these older groups, and had forced them to speculate, or even confidently to predict, that within ten years the Italians would stand first. . . .

It is worth noting that they have been inducted into the industry by contracting stevedores of their own people, who have usually withheld a part of their wages by way of commission. Because of this deduction and because their employment has commonly been less regular than that of the Irish, their earnings, in the period about 1912, were generally as little as $10 or $12 a week.

What is characteristic in the labor of Italian men in North America is nowhere so apparent as on the railways. Both relatively and absolutely, the South Italians, as construction and repair workmen, have there achieved a foremost position. The censuses are but blind aids to tracing these elusive armies. It is true that the category of general steam-railway employees gives to the Italians an altogether exceptional place, but it embraces only a part of them, while the others are mainly and indistinguishably collected in the group of general laborers. . . .

The Italians have succeeded as the predominant unskilled railway laborers of the country. Other people have played important parts—the Chinese, Germans, negroes, Slavs, and Hungarians, more recently the Mexicans and Japanese—but Irish and Italians, in successive epochs, have led all. Thirty odd years ago, when rag pickers and street musicians still seemed to many the very quintessence of Italian immigration, the pick-and-shovel laborers were silently being carried to the remoter places and set to work on the railways. A decade later, a contemporary non-statistical view held that "the Irish have ceased building railroads and doing the hard work of constructing public works. The Italians have taken their place." . . .

In an actual test made by this company to determine the efficiency of Italian laborers, they were shown to have performed in a given time only from 35 percent to 50 percent of the same work done by native laborers.

What clearly emerges from this study is that the Italians are employed in great numbers partly because they are to be had, while other workmen are not, and partly because, in certain kinds of work especially, and with due organization and oversight, they produce good results. While demonstrating less power in accomplishment than some of their harder-fibered predecessors, they have been willing to fag in isolated places for many hours in the day. . . .

A constant source of bodily impairment or death is industrial accident. The occupational concentration of the Italians is precisely such as to subject them to risk; for few are in agriculture or the commercial callings, and many work in an environment of rocks, heavy machinery, sharp implements, and the elemental motive powers. Blasting, concrete mixing, coal gases, and the dangerous seams of coal mines dispose, typically, to many accidents. Ignorance of spoken English, inability to read, fatigue, that uncultivated intelligence which, after a mishap, is only too easily called carelessness, complicate the risk. . . . Now and then, as at Cherry, Illinois, and Dawson, New Mexico, a single accident may destroy a hundred or more Italians. No one can say how many industrial injuries or deaths take place each year in the length and breadth of the land. No one can say how many of those who escape injury in one year will not meet it in five or ten years, or twenty. Once it happened commonly that the worker was known to his employer only by number, so that identificaton was impossible, and friends were uninformed; and even today this occurs, or Pasquale suffers a sea change into Pat![3]

Foerster examines the dualistic aspect of Americanization.

What few Italians understand before they come to the United States—and I speak especially of those who will linger or stay permanently—is that a mysterious process of unmaking and remaking will take place in them. In the older persons the inevitable resistance is greater than in the young. But all have come a long way, and their die is cast. Children of circumstance, they are under a spell of suggestion which makes them fertile ground for the seeds of assimilation—to good elements of our life or bad. America would "Americanize" them. But "Americanization" is a two-edged sword. Some the prodigious conflict will strengthen, others it will weaken. All that moral support that men derive from religious and social ties with the group they have grown up with is imperilled when they find themselves in the maelstrom of a strange land. The Italians are rural dwellers dropped into the unaccustomed brutal parts of great cities. The fascination of the new home may be unwholesome, but it is keen. For many the destiny is one of loneliness, disappointment, demoralization, sometimes transitional in its stay, but often enduring. The immigrant has pressed his steps into a "one-way street."[4]

The Italian laborers are seen as competitors and threats to the nativeborn.

He takes a low wage; even, according to a charge that is common and, I believe, sometimes well founded, a lower wage than others would require for equivalent work. Such is his tractability that strikes for increase of wages and all bargaining for better conditions are through his presence less likely to succeed, and so the general condition remains poor. That employers make capital out of racial rivalries, playing off "Wop" against "Hunkie," for example, and so preventing a united labor front, is well enough established. To American laborers the procedure has naturally been obnoxious, and they have perhaps been more willing to regard the Italian as blameworthy than as victimized. Equally they dislike the Italian's readiness to pay commissions for jobs and to accept a loss from a loose calculation of time served—for example, to take pay for 29½ hours when the work has lasted 30.

Italians have often been strike breakers. They helped to defeat the Pennsylvania coal strike of 1887–88. A few took employment during the longshoremen's strike of 1887, and their increasing numbers became the employers' means of preventing further trouble. The immediate cause of the introduction of Italians into the New York clothing industry is declared to have been the employers' desire to escape trade-union demands. With other workers they helped to break the Chicago meat packing strike of 1904. . . . During the war years, with the tremendous enhancement of the bargaining power of labor, Italians have frequently participated in strikes and at times, as in the case of the coal heavers of the New York piers in 1917, they were the first to quit work.[5]

The reception Italians received in some parts of the United States was violent even to the point of death. The most notorious of these instances was the lynching and shooting of eleven Sicilians in Louisiana in 1891. Against a backdrop of vendettas and violence over control of the local fruit trade, the New Orleans public was sensitive to criminal activities amidst its Italian population. When David Hennessey, the local police chief, was murdered, the public was led to believe that it was surely a crime perpetrated by recent immigrants from Sicily. In vigilante fashion, scores of Italians were arrested and a number were put on trial. Of the latter six were acquitted and a mistrial was declared in the case of three others. The judicial decision, however, only served to anger the populace which took matters into its own hands and killed eleven of them boasting that they had served society well. The following newspaper account reveals the anti-Italian sentiments of a lawyer who led the mob in its vigilantism.

"Your name is very much before the public just now," the correspondent remarked, as he was offered a seat.

"Yes; we had a thirty-minute experience that Saturday," he said with a smile. "The most wonderful thing about it is that it was over so soon. I take more credit for that than anything else." . . .

"Meaning that you would be ready to kill the prisoners."

"That was the feeling, we understood, of the public pulse. On Saturday I came to my office at 8:45, and at 9:45 started for the rendezvous at our friend's room. I was a little ahead of time. Four or five of us went from there to the statue, where we found a muttering mob of many thousands. We walked around outside the railings two or three times to give our own people a chance to fall in. Then I went through the gate of the railings and up the steps. As soon as I took off my hat the people began to cheer. I don't remember exactly what I said, but I made a little speech telling them we had a duty to perform; that it was the most terrible duty I had ever undertaken; that the law had miscarried, and that we were prepared to do whatever they desired. They shouted, 'Come on!'"

"What did you understand from that?"

"That we were to go to the prison."

"Did anybody say so in so many words?". . .

"The crowd was composed of lawyers, doctors, bankers, and prominent citizens generally. It was the most obedient crowd you ever saw. They obeyed me implicitly, just as if I was a military commander. If there was any riff-raff it was all on the outside. The intention had been not to shoot any of them—about fifty of them—they got very furious, and after the first taste of blood it was impossible to keep them back."

"If you did not mean to shoot, why did you take the guns?"

"Because we did not know what resistance we might encounter from the officers in charge—from anybody. We meant to get into the prison, and we would have burned it down if necessary."

"Did you kill anybody with your own hands?"

"No, I did not fire a shot. . . .

"Did it not strike you as not courageous to shoot the lot of unarmed men in a hole?"

"Well," said the young lawyer, quietly, "there was no doubt of the courage of any man in our party. Of course, it is not a courageous thing to attack a man who is not armed, but we looked upon these as so many reptiles. Why, I was told that on Friday, after the verdict, the Italian fruit and oyster schooners along the wharfs hoisted the sicilian flag over the stars and stripes, and the prisoners themselves had an oyster supper."

"Do you regret what you have done?" asked the correspondent after a pause.

"Not a bit," said Parkerson, promptly.[6]

Although anti-Italian sentiments began to change, progress was slow and asocial behavior frequently reappeared. In the highly emotional atmosphere of the early 1920s, prestigious journals such as the *Saturday Evening Post* became notorious for its biased sallies against Americans of Italian descent. It provided ample opportunity for writers whose prejudice caused American readers to conclude that Italians were among the lowest of creatures. In attempting to counter this stereotyping, Luigi Carnovale, an Italian American, published an article designed to demonstrate the important contributions Italians were already making to America. It is of some value to read excerpts from his account.

A conscientious writer ought to set forth not only the "cons" but also the "pros," that is to say, the favorable as well as the unfavorable, especially when subjects of such vital social importance are concerned. Otherwise the reader only sees one side of the truth (if the truth exists in Elizabeth Frazer's article), and it is upon this one and only side that he bases his opinion on the subject discussed by a careless and unjust writer. . . .

I believe I know the Italian immigrants of the United States well enough, having studied their situation for a long time and having published a book covering my impressions entitled. *"The Journal of the Italian Immigrants in North America,"* (Chicago) therefore, I venture to set forth a few facts quite contrary to the foolish, misleading and slanderous assertions of Elizabeth Frazer.

For instance, there are hundreds of thousands of Italians in the United States who are naturalized American citizens.

In agriculture, the industries, in commerce, finance, politics, sports, science, art and education, in fact, in all fields of American activity the Italian immigrants have demonstrated in the past, and will demonstrate more and more, that they know how to Americanize themselves and assimilate to the fullest extent that which America offers them. . . .

Furthermore, the immigrants of today are not like the ones of the old days, to whom, no doubt, Elizabeth Frazer refers with such posthumous zeal.

Immigration: The American Commissioner of Immigration at Ellis Island is an Italian, Mr. Caminetti, who has held the office for years.

Labor: The members of the American labor organizations are a good part Italians.

Agriculture: The vineyards, the orange and lemon orchards, the very finest of their kind in this country, were grown and developed to their present state by Italian immigrants and are in their hands.

Industries: The Boston fisheries, considered among the most important in the United States, were established and developed to their present flourishing state by Italian immigrants and are in their hands. . . .

I could mention many other facts to prove that the Italian immigrants desire and know how to Americanize themselves, that they desire and know how to assimilate the best America has to offer them by securing for themselves American positions of such importance, and in every field imaginable, as to be envied by those Americans whose individuality Elizabeth Frazer so highly praises. Such positions are attained by Italian immigrants notwithstanding the disadvantages they suffer due to the difference in language and more than anything else, to the cruel prejudice held against them such as those found in the lines of Elizabeth Frazer's article.

However, I still want to call attention to the many marriages between high class Americans and Italians in America, which naturally indicates that Italian immigrants do become naturalized American citizens, and, that they assimilate the good America offers to them.

In addition, there is not an Italian newspaper in the United States that does not continually preach to Italian immigrants the gospel of Americanization.

At any rate, if the Italian quarters of any city lack cleanliness the fault lies particularly with the American health authorities who neglect such quarters and do not enforce, with the necessary vigor the observance of the laws covering public hygiene.

One should not entirely condemn the ignorant, the humble, the poor, and insist that they should spontaneously uplift themselves. Instead, the learned and the rich, who generally neglect the ignorant and the poor, should extend to them a helping hand in order to uplift them to a higher standard of living. This ought to be the mission of real civilization.

This is the most sacred and most beautiful mission that America has to accomplish, since she believes herself, nowadays, to be the leading nation of the world.[7]

The religious pattern that emerged for many Italian families who migrated to the United States was often antagonistic to their ancient Catholic religion. For these people who had migrated from their small, peaceful villages, countryside, or mountaintop and who were accustomed to measure their daily routine by the sound of the church bell, the experience of being thrust into the hustle and bustle of a huge and alien metropolis proved to be disturbing and disorienting. A number of them either rebelled or developed habits in which their ties to the Catholic Church atrophied. The experience of Bella V. Dodd, a one-time prominent Communist and later famous convert to her original religion, is perhaps reflective of the pattern that emerged.

We had neighbors all about us—Scotch, Irish, and German families. There were two Catholic churches not far from us. . . . We did not seem to belong to either church and Father and Mother soon ceased to receive the Sacraments and then stopped going to church. But Mother still sang songs of the saints and told us religious stories from the storehouse of her memories.

Though we still considered ours a Catholic family, we were no longer practicing Catholics. Mother urged us children to go to church but we soon followed our parents' example. I think my mother was self-conscious about her poor English and lack of fine clothes. Though the crucifix was still over our beds and Mother burned vigil lights before the statue of Our Lady, we children got the idea that such things were of the Italian past and we wanted to be Americans. Willingly, and yet not knowing what we did, we cut ourselves off from the culture of our own people and set out to find something new.[8]

Almost from the outset of the tidal wave of immigration from Italy, a number of individuals became alarmed at the deplorable religious conditions of the transplanted Italians. At the forefront was Bishop John Scalabrini, whose concern for their material and spiritual welfare prompted him to establish first the St. Raphael Society and then the Missionary Society of St. Charles. Highly conscious of the ethnic sensitivities of the Italian people, the priests of the order made a deep impression among large segments of the Italian population in America. They exhorted their people to remain united in spirit with the land of their birth, while at the same time they fostered a respect for the culture of the new land. They opened national parishes and parochial schools and thereby provided a sense of security for their ethnic group as it began the long journey into the mainstream of American life.

In sum, the experience of the national parishes and their schools served to disprove the conclusion that they hampered assimilation. Quite the contrary, they educated the immigrants and their children to adjust themselves to life in the United States and to become citizens of whom they could be proud.

The national parishes and their schools also sought to keep Italians within the Catholic fold, where for the most part they have remained, although not entirely. But the type of Catholicism which most Italian Americans follow today is a somewhat different model from that which reflected the cultural forms of their forebears. This is the conclusion of one of the more recent observers of Italians on the American scene.

> The greater part of Italians remained at least nominally faithful to the Church. They thus contributed in large measure to the numerical enrichment of American Catholicism without, however, constituting a driving force within it. In other words, Italians have not reached in the American Church the prominence they knew how to attain in other fields. The judgment is valid from the cultural viewpoint and as regards church government. If attenuating circumstances surround the cultural—not the least the priority, given the times, that action had over study—there is no justification for the second, at least not one imputable to Italo-American clergy.
>
> At the end of 1950 not one of the more than 200 American bishops, both residential and titular, was Italian. At the beginning of 1973, only nine bishops were of Italian origin. This is all the more surprising if one remembers that 3/5 ths or so of the Italo-Americans have remained practicing Catholics. . . .
>
> In the long run the Irishman won. Italians of the third and fourth generations are today fully integrated into a Catholicism which was formed more or less on the Irish model. From the end of World War II on, many Italians left the cities, and thus the national parishes, to settle in the suburbs where they have been subjects even more to Hibernization. This is evidenced by the fact that when after Vatican Council II, almost a clean sweep was made of saints' statues, the descendants of those who had so lovingly sent them from Italy did not show much resentment.[9]

THE GREEKS

In most of the important realms of thought—for example, the arts, government, and science—Western civilization has been inspired by the long and glorious history of ancient Greece. The apogee of Greek civilization, however, was followed by decline and subjugation until in 1827 Greece again gained its independence. Its experience with an autocratic monarchy proved to be a disappointment and led to important changes in the Greek government throughout the latter part of the nineteenth century. During that period Greece continued to grow with the accretion of various islands. By the end of the nineteenth century emigration to the United States also became an important feature of Greek society. Admiration for the United States was traceable to Greek gratefulness for American interest and sympathy as the Greeks struggled for independence early in the nineteenth century and to concern for the welfare of Greeks on the island of Crete in the later-nineteenth-century struggle between the Greeks and Turks of that island.

But there were other factors affecting Greek emigration to America. One of the influences was domestic Greek politics in the later nineteenth and early twentieth centuries. Since Greece's entry into the modern world was of relatively recent vintage and since its existence as an independent entity came later than the establishment of the nations of Western and Central Europe, traditional spiritual and economic influences persisted for years after its liberation. The force of Pan-Hellenism emboldened Greece to try to bring under one banner all the Greeks scattered over other parts of Asia Minor and the fading Ottoman Empire. The consequence was numerous conflicts between Greece and neighboring states like Turkey and Bulgaria. Caught in the vortex of these conflicts, many Greek inhabitants of these other countries came to America to escape oppression and persecution.

Unfavorable economic conditions constituted probably the greatest reason for Greek emigration to American shores. A mountainous nation with a primarily farming population, the Greek peninsula was in a backward state. For those aspiring to middle-class status, the home country offered limited possibilities for economic advancement, although a relative degree of prosperity had been reached by the early 1980s. However, before the turn of the century European markets for Greek currants collapsed. For many an enterprising Greek peasant, who despaired of a life of unrewarding toil on the farm which he often did not own, the solution was to migrate to the towns or to embark for the United States. Moreover, as in the case of other immigrants, many had been misled by letters from earlier immigrants from their homeland which exaggerated the ease with which one could achieve economic solvency and security. Even social customs like the dowry system played their role in promoting emigration to America. The custom of expecting substantial dowries from prospective brides often obligated faithful fathers and brothers to secure sizable amounts of money for daughters or sisters, and often this could best be realized by economic opportunities in the United States.

Add to these conditions the desire to avoid military service and the love of adventure that seemed to come naturally to the Greeks, and there emerges a picture of a lively emigration to the United States commencing in the 1890s. In all, over 500,000 Greeks came to live in this country, the peak of immigration coming between 1900 and 1920 when 351,720 transplanted their culture to the Western Hemisphere. (It is to be noted that overall totals are estimates rather than fixed, accurate figures.)

Many of the first emigrants were from the peasant class, mostly illiterate and poor, primarily young men, single or married. They were soon followed by cultivated and educated classes. Despite his background of the soil, the Greek immigrant found it preferable to live in the cities. In a new land, these people faced many hurdles, one of the foremost being the language barrier. Because of this obstacle many Greeks worked at lowly tasks in America, as street vendors or common laborers. Many Greek Americans found their employment through the padrone system, which has been described by the historian Theodore Saloutos as "a modernized version of the indentured-servant system."

The common action of most Greeks on coming to America was to take up residence in a Greek colony. These were distinctive ethnic enclaves within the heart of some of the major American communities. Often this takeover of a geographic region by an ethnic group was accomplished by dispossession of another ethnic group. The new group then started its own ethnic organizations and changed the lifestyle from the previous ethnic orientation to the new one. The way this was accomplished by the Greeks is discussed in the selection below, wherein Fairchild describes the process by which the Greeks replaced the Italians in a section of Chicago early in the twentieth century.

The Greek Colony of Chicago

Five years ago if a visitor to Chicago had alighted from a Blue Island Avenue street car at Polk Street, and had wandered around the neighborhood, along these two streets and South Halsted and Ewing Streets, he might almost have imagined that he was in Italy. The stores, the houses, the people, the sights and sounds all would have suggested a distinctly Italian character. Within the space of five years, an ethnic revolution has been worked in this district, until today it is just as distinctively Greek. Here, in the section of which Hull House is the social center, are gathered the greater part of the 15,000 Greeks who call Chicago their home.

Taking all things into consideration, Chicago is probably the oldest and most important Greek colony in the United States. Here, too, the Greeks have developed their characteristic industries to the fullest extent. Yet the Greek invasion of Chicago is comparatively a recent thing. In 1882 there were very few Greeks in the city, not enough to have a community of their own. But they united with the Slavs to form the "Graeco Slavic Brotherhood," and secured a Greek priest. . . .

As the Greeks became more numerous they began to do what they do in almost every city where they form considerable settlements—they invaded the Italian section and drove the Italians out of their homes and out of their businesses. The district which has been mentioned, around Blue Island Avenue and Polk and South Halsted Streets, is today more typically Greek than some sections of Athens. Practically all the stores bear signs in both Greek and English, coffeehouses flourish on every corner. . . .[10]

Fairchild goes on to express open skepticism about successful Greek (and other) assimilation in the United States. Although a scholar, he placed more emphasis on immigrants' environmental handicaps, poverty, ignorance, and intense nationalism than on their capabilities. To that extent he exemplified the sense of superiority common to the typical Anglo-Saxon of his day.

The great question which, in the case of the Greeks, as well as of every other class of our alien population, is of vital importance and interest to the country, is, Will they make good citizens? The answer to this depends primarily upon one's individual opinion of what is a good American citizen. Some writers go so far as to intimate that there is no such thing as a distinctive American citizen. A large proportion of our population seems to look upon the ideal American citizen as the man who tends strictly to business, makes money, lets other people severely alone and expects them to do the same. If we adopt this point of view, we can have little hesitation in saying that the Greeks answer the requirements, for as we have seen, they are distinctly a money-making class in this country, and if some of the methods by which they do it will not bear investigation—that is nobody's business, according to the hypothesis.

But if we look at the matter more broadly, and think of the ideal American citizen as one who has the higher and better interests of himself, his neighbor and his country at heart, and who believes that he ought to contribute to the general betterment of his community during his lifetime, and give at least as much as he gets—from this point of view the answer to the question is much less certain. In this respect, the effect of the immigrant upon the country is the effect of the country upon the immigrant, viewed from a different angle. If the immigrant finds his change of residence an advantage, if he prospers morally and socially as well as financially, the chances are that he will give back to the country something in return for what he gets. But if the conditions in which he finds himself placed in his new home are such as to cause him to preserve, or even increase, any low ideals, vicious habits or degenerate propensities that he may have, he is, by so much, a hindrance to the country of his adoption.

As far as the Greeks are concerned, at least, it seems undeniable that the determination of the question, into which of these two categories the immigrant shall go, is largely a matter of distribution. It has been frequently remarked in the course of the preceding discussion, that the evil tendencies of Greek life in this country manifest themselves most fully when the immigrants are collected into compact, isolated, distinctively Greek colonies, and that when the Greek is separated from the group and thrown into relations with Americans of the better class, he develops and displays many admirable qualities. Our system and machinery for regulating the admission of aliens is very complete and well-organized. But we do practically nothing for them, after they are once inside the border. We talk with smug complacency of the marvelous assimilative power of America. We are, in fact, by no means sure that these great hordes of foreign nationalities are in any true sense assimilated, even after many years of residence in this country.[11]

J. P. Xenides was a Greek-American clergyman who in 1922 wrote a short but sympathetic work entitled *The Greeks in America*. The result of numerous personal visits to Greek-American communities as well as of questionnaires, this offers some valuable observations into various aspects of Greek-American life at the height of the immigration. Xenides comments on the weak hold America had on some Greeks, while most accepted it as a second fatherland. He also discusses how Americanization will affect Greek family life.

The prosperous will stay.—Those who are accustomed to American ways and ideas with all the rush and hustle of life here, with ever-widening fields of enterprise and efficiency, cannot rest satisfied with the quieter and less active life in the Near East. Besides many own houses and other property. Some are engaged in real estate enterprises or other lines of business. Such will never return. One Greek now in real estate business in Wilmington, Del., owns property worth more than $1,000,000 and he is only one of a class of prosperous Greeks, some of whom started from the very bottom and have risen gradually to prosperity.

Working Greeks will return.—It is different with workers in mills and factories and those who cannot feel at home in America. I asked in 1918 scores of Greeks in Syracuse, N.Y., who were from Broosa and its villages in Asia Minor, if any planned to return home. "All of us," they replied. "Who would not go back to his home and his own? We are strangers in a strange land; we do not know the language of the country; neither can we learn it; we are working hard like slaves and then our earnings fly away from us, everything is so dear. At home we have our houses, fields, vineyards, and our relatives and friends are all there."

In general, however, Greeks are well satisfied with America. They love and adore it. They intend to stay here permanently. They call it "Their second fatherland." . . .

Husband and wife.—Greeks are very much devoted to their families. Whatever freedom may be allowed to men during their pre-marital life, it is understood and expected that, after the marriage, a new chapter is to be opened and strictly clean records are to be entered in it. Women of course have always to be exemplary and pure in every way. Divorce is uncommon among the Greeks. Children are numerous and are regarded as blessings and gifts of God. However poor and ignorant parents may be they are anxious to educate their children in good schools.

There is not much data for comparing the first and the second generations, as to family life, but there are many indications that the new generation is getting Americanized and is learning both the good and bad aspects of American life.

Divorce.—A Greek young man was asked: "Would you marry a Greek or an American?" He replied "American." To the question, "Will you be able to agree together and be happy?" "If we do not, then we get divorced," was his emphatic reply. He would never have thought or said so in Greece or Turkey. There marriage is thought of as a matter of harmony and love to last till death.

Children are devoted to their parents and relatives. Young men gladly undergo many troubles and live a life of thrift and self-denial in order to save, and send money to their parents. They pay the old debts of their parents to keep up their good reputation or save paternal in-heritance. They postpone or even forego marriage in order to get their sisters married. Unfortunately the evil custom of dowry continues in the old country. So fathers and brothers working here must save money in order to provide dowry for daughters and sisters. It is a good thing that the custom of dowry is getting broken in America, though not entirely abandoned.

Neighborhood life.—People from the same town or village in Greece are usually drawn together in America too. The newcomers find out first of all the whereabouts of their relatives and fellow countrymen. In fact they may come directly to them, having already corresponded with them. Even those of different towns are very helpful to one another in finding work and if need be helping each other financially and other-wise. They room together; work together; frequent the same coffee-house, club and restaurant. Thus close attachments are formed.

Here people may live in the same neighborhood (even the same house), and not get acquainted with each other. Not so among the Greeks; they easily get acquainted and are friendly and neighborly to one another.[12]

Xenides speculates on the meaning of assimilation.

Forces of Assimilation

Americanization.—A great deal is being said and written regarding the Americanization or assimilation of the immigrants that seems strange. Some of the heated utterances sound like the nationalistic theories of the Pan-Germans or the Pan-Slavists. If the various races are to be forced to forget all their racial peculiarities and characteristic customs, usages, and language, and to adopt American ways instead, the result will be disappointing. Whenever a people is forced to accept, willingly or unwillingly, a certain course of action, the result has usually been the opposite of what was desired.

But if without being interfered with in their cherished customs, ideas, language and traditions, they are surrounded with a genial American atmosphere and are given suitable opportunities to learn American ways, ideas, language and institutions; in short, if they are gradually taught what is good in their new surroundings, while they retain what was good and useful in their former life, all the immigrants will be Americanized in due time.

Even the word "Americanization" sounds strange to many ears; it sounds like suppression, force. Let the immigrant have freedom to contribute his best to the welfare of America. As the various races have brought their national dishes, customs and usages, so let each contribute his peculiar talent and accomplishment in art, letters or business, though he may be deficient in the knowledge of the English language.

Americanization of the children.—Many a simple illiterate immigrant may turn out to be more loyal to America, than the so called cultivated theorists who can chatter, parrot-like, good English, but are unsound in morals and unprincipled in action. It is difficult and in some cases impossible to change the habits of the adults. It is different with the young and the children. They are open to impressions, and the future lies with them. They will all get Americanized through education. The public school is the melting pot where children of all races are being assimilated. Many Greek children who are being educated in American schools, answer their parents in English who speak to them in Greek.

The evening schools are of immense value. Both men and women are attending evening classes, in the public schools, Y.M.C.A. and the various Greek societies.[13]

If it is true that every ethnic-immigrant group transplanted its own unique institutions, then a discussion of the Greek coffeehouse (kaffeneion) is in order. Indeed no Greek community was without its kaffeneion, for it was to the coffeehouse that newly arrived Greeks would repair in order to seek out acquaintances, addresses, jobs, solace, the familiar companionship which cushioned the otherwise solitary feeling experienced in a new land.

Wherever there was a sufficient number of Greeks, the coffeehouse made its appearance. With the minimum of capital, a store could be rented, a few tables and chairs put in place; several pounds of coffee, a few nargilehs, and several decks of playing cards could be purchased—all the necessary appurtenances required for operation. Of course the place would be suitably decorated with pictures of Greek kings and political leaders, victorious battle scenes or historic monuments.

This was the place where men came after a long day's work and on weekends to sip thick black Turkish coffee, smoke nargilehs, and play cards. Here, oblivious to the clouds of the smoke, they animatedly discussed the latest politics and traded the most recent gossip. It was in truth a genuine social center.

Greeks remained an intensely religious people, at least in the early years, with women paying particular attention to Sundays and saints days. Many also went to church on weekdays. The name day—the feast of a saint for whom someone is named—was of special importance to Greeks. In accordance with Old World customs, the name day rather than the birthday was the occasion for family celebrations, replete with music, dancing, and food. In America the tradition continued but with declining regularity.

Other important days in the religious calendar were Christmas, treated more as a religious celebration than a fun-giving day, St. Basil's Day, and Easter. The latter was the most important of all. This was the day that the once-a-year church goers came out.[14]

Greeks continue to emigrate to America, with the newer, post-1960 immigrants manifesting certain differences from the earlier comers. Thus whereas the pre-1960 immigrants came primarily from villages and had little formal education, the more recent arrivals have come mostly from cities and are more educated than their predecessors. The latter, furthermore, tend to be more liberal politically.

Greek-American ethnicity, therefore, is a continuing phenomenon. Although one of the smaller ethnic groups, there are today about a million first- and second-generation Americans of Greek descent. In general they can be divided into three basic groups: the old Greeks, the new Greeks, and the American-born Greeks, each with its own attitudes and lifestyles. About a third of them live in the New York metropolitan area where they have gained the positive attention and approbation of their neighbors. As one newspaper reporter put it:

> In the last few years a strange thing has been noticed by Americans of Greek descent, from the hot-dog vendor on the corner to Telly Savalas—it's chic to be Greek.
> Anyone who can do the syrtaki (Zorba's dance) can gather a crowd at a party. In many cities the gyro sandwich is nearly as common luncheon fare as tuna on rye. While some New York night spots are dying, Greek clubs like Dionysos and Sirocco are packed every night.

It has come as quite a surprise to all those immigrants with the un-
pronounceable names to discover that they are now admired and im-
itated by their fellow Americans.[15]

This acceptance incorporates inevitable stereotypes: free spirits,
unfettered, unneurotic. But the observer is also impressed by a commitment to hard work which has rewarded more than a few with
thriving businesses. It would be misleading, however, to portray
Greek Americans as universally successful. Some who came here and
started out as dishwashers continue in the same job many years later.
Problems of adjustment between two diverse cultures persist, particularly for the second generation. Thus the women's liberation
movement has had little impact within Greek-American enclaves. Life
within these enclaves still revolves largely around the traditional institutions and Greeks in America continue to enjoy the old customs
and pastimes. Name days are still occasions of major celebrations.
Gambling in various coffeehouses for immigrants from different sections of the old country is widespread in the enclave, and the church
continues to be the center of social and religious life. Church-
sponsored dances afford opportunities for young Greek Americans to
meet and form relationships which hopefully will lead to marriages
within the group.

For all their intragroup ethnic life, increasingly large numbers of
Greek Americans are attracted to public life. In recent years this has
led them to become governors of states, mayors of large cities, congressmen, senators and even a vice-president of the United States.
Thus although a small ethnic group, Americans of Greek descent are
making unique contributions to American life.

THE PORTUGUESE

Portugese influence in the United States, although moderate, has
been of long duration. Portuguese explorers charted the California
coast in the sixteenth century, and small numbers of colonists settled
in the eighteenth century. This latter migration was largely from Portugal's Azores Islands, and these early immigrants worked primarily
in the American fishing industry. There are records of some Portuguese migrating to California during the gold rush of 1849.
However, it was not until the last years of the nineteenth century that
a significant number of Portuguese entered this country, with even
greater numbers coming in during the first three decades of the twentieth century. By 1920 Portuguese stock in the United States was

estimated to be 126,000, of whom two-thirds resided in several New England cities. The bulk of the remainder settled in California and Hawaii. The 1940 census gives a figure of 176,407 Portuguese Americans.

Whereas stringent immigration laws limited Portuguese emigration to the United States in the 1930-1960 period, the following decades found impressive increases in the movement. By the end of the 1970s they have come to constitute one of the largest ongoing immigrant groups from the European continent. Altogether statistics show approximately 400,000 Portuguese having emigrated to the United States since 1820. Together with descendants from earlier generations, the Portuguese stock probably numbers a few hundred thousand, although accurate figures are not available.

The social and cultural backgrounds of these people forecast divergencies between them and the majority of older inhabitants in the United States. In addition, Portuguese Americans themselves did not possess homogeneity, as they were composed of several distinct groups. Those from mainland Portugal included Portuguese of Moorish or Negro admixture, while the Flemish element was featured in the Azores. Steeped in backgrounds of agriculture and fishing, a significant number of Portuguese Americans carried on their pursuits in the New World as hardworking farmers in California or in the fishing communities of New England. However, for perhaps most of them the mills in Massachusetts and Rhode Island were the economic support. As for other immigrants, life for these people in a new country was hard. In addition, Portuguese Americans were burdened by other problems—they had an excessive infant mortality rate compared to other nationalities, and they took less advantage of education than most of the other national groups.

Attachment to ethnic Old World patterns continues in many Portuguese American homes. In the areas of language, religion, education, marriage, the family, and social relations, they remain strongly ethnically oriented.

Donald R. Taft's *Two Portuguese Communities in New England*, first published in 1923, is the pioneer work about Portuguese Americans in the English language. Taft concentrated on two communities with a high percentage of Portuguese, Fall River and Portsmouth, one urban, the other rural. He was able to examine the social contacts they had as one of many immigrant elements in Fall River and such contacts as they had with primarily native-born non-Portuguese in Portsmouth. Taft's description of the Portuguese immigrants' first contact with Americans is revealing for its exposure of economic hardship and social isolation.

Contacts with Americans

When the peasant from St. Michael's arrives either in Portsmouth or in Fall River, he finds himself in America but not of America. The innumerable differences between himself and the native-born American isolate him; and this isolation is also promoted by peculiar conditions of the environment in which he finds himself.

In Portsmouth the Portuguese immigrant is fortunate if he begins as a farm laborer for one of the more progressive American farmers or for a fellow-countryman who knows the farming and marketing methods of the community. The Portuguese bring with them patient industry and some knowledge of cultivation, but there is much to learn under new conditions.

Work as a laborer is only an apprenticeship, however, for every true Portuguese is ambitious to farm for himself, and his next step is to rent a farm from a native family where the man has either died or moved to the city. The Portuguese immigrant sends for his wife, if she has not already come, and a life of real isolation begins. This isolation is especially pronounced if he has chosen a farm off from the main highway as is frequently the case. Even then he has some contacts, of course, when he takes his vegetables to market, purchases seed or supplies, or goes to the town hall to procure a license for the inevitable dog. But these contacts are for the new-comer very transitory and he has no share in such active community life as there is. For his wife the isolation is well-nigh complete for she toils all day in the fields, bends over the wash-tub in the yard, or minds or neglects the rapidly accumulating brood of children. About every year she gets a very few days vacation from these occupations to bear another child. Her life is altogether at home and she seldom talks with a native woman and never on the same social plane. As for the children, they run wild until the school age is reached when the mother is only too glad to get them out from under foot until they are strong enough to work in the fields, when their attendance becomes less regular. If a visitor drives up to such a secluded farm house these younger children may be seen peeking out from behind the curtains or from around corners. On the visitor's nearer approach they scurry away like rabbits, to return, perhaps, when the conversation with the mother reassures them. In school, of course, they do learn American ways and see some American children, but there is some evidence that they tend to form separate play groups. In one school, as we shall see, there are but two non-Portuguese children; but this is unusual and to some "Ports" school opens a new world. In general, however, life for the new-comer in Portsmouth is one of isolation. His illiteracy, foreign ways, and inability to speak English would create this isolation even if he were welcomed by the old stock. As compared with some other foreign communities Portsmouth evidences remarkably little open hostility to the Portuguese, but they certainly are not "of" the community which, though fast going to seed, is nevertheless Yankee, Protestant, relatively clean and just a little self-satisfied.

The isolation we have just described applies to new-comers. After considerable time has elapsed and the Portuguese have become semi-"Americanized" the isolation decreases. Not a few Portuguese farmers are respected, some even admired, by the older native stock. One resident of long standing delights in telling of kindly neighborly acts by the Portuguese nearby. On the occasion of illness one of them did all the farm chores for a considerable period and refused to accept payment for his work. The fact, also, that there is but one Catholic church in the town brings the few non-Portuguese Catholics into contact with the Azoreans and contacts reach even the women. . . .[16]

To test the persistency of cultural patterns in the face of acculturative processes, Hans Howard Leder undertook an in-depth study of a Portuguese-American enclave in Bayside, California. As a result of extensive field work, Leder became an active participant in the life of that ethnically heterogeneous community. The typical resident of the area was aware of ethnically identifiable groups, such as Italian Americans or Mexicans, usually living in a given section. Although this residential pattern, presenting a picture of a hermetically sealed people living and working totally within a single neighborhood, did not apply to the area's Portuguese Americans, they nevertheless presented ample examples of ethnic persistence. In the extracts that follow, we see descriptions and evaluations of these people in regard to working practices, for which they were held in high regard; aspects of social life, such as the great emphasis on the *compradrazoo* (godparent system); and the existence of ethnic voluntary organization that satisfied their associative needs.

In the offices of the city's planning commission, where I had gone to obtain general information on the demography of Bayside, the Anglos with whom I discussed this subject definitely felt that, despite their lack of advanced education and their following of "lower status" occupations, the Portuguese-Americans were "definitely middle class," had "high standards" (i.e., morally and ethically), and, in general, were among "the best people in Bayside." Representative of the conversations I am referring to are these excerpts from a talk I had with the planning commission's senior statistician:

We have some younger men of Portuguese descent on the staff here. None in my own department, so I can't tell you anything there that you might want to know. They are not attracted to work of this kind, under these conditions; furthermore, there are not many who are qualified educationally to step in even at a trainee level. . . . There were any number of Portuguese youngsters in my class at High School, but I don't recall that any of them went on to college. They were quiet, polite, did their work. No scholars, but no dunces either. . . . Of course you know a lot more about this than I do, but I would say that most of them, after High School—that is, the group I am familiar with—joined some sort of family enterprise, or followed in their fathers' footsteps. Agriculture is their big vocation. I say "vocation" because that is what it is with them. With the Mexicans—and you could even say with the Italians—a job in agriculture is just that, a job, to work at because nothing else is available. . . . The Portuguese have done their share of stoop labor in California, but with them it was a means to an end. Now you'll see their children out there picking, but on their own land. . . . They have a dignity about their work, whatever it happens to be.

I discussed this one evening with a group of people who had gathered in the Sameiro home to view my slides of Portugal, and there was general agreement with the host's view that

No matter what we might think, when it comes right down to it, where something is really needed—money, advice, I don't care what—the Portuguese will think first of his *compadre*. Or, if it's a young man, of his *padrinho*. Even where there is a rich father, say, or uncle. One big reason is because—to speak for myself and Mr. Freitas, here—because we know that the spirit is the same for both of us.[17]

Portuguese emigration has continued in recent years as these newcomers move not only into the older established ethnic enclaves of yesteryear, but also into the expanding suburban communities. One case in point is that of Mineola, Long Island, New York. The best evidence is that Portuguese began to appear in that community in 1919 when a Portuguese American left the ethnic community in New Bedford, Massachusetts, for the Long Island community. He was soon followed by others so that within a decade a small, but identifiable Portuguese enclave could be detected in Mineola. As a result of changes in the basic immigration laws in 1965, additional Portuguese moved into the suburban locale. The following excerpts discuss the contemporary group life of the four to five thousand Portuguese Americans of Mineola.

Focusing on the Mineola School District for a moment, it should be noted that it now employs a number of bilingual teachers, resource specialists and aides under the direct supervision of Mrs. Florence Band. Each professional involved in the program has it in mind to stress a positive self-concept on the part of the students, as well as work on improving the students' skills in the subject areas in both English and Portuguese. The program is supported by both local and government funding and has the backing of the community and other school personnel. Also of interest is the fact that Adelphi University, with the only full University program of Portuguese Studies in Nassau and Suffolk Counties, is also involved in the Portuguese Community, having sponsored symposia on the Portuguese experience in the U.S. and including Portuguese among the various components of its Bilingual Teacher Training Program. BOCES-Nassau has also been involved in the above. . . .

Family and Tradition

Portuguese family ties in the various Long Island communities are not much different than those of other Portuguese communities. In fact, many characteristics are similar to those of other immigrant groups. The family unit is a very closely-knit one. Each generation still transmits the pride it has in its heritage to succeeding generations. With respect to this matter of identity, we might classify our Portuguese into three groups. The first consists of those who obviously maintain a very strong Portuguese identity, both in public and at home. The second consists of those who maintain a more Americanized appearance in public, but whose home life is traditionally Portuguese. These two groups are by far the largest. The third consists of those who prefer to become totally assimilated into the American way of life and who, while not denying their heritage, do not relate to it as readily as others.

The role of each member of the family is, once again, typically Portuguese. The father is the head of the family and the mother is the one most responsible for maintaining traditions and family ties. She is also a link between families. In describing the parents' attitude towards raising children, strictness would be quite appropriate. The parents are also more protective of and give less liberty to their daughters, while the sons, once attaining a certain age, are somewhat less restricted. One additional characteristic of this family relationship is mutual respect.

The proverbial generation gap exists in the Portuguese community, as it does elsewhere, although more between more recent generations than between the original immigrants and their children. However, this is more of a societal phenomenon and not one which can be characterized as Portuguese.

Within the community, especially on Sundays and holidays, many families continue to get together for large meals and long conversations. It is not uncommon for grandparents, children, and grandchildren to be extremely close, sometimes living near each other and, in some cases, under the same roof. Because it was the aforementioned word of mouth which brought many of Mineola's Portuguese residents together from various parts of the Northeast, not to mention other parts of the world, it is also not uncommon for many families to have numerous members in the community. Ida Paes, the daughter of Mineola Portuguese pioneer Antonio, for example, has sixty-three relatives living in Mineola.

Families tend to continue traditions begun in Portugal. Skills, beliefs, and customs are passed along from generation to generation. Even the celebration of certain events, including Christmas and other holidays, still maintains the touch of old Portugal. Traditions are also maintained where religion is concerned. While the extent to which one family or another actually practices its religion may vary, there is no doubt that the Portuguese people of Mineola can generally be considered religious. Holidays and celebrations, including Nossa Senhora de Fatima, October 13, and Carnival, as well as Christmas and Easter, often center around the Church. In the case of the Portuguese of Mineola, that Church is the Corpus Christi Church on Willis Avenue. It is near the center of the community and has been the "Portuguese Church," as well as that of others, for a long time. However, it was not until September 15, 1976, with appointment of a Portuguese-speaking priest, that thought was given to a regular Sunday morning Portuguese mass. This was begun in February, 1977. It is the goal of Brazilian-born

Father Tomas Gomide to continue this practice and to make the Corpus Christi Church one where Portuguese from different parts of the area will want to come. Father Gomide, who happens to have a Brazilian law degree and a canonical law degree from Rome, is interested in meeting as many needs of the community as possible. He has already begun to do so. The Saint Pius Church in Jamaica also has a Portuguese Mass on Sundays and participates in the yearly festivals of both Sao Caetano, celebrated by the Portuguese of Tras-os-Montes, and Sao Paio, celebrated by those of Murtosa. The Portuguese of the Farmingville area do not yet have a Portuguese Mass, but have expressed the hope of having one in the not too distant future. . . .

No Portuguese community would be complete without its soccer club. Mineola now has two of them. The Mineola Soccer Club is sponsored by the Portuguese American Club and is now more than thirty years old. A more recent addition is the Lusitano Soccer Club, sponsored by a local Portuguese restaurant. It has been in existence for only two years. Both clubs are members of the Long Island Soccer League, although they play in different divisions. Jamaica's entrants in the above leagues include the Jamaica Portuguese Tigers, and Club de Futebol and the Jamaica Portuguese Soccer Team.

Another organization which should be mentioned is the Portuguese Civic Association. This is an organization which consists of most of the Portuguese clubs in New York State. Each individual club must be represented and elects one representative, who will then be a Vice-president of the Association, and one Trustee. All of the clubs elect the officers of the organization. The purpose of the Association is to bring together Portuguese people from all over New York. The members share common ideas and goals for the betterment of the community at large. In addition, the Association would like to be recognized as an organization to which recent immigrants, as well as already established ones, can go for advice with respect to educational and cultural matters, among others. . . .

Language

In general, most of the Portuguese on Long Island certainly do speak the Portuguese language. This is even true of those of the second and third generation. It is part of the heritage transmitted from the original members of the community to those who have followed. However, the extent of which the members of the younger generations speak the language may vary. Those born in the United States, for example, may be less fluent than their colleagues born in Portugal. Once again it depends on the particular goals of each individual family.

One pheomenon studied that is common to a large number of the Portuguese residents is Portuguese-American speech. Although this general subject has been studied before, it is included here because of the interest and curiosity it always arouses. It is a commonly accepted fact that when two cultures come in contact with one another, the languages spoken by the members of both will have some type of effect on each other. This occurs in most immigrant groups.

In the case of the Portuguese, their contact with those speaking the English language has produced what has been called both Portuguese-American speech and, more colloquially, Porch English (not much different from the case of Spanglish, created from a combination of Spanish and English). What happens, in effect, is that the Portuguese-speaking person, upon hearing certain terms in English, will, in time, begin to incorporate those terms into his or her vocabulary. These words will eventually be used as though they were perfectly correct Portuguese words. In the few examples which follow, all of which have been heard in Mineola, first listed is the English word, then the Portuguese-American word, and finally the correct Portuguese word:[18]

English	Portuguese American	Portuguese
store	estoa	loja
roof	rufo	telhado
couch	caixo	sofa
room	rumo	quarto
blanket	blanqueta	cobertor
drive	drivar	conduzir
shovel	chovela	pa
desk	desca	escrivaninha
gas station	gasteixa	estação de serviço
cellar	cela	adega
truck	troque	camião
market	marqueta	mercado
nice	naice	bom
television	televeja	televisão
factory	factoria	fabrica
teacher	ticha	professor

1. Renzo De Felice, "L'emigrazione egli emigrante nell' ultima secolo," in *Terzo Programma*, ERI Edizione, N. 3, 1964, p. 176.

2. For an excellent history of the Italians in the western part of the United States, see Andrew F. Rolle, *The Immigrant Upraised* (Norman: University of Oklahoma Press, 1966).

3. Reprinted from *The Italian Emigration of Our Times* by Robert F. Foerster (Cambridge, Mass.: Harvard University Press, 1919), pp. 356-58, 362, 389.

4. Ibid., p. 394.

5. Ibid., pp. 402-404.

6. *New York Illustrated American*, April 4, 1891.

7. *La Fiama*, November 1923, as reprinted in Wayne Moquin, Charles Van Doren, Francis A. J. Ianni, *A Documentary History of Italian Americans* (New York, 1974), pp. 283, 284, 286.

8. Bella Dodd, *School of Darkness* (New York: P.J. Kenedy & Sons, 1954), p. 15.

9. Alberto Giovanetti, *The Italians of America*, (New York, 1979), pp. 268-69.

10. Reprinted from Henry Pratt Fairchild, *Greek Immigration* (New Haven: Yale University Press, 1911), pp. 122-123.

11. Ibid.

12. Reprinted from J.P. Xenides, *The Greeks in America* (New York: Doran, 1922), pp. 78-79, 91-92.

13. Ibid., pp. 112-13.

14. Theodore Saloutos, *The Greeks in the United States* (Cambridge: Harvard University Press, 1964), pp. 78-79.

15. Nicholas Gage, *New York Times*, December 26, 1975.

16. Reprinted from Donald R. Taft, *Two Portuguese Communities in New England* (reprint ed., New York: Arno Press, Inc., 1969), pp. 205-207.

17. Reprinted from Hans Howard Leder, "Cultural Persistence in a Portuguese-American Community" (Ph.D. diss., Stanford University, 1968), pp. 56-57, 75-76, 79, 87-88.

18. Neil Miller, "The Portuguese of Long Island," in *Ethnicity in Suburbia: The Long Island Experience*, edit. by Salvatore J. LaGumina (Garden City, New York: 1980), pp. 30-33.

KEY QUESTIONS

1. Analyze and compare America's views of Italians and Greeks as workers (favorable or unfavorable impressions) and their impact on the labor movement.

2. In what important respects did Italian and Greek colonies in America manifest similarities and differences?

3. Compare and contrast the experiences of the Italians, Greeks, Portuguese, and Syrians in America by commenting on the durability of their traditions and how these served to keep them aloof from American influences.

4. Compare and contrast the causes for emigration to America on the part of Greeks and Portuguese.

5. Could it be said that the sense of inferiority strengthened when immigrant children entered the American public school atmosphere? Answer this by reference to the Italian experience and by comparing it with the Portuguese experience.

6. If the Greek experience in America is taken as an example, what was encompassed by the term "Americanization"?

7. The ongoingness of ethnic group life is reflected in the excerpt on the Portuguese on Long Island. By reference to this excerpt, comment on the uniqueness of language retention.

FIVE

The Asians: The Chinese, Japanese Filipinos, Indochinese, and Koreans

The Asians in the United States have experienced nearly insurmountable obstacles in their attempt to move from the periphery to the center of American life. In grappling with the question of race and nationality, Henry Pratt Fairchild provided a clue to the cause of prejudice:

> But group feeling is not based solely on characteristics of individuals. Like all true race and nationality matters it has a mass aspect. There is undoubtedly a definite quantitative factor involved in it. An increase in the numbers of strangers does not merely intensify the antipathy proportionately, it may even cause an actual reversal of sentiment. The first two or three representatives of a foreign type frequently arouse no actual antagonism whatever. They are regarded as interesting, quaint, exotic.[1]

White America regarded the physical and cultural differences of the Asians as handicaps, and even failed to distinguish the vast diversity among the Asian immigrants. Because they were subjected to racial discrimination and were not generally appreciated for their ethnic heritage, Asian Americans today tend to regard their earlier designation of "Orientals" as an ethnic slur. As with American blacks, prejudice toward Asians could be traced to skin color. Economic competition also caused nativists to react negatively, often violently against the newcomers.

THE CHINESE

Anti-Chinese discrimination increased in the nineteenth century as their numbers increased, especially in the West. They developed their own communities, maintained their own customs, and competed for jobs. The Chinese helped fill the need for cheap labor in a growing industrial America. They worked the gold mines in California, built the railroads, labored in factories, and started businesses of their own.

113

Nevertheless, they were exploited by their employers who gave them lower wages than the Caucasian workers.

Anti-Chinese sentiment increased to fever pitch on the West Coast in the 1870s during the Sandlot Riots in San Francisco. There were other numerous examples of prejudicial legislation, segregation, and physical violence. Caucasian leaders alleged that the Chinese depressed wages, lowered the standards of work, and were servile and unassimilable. All of this culminated in the Exclusion Law of 1882 which prohibited the entry of Chinese laborers to the United States. The exclusion principle was to be renewed and extended to 1943. Singling them out for prejudicial treatment served to reenforce Chinese institutions in the many Chinatowns throughout America, thereby keeping them on the periphery.

The period following World War II witnessed an increase in status and power for the Chinese. They had proven their loyalty by serving in the Armed Forces and working in the war industries. Discriminatory laws were abolished, although discrimination itself would become more subtle, and they did participate in the postwar prosperity.

The Immigration Law of 1965 benefited the Chinese on the mainland and Taiwan. Most of the new immigrants settled in the Chinatowns in San Francisco, Los Angeles, and New York, causing a further demand for Chinese goods and services. Many problems developed: overcrowding, crime, juvenile delinquency, generational conflict, and economic exploitation. Chinese Americans who were socially and economically mobile moved to suburban communities to escape the stigma of the ghetto. Approximately 510,000 Chinese migrated to the United States during the period from 1820 to 1977. These figures include those who came from Taiwan since 1957. From 1951 through 1977, 103,800 Chinese have settled in the United States.[2] The official Chinese population in 1980 was 806,027, the largest of any Asian group in the United States.[3]

In a revised interpretation, Betty Lee Sung has pointed out the changing pattern of Chinese-American life. Writing in 1967 she asserted that family circles provided the security and companionship formerly found in Chinatowns. There was little or no discrimination against the Chinese Americans' choice of residence because of their financial gains and their adaptation to American society. "The social climate and general attitude toward the Chinese have changed so rapidly in recent years that the Chinese actually encounter little or no discrimination in their choice of place to live. In fact, only a small percentage of Chinese in the United States live in Chinatowns, and the old-time residents have practically all moved away." The larger Chinatowns expanded because of the increased numbers of immigrants, but the new Chinatowns differ from the old because the old bonds are gone and the "communal organizations have lost their leadership and their functions."[4]

The increasing Chinese population in the United States has caused pressures to build in the old Chinatowns. As was the case for the earlier ethnic groups, the Chinese have been experiencing social and geographical mobility. On the Lower East Side of New York City they have extended themselves northward into Little Italy, putting pressure on the older Italian-American population on Mulberry Street, thereby altering traditional residential life there. They have also migrated to such places as Flushing in Queens County, contributing to the development of a vibrant Asian community.

The following poetic statement poignantly expresses the loneliness of early Chinese immigrants. Translated from a Chinese calligraphy, it was found on a wall of the barracks at Angel Island, California, where first-generation Chinese passed through. It was written early in the twentieth century.

> I have always admired America as a land of promise.
> Immediately I raised money and set out on my journey.
> I endured rough winds and waves for more than a month;
> Now I am trapped in this prison place.
> I look out and see Oakland so close, yet I cannot go there.
> I wish I could go home and be a farmer again.
> My heart is filled with sorrow and I cannot sleep.
> I write these words to express my sadness.[5]

The Chinese have undergone a wide variety of ethnic experiences in the United States. After the Civil War, an increase in Chinese immigration paved the way for discriminatory treatment by Californians. This prejudice, strong at the turn of the century, is illustrated by the unsuccessful attempt of a prominent Presbyterian and editor of a Chinese daily newspaper to move out of Chinatown to a white neighborhood.

> The story of the attempts of one Chinaman to find a place to live outside of Chinatown, in order that he might bring up his children as Christians and good Americans, will serve better than any abstract statement, to illustrate the difficulties produced by anti-Chinese prejudice. The writer of this story is a prominent member of a Presbyterian Church and the Editor of a Chinese Daily paper. He and his family speak excellent English, dress in American clothes and his children are being educated carefully after the manner of well-to-do Americans:

In the summer of 1901 I proposed to bring my family from Los Angeles to San Francisco. I tried many times to find a suitable house outside of Chinatown so that my children might be properly brought up in the ways of the Americans, that in the years to come they may perform the duties of American citizenship.

I found a good flat with five rooms and bath and the rent was within my ability to pay. The landlady was willing also to rent the house to me after having heard the explanation I made regarding myself. The rent was paid and preparation was made for moving in, but after two days the landlady came to my office and returned the money to me and explained the situation: the whole neighborhood had risen in arms against the idea of having a Chinese family in their midst, and since the landlady would not give up the house to me it was out of the question to move in, so my first attempt to find a home outside of the district where my own people live was a flat failure.

A few weeks later I again tried my luck, and in the course of an afternoon, I found two houses which I thought would be suitable to me, since they were not far from Chinatown and rent was not exorbitant. The agents kindly made arrangements to rent the premises to me but when the landlords were apprised of the nationality of their prospective tenants all arrangements were annulled.

After all these failures, I was not yet dismayed, I resolved, to try again and hoped for better results. Accordingly one ideal afternoon, after having gone through the rush of business, I sallied forth putting aside the memory of all previous defeats from my mind. I found a flat on Mason Street near Sacramento, which I thought was the ideal place for a home. The landlord was a good-natured Frenchman. He had no race prejudice in his mind and what he had there was only dollars and cents. So he agreed to rent the place to me provided his other tenants would not object and that he would let me know one way or the other in two days. At the end of the two days I called at his house and he told me that it was out of the question to rent me the house since the other tenants objected strenuously to renting the flat to a Chinese family. I was greatly disappointed but not the least surprised. I had the temerity to ask him what family objected to my living there, and he replied that it was a family of negroes. That was the last straw that broke the back of my buoyancy of hope. I then repeated again and again to myself saying, if negroes even object to my getting a house outside of Chinatown, how can I ever succeed in getting a place where no one objects. From that time on I never made another move. The proverbial Chinese perseverance seemed to have left me for good.[6]

Despite the strong prejudice against the Chinese and against the Chinatowns that developed in the major cities they inhabited, there is much evidence to indicate that the Chinese became Americanized quite rapidly. In her excellent study, Mary Roberts Coolidge dramatizes the desire of the Chinese to adopt American life patterns.

The Chinaman is above all, a lover of home and children and if married men were allowed to bring in their wives freely the conditions of life of the Chinese entitled to live in this country would become much more normal. In no one respect have the Chinese in America altered more than in their ideas about women. Wives have a far greater amount of freedom in America than in China; daughters are no longer unwelcome. The Chinese have repeatedly tried to adopt white children and half-bloods of other races from the asylums, but the anti-Chinese prejudice is so strong as to make it impossible. It has often been rumored that the Chinese sell children in San Francisco. This idea probably arose from their custom of binding any bargain with a money payment. The contract of adoption is made final among them by the payment of a small sum of money.

On account of the difficulty and expense of bringing in Chinese wives, there have been a number of marriages between the laboring Chinese and women of the darker foreign-blood—Indian and Mexican and even Europeans. A number of native-born Chinese have married American women, and the children, so far from being the "monstrosities" predicted by early Californians, are superior, both physically and mentally. In the Southwest, the offspring of marriages between Chinese and Mexican women are conspicuously superior; but the prejudice against the mixture of North-European whites and Chinese is extreme and has resulted in an amendment adding the word Mongolians, to the law prohibiting intermarriage of white persons and negroes, in several states and territories.

It was assumed for many years that the Chinese were unassimilable and their clannishness, the slowness with which they adopted American dress and the English language lent color to the assumption. But a comparison of the Chinese with other aliens, particularly with the Italians, Mexicans and Greeks in San Francisco, discloses the fact that they are being Americanized quite as rapidly, and in some respects, make better citizens because of their superior intellectual capacity. At the time of the first Restriction act very few Chinese had cut their queues and adopted American clothes, and they chiefly because they were converts to Christianity; but since 1900 the movement in this direction has been very rapid. Only about one boy in six in the graded school wears a queue and there are now four barbers in Chinatown itself who advertise to do queue-cutting. Those who still wear the queue do so because they mean to return to China to live or to visit their parents. One very much Americanized Chinamen said that his aged mother in China would be so shocked to see him without it that he would not have it cut till he returned from the visit home which would probably be his last.

The majority of Chinese immigrants some time ago exchanged their baggy pantaloons for American trousers, but like many other foreigners they have not yet compassed the idea that the cut of them must be changed frequently to be truly in the American fashion. Nor have they yet generally adopted in place of the soft cotton or silk shirt the starched garment, nor in place of the loose linen or wadded silk tunic the conventional tailor-made vest and coat; although a considerable number of the educated Chinese now wear the conventional business man's dress; and the native-born Chinese of the second generation are extremely American in their clothing.

To an Oriental the mastery of English is necessarily much more difficult than to a European, but it may be set down that every

Chinaman who has cut his queue and every Christian Chinaman, speaks English, and many others speak it a little. Some who speak badly have nevertheless learned to read the American papers. Just as in the case of other foreigners, if the Chinaman came to the United States when he was a little boy or if he has a wife and children here, he speaks English and is Americanized to a considerable degree; and the native-born boys are, almost without exception, fully Americanized in speech as well as in dress.

Among the few hundred men who have families in this country not many care to vote themselves, but all of them are proud of the fact that their sons can vote. One old Chinaman said: "I no care much about vote—my son, I make him vote." The older Chinese are sensitive about the denial of naturalization because it is a discrimination against their race, and the native-born are proportionately proud of the privelege. More than a hundred native-born Chinese registered in San Francisco as voters in 1904; and in that campaign the anomalous spectacle was presented of a Union-Labor candidate for Mayor making election speeches in Chinatown. There is abundant evidence that the Chinese of the second generation mean to claim their citizenship. In the smaller towns of California and in some other states they show strong patriotism, marching in Fourth of July parades and even drilling and volunteering for the army.[7]

The next author engages in a friendly criticism of American civilization. No-Yong Park, a Harvard Ph.D., admits to being a "Chinese recipient of American kindness and hospitality." Yet he presents a frank evaluation of various aspects of American life: the fast-paced pattern of behavior, the moral standards, materialism, commercialism, race prejudice, "boostmanship," and the press. No-Yong Park's observations get to the substance of American lifestyles.

Take another illustration: The Americans "rush." Look at them; how they hurry! They rush all the way from the maternity hospital to the graveyard. . . Undoubtedly it is the machine which makes the speedy Americans speedier, but their rush is too much rush. They burn up their energy, life and all in the "pursuit of happiness" but never have time to enjoy happiness itself. But what one would say if the Americans were extremely slow and inactive and, like the classical Chinese scholars, sought contentment in all things, including "cold water to drink and coarse rice to eat"!. . .

"American materialism" is probably the strongest case against the United States. In taking up this point, however, I must admit frankly that it is not a proper time for us Chinese to condemn American materialism, for what we need in China today is American science, American industry, and many other things which might be branded as American materialism. But, as a citizen of the world at large, I cannot help feeling that American civilization is too materialistic to be described as an ideal civilization. . . Man is more or less materialistic, but the American is too much so. If the ancient Chinese philosophers have gone to one extreme by condemning everything that is materialistic, the modern American has gone to the opposite extreme. He has abandoned cultural and spiritual values, and has given himself up to the gods of materialism and commercialism. He has let the blind forces of materialism and commercialism dominate himself and his institutions, and control every move he makes. He can hardly listen to the radio three minutes without being interrupted by the voice of commercialism. He can hardly travel a mile on the highway without being confronted by the sticky hands of commercialism. He can hardly sleep at night without being haunted by the ghost of commercialism, hovering over his head and peeking into his purse. Thus the inevitable commercialism manifests itself in everything in America.

Money, money, money,—that is the alpha and omega in America; it is the master of all things and the measure of all values. Money does not exist for man, man exists for money. He works, toils and struggles for money and more of it. He conquers the sky, levels the mountains and wrecks the earth, for money. He exploits his woman, makes her smoke, makes her wear all sorts of laughable clothes year after year, all for the purpose of making money. Money is his strength; it is his weakness, too. To the God of Gold he offers for sale all his morals, his character, his culture and his life itself. . . .

Race prejudice is probably one of the ugliest scars on American civilization. Nowhere in the world is it more outspoken and more deeply rooted than in America, perhaps with the exception of Hitler's Germany. Truly, this land of the free deserves the appellation "a land of race prejudice." A little sense of preference for one's own race is not only harmless, but would be considered desirable. How tragic would it be if we all treated unknown strangers as our wives or sisters! How dangerous would it be if we treated tigers and serpents as our brethren! We should have kinder feelings for our relatives and friends, our own nationals and races, than we have for others. But American race prejudice has gone a little too far. This prejudice is most strongly manifested against the Jews, the Negroes and the Orientals. Their ostracism of the Jews, their condemnation of the Negroes and their discrimination against the Orientals make it difficult for the Americans to laugh at the Indians for their caste system. . . .

With such a pride and optimism and ever-progressive frame of mind, the American cannot help being a "booster." . . .He will tell you that his people are the most civilized and his country the best in the world. He will also tell you that his state is the best in the Union and his town is the best in the state. You will hear the same statement in every state and in every town, hence all the states and all the towns in America are the best. In a small town in North Dakota, I was talking to an undertaker. Even that undertaker was boosting his town before me. He said that his town was the best in the state, business was better than in other towns, and more people died there than in any other town in the state! The booster looks at times very childish, and often foolish. . . .

The American does not stop with boosting. He works, works and works. I have never seen any one who likes to work more than he. To him work is his religion, his recreation and his life. You take work away from him, and you will kill him. He is born to work, he lives to work, and he dies for his work. He works when he has something to do; he works when he has nothing to do. He builds up when he can and he tears down when he has nothing to build. He has no time to be graceful, polite and stylish. He is always on the go. He runs, jumps and hops back and forth like a rabbit. Speed! Speed! Speed! It gets on one's nerves. But that is better than being lazy, idle and mischievous.[8] . . .

THE JAPANESE

Japanese immigration began in large numbers after 1890, there being only 3,000 living in the United States at that time, with most living in California. In fact, most Japanese settlement took place in California and Hawaii until recently. By the Gentlemen's Agreement of 1907, Japan agreed to prohibit emigration of laborers to the United States. In 1924 a new arrangement excluded Japanese as "aliens ineligible to citizenship." In 1952 the MaCarran-Walter Act ended both the policy of denial of citizenship to Japanese residents and racial discrimination in immigration. The 1965 immigration law eliminated the discriminatory national origins quota system.

One of the most unsavory incidents in the treatment of an ethnic group occurred after the attack on Pearl Harbor, when 110,000 Japanese Americans, two-thirds of them American citizens, were taken from their homes on the West Coast and placed in ten "relocation centers." Bolstered by the anger from the sudden attack on Pearl Harbor, coupled with the deep-seated animosity against the Japanese, the Western Defense Command, the President, Congress, and the Supreme Court all sanctioned the Japanese internment. The German Americans and the Italian Americans received no such treatment. Nevertheless, the Japanese Americans remained loyal to the American cause during the war. After World War II the United States compensated the Japanese Americans who were forcibly relocated, although the matter was never, and could never be, fully satisfied.

The Japanese Americans have displayed a resiliency in spite of the discriminatory treatment received in this country. Such ethnic strength has resulted from group loyalty, strong family ties, reverence for work, respect for authority, and moral training. As peripheral Americans they have maintained effective ethnic institutions and communities. More recently, facing less prejudice, they have readily adapted to American society. Relations between the United States and Japan have improved, and from 1946 to 1976 over 116,000 Japanese have settled here. From 1820 to 1977, 402,938 have been recorded as having migrated to the United States.[9] The 1980 census recorded 700,747 Japanese Americans.[10]

"No immigrant group encountered higher walls of prejudice and discrimination than did the Jaspanese." Edwin O. Reschauer's assessment in the foreword to *Nisei* by Bill Hosokawa, (New York; William Morrow, 1969), points up the extreme ethnic difficulties experienced by the Japanese Americans. The thread of hostility toward the Japanese minority runs continuously from the time of their arrival in large numbers around the turn of the twentieth century to the end of World War II.

The following abstract examines the anti-Japanese movement on the West Coast. A pivotal event in this saga was the San Francisco earthquake in April 1906, which led to the famous school segregation issue.

As soon as Japanese immigration assumed a larger proportion in the late '90's, there appeared expressions against it. This was inevitable in view of the long-continued agitation against the Chinese in an earlier period, which culminated in the enactment of a Chinese exclusion law in 1882. But anti-Japanese utterances were sporadic, and did not assume concrete form until the beginning of the present century. Still nothing was achieved.

In the beginning of 1905 a San Francisco newspaper started to publish a series of articles against Japanese immigration, and in the spring of the same year the so-called Japanese and Korean Exclusion League was organized. These two combined in effect to demand of Congress that it adopt a measure to restrict Japanese immigration. In May 1905 the San Francisco Board of Education passed a resolution to establish separate schools for Chinese and Japanese children, but no action followed it. In April 1906 San Francisco was visited by an earthquake, which together with subsequent fires devastated a large area of the city. In the resulting general chaos, Japanese persons and business establishments were menaced and attacked by hoodlums, who were encouraged in their acts by a prevalent anti-Japanese attitude. In the midst of this unfortunate situation, the school board issued, on October 11, its order compelling Japanese school children to attend the Oriental School located near the devastated Chinatown. Thus began the famous school question which was settled by the prohibition of Japanese migration from Hawaii, Mexico, and Canada, and by the Gentlemen's Agreement, stopping fresh labor immigration from Japan. These measures proved to be effective. But the anti-Japanists in California desirous of the exclusion of Japanese were dissatisfied. The state legislature was flooded with anti-Japanese bills, none of which, however, became law until 1913, when an alien land law was enacted. Similar laws were adopted in Washington, Oregon, Arizona, and other states where Japanese were engaged in agriculture.[11]

The War Relocation Authority was established by President Franklin D. Roosevelt in 1942 for the purpose of ensuring the welfare of the evacuated Japanese Americans. Throughout most of that year the WRA people worked at setting up living quarters, hospitals, schools, farms, and other businesses in the relocation centers for the evacuees. The Manzanar Relocation Center in southern California, from which the following extract is taken, was one of the ten centers, all west of the Mississippi. The account is an actual transcription from a Nisei (American-born children of immigrant Japanese) who refused to swear an oath of allegiance to the United States. It describes vividly the firsthand experiences and impressions of a Nisei's evacuation.

Hearing Board Member: I see you have always lived in this country.

Nisei: Yes.

HBM: Are you a dual citizen?

Nisei: No, I am an American citizen only.

HBM: In February, during the army registration, you said "No" to Question 28 according to our record. Did you understand the question?

Nisei: I guess I did understand the question.

HBM: And do you want to change the answer or do you want the "No" to stand?

Nisei: I'll keep it "No."

HBM: What does that mean?

(The boy stands there. His lips are quivering but he does not speak.)

HBM: Do you want to talk about it? Something is bothering you.

Nisei: What is bothering me could not be answered by any one person in particular.

HBM: Don't you want to tell us? Perhaps there is something that we can do. If you say "No," you are giving away your American citizenship. Is that what you want to do? Feel free to talk. We're not here to argue with you but we want to help you.

Nisei: What I was thinking, I thought that since there is a war on between Japan and America, since the people of this country have to be geared up to fight against Japan, they are taught to hate us. So they don't accept us. First I wanted to help this country, but they evacuated us instead of giving us a chance. Then I wanted to be neutral, but now that you force a decision, I have to say this. We have a Japanese face. Even if I try to be American I won't be entirely accepted.

HBM: What is this about "the Japanese face" deal? Up to today we haven't heard this expression, and today we hear it all over this block. Have you been reading Mary Oyama's article in *Liberty*?

Nisei: I read Mary's article. It doesn't say much. It just tells about the conditions of leaving our homes, about the hardships we suffered and how well we took them. But that was just the beginning. A great deal has happened since then that she says nothing about.

HBM: What do you plan to do?

Nisei: I planned to stay in this country before the war. I planned to be a farmer.

HBM: What about your folks?

Nisei: They figure they'll stay here if I do or they'll go Tule Lake if I do.

HBM: Is it that some of your friends are going to Tule Lake? Are you being influenced by the talk of friends?

Nisei: No, my best friend is going to stay here.

HBM: Then what is at the bottom of this?

Nisei: If I would say "Yes," I'd be expected to say that I'd give up my life for this country. I don't think I could say that because this country has not treated me as a citizen. I could go three-quarters of the way but not all the way after what has happened.

HBM: Would you be willing to be drafted?

Nisei: No, I couldn't do that.

HBM: That's all. I see that you have thought about it and that your mind is made up. (Nisei goes out).

HBM: I feel sorry for that boy. Some of them I don't feel sorry for.

Later I contacted this young man and asked him for a fuller statement of his views. The following is what he told me:

I'm just a fellow who has always worked as a farmer. I've never met the real community yet. When I was at home, I thought about this hearing and how to explain my feelings. But you come before a board like this. I'm not used to it. I couldn't say it the way I meant it.

Back home, before evacuation, when fellows were drafted for the United States Army, that was good. The Japanese gave a party for them, a big sendoff. It was not a party for them all together but for each one individually. There were fifty people or more at the bus to see each one of them off. You saw the white American boys there who were going too. In most cases no one would be there to see them off but the immediate family. We were glad to serve in the American Army then. We thought it was right because we lived here.

Before evacuation, all our parents thought that since they were aliens they would probably have to go to a camp. That was only natural—they were enemy aliens. But they never thought that it would come to the place where their sons, who were born in America and were American citizens would be evacuated. We citizens had hopes of staying there because President Roosevelt and Attorney General Biddle said it was not a military necessity to evacuate American citizens of Japanese ancestry.

So we went ahead and planted our crops. If anyone didn't believe it and didn't plant, everyone said it was sabotage. So we lost a lot of money that we wouldn't have had to lose if we had not put the crop in and had been told in the first place that we were going to be evacuated. Then we came up to Manzanar. It was just the same whether you were alien or citizen. When they asked for people to go on furlough, it was not only the citizen but the alien who could go out if he wanted to.

At first when we go here, when people thought we were dangerous, that should have been the time where we should have been guarded. But it was about a half a year afterwards that they thought those things up. Then they put up the fence and the towers. When we first came here, if you had business to do you could go to Lone Pine or Independence. But afterwards you couldn't go anywhere, even with a military guard. . .

In religion our family is Buddhist. I don't make too much of this. I believe that when you get down to the central part every religion stands for much the same thing. But they say this about those who change from Buddhism to Christianity lately and I notice that it is true. The ones who do something wrong, who get into trouble, are the ones who change. They become Christians and then they say that the past is all wiped out and they don't have to worry about what they did in the past. There is one part of the Bible they depend on, the part that says "Forgive the transgressors." They take this literally and hang on to it, but they don't pay much attention to the rest of the Bible.

I appreciate this talk with you. But my mind is made up. I know my father is planning to return to Japan. I know he expects me to say "No" so there will be no possibility that the family will be separated. There isn't much I can do for my father any more; I can't work for him the way I used to. But I can at least quiet his mind on this.[12]

Social psychologist Harry H. L. Kitano of the University of California in Los Angeles has studied the Japanese-American sub-culture in the context of American civilization. He based many of his conclusions on personal interviews with Japanese Americans. The following account describes the discrimination against and eventual acceptance of a Nisei in the teaching profession.

Today the Japanese have made rapid progress in the teaching field. A successful Nisei teacher told us:

When I came to UCLA (1936) I had to pick a college major so I chose elementary education. I always wanted to be a teacher, so even when they told me there would never be a job for me, I went ahead to work for my teacher's certificate. Actually, some of the other girls were in sociology, or economics and they'd never be able to jet a job either. So I guess you can say we were all even.

After I got my degree in 1940, I didn't even look for a job in teaching since there were no openings for Japanese. Soon after, I was evacuated. While in camp, they neded teachers very badly and somehow or other, they knew I had teacher training and the state sent over a teaching certificate. So I taught for several years in camp—when I relocated to Idaho, that state kept after me to teach.

I came back to California in 1946 and tried to find a teaching job. It was still discouraging but I stuck to it and finally landed a position. I still remember the first day. . .as I was walking into the teachers' lunch-room, one of the teachers said in a low voice loud enough so that I could hear, "Look who we're hiring now, we really must be hard up."

It wasn't a pleasant situation but I knew I could teach and my experiences in camp helped out. Now that I look back on it, I always wanted to teach, I finally got the opportunity, and I'm glad I stuck it out.[13]

From his own private interviews with Japanese Americans, Professor Kitano found that the Sansei (third-generation Japanese born in the United States) faced the real problem of alienation simultaneously with their acceptance into the larger community. A Sansei high school student on the West Coast expressed the social gap between the oriental and western cultures.

> The loneliest time for some of us is the Easter recess. We're pretty well accepted in the classroom and some of the social and athletic groups. But it gets kind of hard at Easter; most of the guys and gals (white) take off for Newport or some place like that. . . . There are two problems. One is I don't know whether my parents will let me go. But the main problem is what would happen if I went. One Sansei went with a (non-Japanese) group last year and he told me he felt left out on certain things. . . . He didn't have a good time so he's not going this year. . . . But, I don't want to go out with an all-Japanese group either.[14]

THE FILIPINOS

Since most Filipinos have arrived in the past two decades, they have not suffered as much discrimination as their predecessors because of the greater protection afforded to minorities in American society. Contributing to their earlier problems and confused status was their Spanish heritage. The Filipinos had not considered themselves Orientals, but local officials in the Western states, interpeting their ethnicity according to local tradition, looked on them as Asians. On the West Coast they were discriminated against; if seen on the street in the evenings, they were stopped by police, States passed laws prohibiting marriage between Caucasians and Asians.

When it became evident that hostility would not completely subside, the Filipinos organized the Filipino Federation of America in 1925 in Stockton, California. The Stockton Center was bombed in the 1930s and rebuilt in 1962, a decidedly less hostile period.

The Filipinos first started to come to the United States around 1906, but as late at 1920 they numbered only 5,000. A large influx arrived in the 1920s as a consequence of the need for workers on the West Coast and the exclusion of the Filipinos from the newly adopted quota system. In fact, they were the only Asian people not restricted from immigrating. However, the Exclusion Act of 1924 prohibited the Filipinos from becoming citizens, although they were not regarded as aliens. Their unique status resulted from the fact that the United States owned the Philippine Islands. They were considered nationals but not subject to the quota system. As a result of anti-Filipino agitation of the Pacific coast, demands for exclusion grew. The Philippine Independence Act of 1934 provided for an annual quota of 50, and when independence became a reality on July 4, 1946, the annual quota was raised to 100. Today there are 774,640 living in the United States.[15]

The 1965 Immigration Law abolished the national origins quota system and benefited Filipino immigration. Thousands entered the United States under the category of professional and skilled workers. Many arrived as doctors, dentists, nurses, and pharmacists. Most settled in such major cities as Honolulu, Los Angeles, Chicago, and New York. The following figures reflect the impact of the new law.

1966 - 6,093
1967 - 10,865
1968 - 16,731
1969 - 20,744
1970 - 31,203
1971 - 28,471
1972 - 29,376
1973 - 30,799
1974 - 32,857
1975 - 31,751
1976 - 37,281
1977 - 38,500[16]

The following descriptions of the Filipinos' ethnic experiences touch upon the following: the position of Filipinos in the United States; state laws forbidding marriage between Filipinos and Caucasians during World War II; mistreatment by police; the high caliber of work performed by Filipino workers; and Americans' tolerant attitude toward and treatment of Filipinos after World War II.

The demand by various labor organizations, patriotic groups such as the American Legion, and finally the California state legislature for exclusion of Filipino immigration prompted a study of this ethnic group from the Pacific. Bruno Lasker collected extensive firsthand data while analyzing the status of the Filipino immigrants on the American mainland. Below, Lasker summarizes the many problems experienced by the Filipinos.

No attempt has been made in the preceding pages to depict those problems which all immigrant groups, in their first phase of contact with the special conditions of new country, have to meet. Whether due to the lack of facilities in virgin territory or to the necessity of adjustment to a fully developed civilization, these problems are inherent in the circumstances and readily recognized by those who have studied the history of migrations. But there are several novelties in this latest large-scale influx. One of them is precisely that it is the latest, that it inherits all the defenses which a people has built up in its institutions and in its attitudes after a period of enormous population mixture from which it is only just emerging into an era of difficult assimilation. As the latest comer, the Filipino encounters checks in national and state laws, in the percedents of discriminatory treatment set by custom, in the prejudices built up by previous race contacts of the dominant group. Thus, a comparison of the Filipino influx with the earlier Japanese wave of immigration is misleading unless one remembers that while the earlier Japanese immigrants, welcomed to this country, were able by their competency to establish a high degree of prosperity which later became an important factor in fortifying the position of the larger group, the Filipinos were not privileged to establish such a pioneer colony that might later take up the advancement and protection of the national group as a whole. The result is a lack of responsible, economically anchored leadership, which constitutes one of the greatest concrete obstacles to the success of the Filipino group in America as a whole.

The Filipino immigrant is further handicapped by the distance of his homeland, which necessitates considerable sacrifice, on his own part or that of his family, before he can make the expensive trip, and usually lands him at his goal without further resources. This distance also makes impossible a rapid adaptation of the current of emigration to the employment conditions in the receiving country and prevents the return of those who, either for personal reasons or because of a choked labor market, find it difficult to make a living.

The limitations of the Filipino are partly physical and partly cultural. His smallness of stature makes him unsuitable in the eyes of employers for work requiring hard muscular exertion. Bad dietary habits often render him much weaker than organically he need be. Overcrowding, the frequenting of smoke-filled poolrooms and insufficient sleep also impair his physical efficiency. Mentally, the Filipino worker is alert enough to take his place beside other national groups; but his vocabulary usually is limited and, unless a Filipino foremanship should grow up from among the more experienced workers, employers have difficulty in handling this class of foreigners.

Against the Filipino's chances in competition for work are further his temperament (sometimes) and his reputation. While as an individual the Filipino is considered docile, he often finds himself barred from employment because of the assumption that, as a group, Filipinos are temperamental, prone to take offense easily and to walk out on an employer at small provocation, quarrelsome among themselves and revengeful when considering themselves injured. Moreover, employers, especially in small and rural communities, are influenced more largely by non-economic motivations than in large cities and industrial plants: It is sometimes considered unwise to employ Filipinos where there are women around or where their work may be regarded as in competition with that of white Americans, even when there are no complaints on either score. Again, in the hotel and restaurant trades and retail business, employers are obliged to consider the prejudices of their patrons; and Filipinos find themselves debarred from promotion to positions as waiters or salesmen even when their own employer would consider them qualified and desirable.

Like other newcomers, Filipinos find themselve the victims of many forms of exploitation by labor agents and contractors, by foremen and straw bosses, by venders of goods and of transportation, by gamblers and racketeers. Ignorance of work opportunities, of their rights when employed, of means to gain legal redress, of prices and charges, of the functions and duties of officials, of American customs; often a childlike faith in the printed word or misplaced confidence in a countryman, romantic hero-worship, inability to resist argument when couched in flamboyant terms—all these handicaps make it difficult for the Filipino immigrant worker to prosper and to realize his economic ambitions on coming to the American mainland. Moreover, he does not know how to avail himself of such protection as American community organization and state legislation afford.

But there are other difficulties not shared by earlier immigrant groups. The permanent settlement of the Filipinos is feared; and this fear reacts against them. In vain do they point out that they have not come here to stay and settle. Just because they are ever conscious of the temporary nature of their stay, they find it harder than those who come for permanent residence to make those adjustments of habits and tastes that would ensure a rapid assimilation.

This statement may seem contradicted by the actual ease with which Filipinos seem to adopt American ideas; but observation here is often at fault: The tastes and notions which the Filipino immigrant endeavors to express through his mode of living are those of his own country with its long history of Spanish cultural domination, modified, to be sure, by an aggressive North American impact during the last thirty years. A bird of passage, the Filipino in his attitude to American life is comparable with other transients rather than with those who came here to settle and throw in their fortunes with native Americans. This makes for a certain aloofness which is only partially disguised by the Filipino's desire for social recognition and the company of American men and women. He wishes to learn from these contacts, not to become one of us.

Closely linked with these conditions, there is the Filipino's youthfulness—, or, if you will, immaturity. This is not merely a matter of age composition of the Filipino group, which is lower than that of any other wave of immigration this country has ever had. Employers, college deans, social workers and public officials frequently comment upon the seeming inability of Filipinos, well in the higher twenties and in the thirties, to take a responsible attitude toward their obligations to others. More specifically we have found, in the preceding pages, as militating against the Filipino's success as an immigrant the absence of a normal home life, the excessive mobility that prevents the formation of close ties within a community, even within his own national group.

Bad housing conditions, limitation of vocational opportunites, exposure to unscrupulous profiteers, especially of their own nationality, ignorance of their legal rights and obligations, the general neglect of the community—these are evils which every newly arriving group of immigrants has had to face. In the case of the Filipinos they are aggravated by lack of experience and the absence of those checks which a normal age- and sex-composition place upon individual recklessness. The very adventurousness which makes it possible to suffer temporary misfortune, in the case of the Filipinos, is producing an unusual crop of evils; it encourages an instability which stands in the way of those opportunities which only the growth of a reputation for sustained effort opens to newcomers. Thus criticism by employers and by teachers helps to give substance to the inevitable popular verdict that the newcomers are "undesirable."[17]

The laws of the Western states that prohibited marriage between Filipinos and Caucasians pointed up one of the cruelest ironies in American history. During World War II the Philippine Islands was a staunch ally much praised in the popular media for its loyalty to the American cause. But certain states restricted Filipino marriages, thereby denying these people their equal rights before the law, to say nothing of making them suffer humiliation. Mrs. Iris B. Buaken, an American Caucasian married to the Filipino Manuel Buaken, relates a poignant account of these restrictive marriage laws, their meaning, attempts to get them changed, and their relation to American democracy.

Have you heard what the Catholic Chaplain said to the Governor of California? Do you know of the deadlock that has existed for years in California in which thousands of men have been denied the right to marry and told to resort to prostitution? Did you know that of all Christians on the Pacific Coast, only Catholic priests have lifted their voices in defense of the right of Filipinos to have a normal home and family life?

It is a deadlock that has poisoned democracy and Christianity for years. On one side are the Filipinos of the United States—young, loyal Christians brought to this country by the glowing legend of the land of opportunity and equality—in search of education in the modern Christian way. They were not accompanied by Filipino women. The Immigration Service has made that nearly impossible. There is in the Philippines a tradition of inter-marriage. The great leaders of the country have been men of mixed blood—the late President Quezon, Sergio Osmena, President of the Philippines, are good representatives of the vigorous, socially-honored mestizo class. The Filipinos of the U.S. have been firm in their determination to marry here, for economic and social conditions have generally made it impossible for them to return to the Philippines. They are determined not to go home without the training they came here for, and the path of education for Filipinos in the U.S. has been strewn with thorns. Many educational institutions have raised tuitional and other barriers against Filipinos, in specific race discrimination. Filipinos have been determined to marry and enjoy the companionship of decent women. They brought high ideals and Christian up-bringing. They have been attracted to and have attracted many fine white girls.

But California had a race marriage law that prevents the marriage of Filipinos to "Caucasians" on the ground that Filipinos are Mongolians. Resourceful Salvador Roldan successfully disputed this myth in 1933, and forced the state of California to give him a license to marry his white wife.

Immediately the legislature of California passed a law specifically forbidding the marriage of whites and Filipinos.

There has been also great economic discrimination. Filipinos have not been allowed to practice law or medicine in California, or to belong to the majority of unions, or to have skilled industrial employment. They have not been allowed to buy real property so that they could own homes; they have been required to rent in slum districts.

This combination squeeze play has prevented many Filipinos from taking the trip necessary for marriage. So if they are able to win and keep the love of white girls who become their wives, in affection and faithfulness, till death do them part, they have to do so without benefit of clergy or county.

We were among these couples, Manuel and I. My husband is a person of high moral standards, of keenly logical mind, of charm and humor. Sadly for us, we have no children. If we had, we would have made the desperate sacrifice required to get to a state where we could be "married." But "marriage" as a ceremony becomes cynical double-talk and a farcical specimen of legal quibbling under our state regime.

Prostitution, of course, has had no such legal persecution. Organized vice has sent its armies cruising through regions where Filipinos, denied homes and marriage, have been herded together in labor camps. Venereal disease came hand in hand with this state sponsored prostitution.

Our church had nothing to say about all this. Corporal Manuel Buaken, my husband, is son of a Methodist minister. I am a graduate of a Methodist university. The church had for us only ineffectual glares, or angry, or embarrassed stares. One ray of hope! We heard that some Catholic priests were performing Filipino-white marriages in California, that for Catholics they would "go to bat" with the license bureau. But we aren't Catholics, and anyway, we doubted the legal validity of such marriages.

War came. But first came November, 1941, when Filipinos were required to register as aliens, in spite of their years of unwavering loyalty to the U.S. and its ideals, in spite of their status as "nationals" of a country under the jurisdiction of the U.S., in spite of all the golden promises that America took to the Philippines.

Within a few months, Selective Service took them in. This was the achievement of Bataan! In April, 1942, the First Filipino Infantry was activated. Later a second all-Filipino regiment was organized. Thise Filipino members of the United States Army were made citizens in mass ceremonies. It was a belated legal recognition of what had been true in fact—that they were and are loyal Americans. . . .

Many Filipinos thought citizenship meant equality before the law. They were bitterly diappointed. They were still denied the right to marry, and their right to real property is still in doubt. The Army had their services, their lives to use, but the Army could not give them the service of family allowances or insurance for wives or children. California, Arizona, Utah, Nevada and Wyoming are the saboteur states of this region, refusing the right to marry.

Then Chaplain Eugene C. Noury became the regimental chaplain of the First Filipino Infantry. Its commanding officer is Colonel Robert H. Offley, a man born and raised in the Philippines, a man who feels himself truly a brother of the Filipinos. Finally there was Mr. E.W. Zueger, a Red Cross worker assigned to the First Filipino Infantry—a man to whom the Filipinos demonstrated their eager loyalty by establishing a national record for per capita contributions to the Red Cross, being leaders among all the soldiers of the U.S. Army in this field.

Mr. Zueger began to receive calls for emergency aid to families of Filipino soldiers denied family allowances. At Colonel Offley's request, he made a survey to determine the number of such cases—of unlegalized though true marriages—and found them to be extremely numerous. He learned of the heavy burden of unnecessary worry, of cynicism and of despair, of democracy and Christianity borne by these loyal American soldiers—these Filipinos of the United States Army. So the Red Cross, under the sponsorship of the Army, began its effort to make it possible for Filipino soldiers to make the long trip to some other state—Washington, or New Mexico, to be "married" to their white wives. The Red Cross made loans for funds needed, and asked the Army for emergency furloughs for such Filipino soldiers. My husband and I were among these couples, and we are very grateful to those loyal Americans who made it possible for us.[18]

INDOCHINESE REFUGEES

Over 170,000 Indochinese refugees were settled in the United States as a result of the collapse of South Vietnam in April 1975, and similar dislocations in Cambodia and Laos. The bulk of this migration—90 percent—was Vietnamese. Only 20,038 Vietnamese had come to the United States from 1966 to 1975.

The United States adopted a policy of dispersing the Vietnamese migrants to the fifty states to avoid American hostility at a time of rising unemployment. Moreover, the Vietnamese and others from Indochina reminded Americans of their tragic involvement in a war they wanted to forget. This dispersion broke up the extended families of the Vietmanese and prevented development of viable ethnic organizational support systems. The U.S. Department of Health, Education, and Welfare reported that one-third of the Vietnamese had settled in California and Texas by the end of 1978, because of the agreeable climate, proximity to the old country, and economic opportunities.

The following article focuses on the trauma experienced by the Vietnamese refugees. Note the comparisons of this ethnic migration with those of other immigrant groups. The author, Tran Truong Nhu, is a consultant with the American Friends Committee Service and Indochina Coordinator for the International Children's Fund.

On April 30, 1975, after 30 years of involvement, the United States pulled out of Indochina, thereby ending a long and tragic war. In the course of withdrawal, more than 130,000 Vietnamese, Khmer, and Lao, along with some tribal minorities, were brought to this country in a dramatic exodus which seemed to eclipse even the end of the war. The refugees arrived in a daze and were processed through four resettlement camps around the country as they waited for Americans to "sponsor" them.

Unlike previous migrants, these people were deliberately separated from the very ethnic unity they needed. Previous immigrants—Eastern Europeans, Italians, Irish, Jews, Chinese—lived together, albiet in ghettos, but from such concentration drew strength through mutual self-help to "make it" in American society. The enforced diaspora resulted in widespread depression in the camps that was reflected in a reluctance to leave the safety of the group for the unknown of American society.

While in camp, refugees were briefed on aspects of American life by people from voluntary agencies and the U.S. State Department who told them, among other things, that they should not attempt to communicate with their families and friends in Vietnam lest the Communists harm them. Many reported being told to stay away from blacks, reinforcing fear and prejudice. They were also told that accepting welfare would have an adverse effect on later employment.

Naturally, these warnings depressed the refugees all the more. The admonition not to communicate with their families made them feel lost, without roots or soul. The intimation that another ethnic group was already hostile frightenend them. Thus people were in shock, confused, and deeply despondent after they first arrived.

During the first year, refugees I met would blurt out the story of their departure whenever they had the chance. Each time I met a Vietnamese, our conversations became a catharsis, accompanied often by bitter tears and regret. Had they done the right thing? What had they left behind? There were so many unknowns about the U.S., and the knowledge that they would never quite be at home again weighed heavily.

Most refugees were ill-equipped to leave Vietnam, as many spoke no English and had no motive to leave except fear. From eyewitness accounts by two American brothers who stayed in Saigon beyond the end of the war, Richard and Joseph Hughes, the people of Saigon watched while the rich scrambled for a way out. Or, as one student put it: "You had to be privileged to riot at the airport." People who left by sea, however—fishermen, airforce and navy personnel and their families (army members who did not have access to planes and boats stayed behind)—were not so well-to-do.

Those who were able to leave by plane did so under the auspices of the American Government and American companies were they had been employed. They were the only one guaranteed a way out. Most of the Saigon bourgeoisie—the merchants, civil servants, professionals, teachers—had no direct American connections and could not go. An apparent exception were physicians; of 2,500 physicians in South Vietnam, 660 came to the U.S.

A woman I knew in Saigon, whose husband was a businessman, told me that to her surprise she hardly knew anyone at the camp where she was processed. Her friends, she said, had not realized that the war was ending, and even if they had, they would have been unable to leave since they knew few Americans.

The exit from Saigon was conducted in utmost secrecy. People dared not tell their siblings or neighbors and would steal away without saying good-bye. Saigon was fraught with fear and paranoia. Another Phnom Penh situation where the city might be under siege for months was feared. . . .

Vietnamese were extremely sentimental by nature, with a deep attachment to Viet-nam. It is not just the beauty of the land which has been ruined by the war, but a profound appreciation of family relationships, friends, society, and all the ramifications of that closeness. The American family is nuclear and therefore impersonal from a Vietnamese perspective. The Vietnamese have always lived in an extended family system, in a tight network of solicitude and awareness of others. This is why Vietnamese are always considerate, polite, ever alert to the need of others.

When they arrived in this country, the refugees were scattered throughout the 50 States in an attempt to absorb them quietly into the mythical melting pot. Between 40,000 to 50,000 were sponsored privately without adequate safeguards, and many sponsorships have not worked out. Besides the limited resources of most sponsors, unfamiliarity and anxiety made these arrangements untenable. Most refugees are on their own now, according to the U.S. Department of Health, Education, and Welfare (HEW).

Although in most cases sponsors were well-meaning, some were abusive, and some Vietnamese found themselves indentured servants on isolated farms, especially in Southern States. The sponsors frequently reinforced the refugees' uneasiness by their ignorance of Vietnamese culture.

Some Vietnamese complained to me that although Americans were well-intentioned, they are impersonal. Because Vietnamese are meticulous in regard for detail, American casualness seems barbaric. Thus it is in relationships too. For Vietnamese, friendship is never casual, yet it is not very formal, so the American concept of friendship, seeing each other occasionally (especially family) and calling before visiting, seems cold and distant. Vietnamese love to visit and just drop in. Vietnamese talk about "tinh căm" and "thông căm"—love and sympathy—as the two missing notions in American society thay they cannot live without. So they are regrouping, despite government efforts to separate them, joining each other in California, Washington, D.C., Texas, and Florida to find comfort.

California has the largest Vietnamese population and nearly 80,000 are expected there by the end of this year. The State already has a large Asian population, the climate is temperate, and, one suspects, many come becaue it is the closest shore to home. In general they are doing well, considering they they have been here just over a year. Vietnamese children are scoring in the 90th percentile in math and doing well in verbal tests.

It is important to remember that 45 percent of the refugees are under the age of 18 and it is for their children that parents are willing to make sacrifices—not unlike immigrants before them. Education is the main reason people cite for remaining in the U.S. As long as they are here, they reason, they might as well take advantage of the opportunity to receive an education—which is paramount in Vietnamese culture.

As a rule, Vietnamese are not goal- or success-oriented, which makes them particularly unsuited for the rhythm of American life. Most are not pushy, most do not know what it means to "get ahead," and most are not aggressive (although it was their compatriots who won the war). This lack of aggression has been interpreted as a lack of drive by the Americans who used to work in Vietnam, but it is merely an expression of a different approach and outlook, as well as a reaction at times to their treatment by Americans. Americans like to see tangibles and the immediate consequence of their actions. Vietnamese know that everything takes time and they are used to waiting. They are also used to hardship and used to not having their own way, at least not right away. This is what has enabled them to endure and made them patient.

Almost every Vietnamese dreams secretly of going home some day. People tell me that when their children obtain their education, and when all have their American passports, they will return home—for a visit.[20]

THE KOREANS

Koreans represent one of the fastest growing ethnic groups today in the United States. Population estimates ran as high as 300,000 by the end of the 1970s. Of these, 90 percent have arrived here since the passage of the Immigration Reform Law of 1965 which allows 20,000 to enter annually, and special exemptions can permit even further immigration.

Few Koreans came to the United States mainland in the nineteenth century, but by 1905 more than 7,226 had gone to Hawaii to work on the sugar plantations. Japan, which controlled Korea, and the United States restricted Korean immigration. In 1910 the census reported 461 on the mainland and 4,533 in Hawaii. In 1920 there were 1,677 on the mainland and 4,950 in Hawaii. Ten years later the number increased to 1,860 and 6,461 respectively, and in 1940 the number was 1,711 on the mainland and 6,851 in Hawaii, After World War II and Korean independence in 1945, immigration increased dramatically as many Koreans were allowed to enter the United States as nonquota immigrants, such as orphans, refugees, and war brides. The Korean war had caused considerable population displacement. The rise of General Park Chung Hee to despotic power in 1967 forced many to leave the homeland. The Immigration and Naturalization Service reported more than 175,000 Koreans had been admitted from 1965 to 1976. According to the 1980 census, there were 354,529 Korean Americans in the United States.[21]

As with other ethnic groups, the Korean Americans have established their own institutions to replicate their old lifestyle and customs. The Korean-American capital is Los Angeles with a population in excess of 150,000. Fifty nonprofit organizations over eighty churches, and over fifty Korean high school and college alumni associations attest to the ethnic vitality of these peripheral Americans in the Los Angeles area. Other major cities that contain large clusters of Korean Americans are New York City, Honolulu, and Chicago. Radio and televisions stations broadcast special programs in the native language. News of the homeland and the Korean-American communities is reported in newspapers and other publications.[22]

Official and census reports have depicted the Korean Americans as well-educated, highly mobile, young to middle-age persons in their most productive years. They are regarded as exemplars of Asian immigrants who, according to the United States Bureau of the Census, have succeeded and have attained the highest median family income of any ethnic group in this country. They have also accomplished higher levels of formal education than other ethnic groups.

Part of the problem with this picture is that it is based on an earlier wave of Asian immigration. The latest wave, which has arrived in the last several years, is often made up of a populace of unskilled, poor immigrants, illiterate even in their own language. Thus on closer examination the highly favorable picture of the Asians is open to challenge as indicated in the following abstract. Many problems persist which will inevitably keep Korean Americans on the periphery of American life at least for the foreseeable future.

> Underemployment of highly trained and educated Korean Americans represents a waste of valuable human resources as well as the deprivation of needed services from the Korean American community and society at large. Underemployment is severe among professionals in the fields of health, engineering, law, and education. Such professionals find that their credentials and work experiences in Korea as well as their education in the United States are often ignored by potential employers and licensing bodies. . . .
>
> Problems encountered by Korean women married to U.S. servicemen are less visible and consequently are poorly understood by both the Korean ethnic community and the majority population. Since 1950 nearly 30,000 Korean women emigrated to the United States as

wives of American servicemen. An indeterminate number of them suffer from physical abuse, neglect, and desertion. Many more suffer from isolation and alienation. There is an urgent need to identify such women and develop programs to assist them.

English classes are needed for most foreign-born Korean Americans irrespective of age and level of education. The Korean language is structurally different from English and most Korean Americans find mastery of the English language to be a most difficult task. A lack of English proficiency has far-reaching tangible and intangible consequences: English language deficiency affects the type of jobs available and the rate of promotion for Korean Americans; racist employers use language as an excuse not to hire or promote Koreans; Korean American children with a lack of English skills find that it affects academic learning and performance in school as well as relationships with teachers and peers. On the intangible side, English deficiency affects the self-esteem of Korean Americans; many speak of losing their self-confidence after repeated experiences of being misunderstood or mistreated by unsympathetic Americans. Several studies carried out within the Korean American community emphasize the need for several levels of English classes to be taught by bilingual and bicultural teachers to assure the most effective language learning.

A recent survey of Asian Americans in Chicago indicates that Korean Americans express a desire for legal services, English classes, child care facilities, and bilingually staffed medical care and referral services, in that order of priority. The findings of one such study can obviously not be generalized to all other areas. However, a few additional studies from other regions offer evidence in support of the Chicago conclusions.[23]

As an organizer and director of the Korean Community Service Center in San Francisco, Tom Kim makes use of his background by presenting firsthand observations of his peoples' experiences in the United States. Moreover, he is critical of the Census Bureau's 1970 negligence toward the Korean American population. But he is gratified that his eighteen-year old son, a fourth-generation Korean American, would be included in the 1980 census count. Kim's analysis of Korean Americans as an emerging community is insightful, as is his comparison of other Asian Americans.

It is clear that the Korean American community is an emerging community that does not yet have either the external visibility or the developed social support systems of the other minority communities. As Dr. Bok-Lim C. Kim has pointed out, probably less is known about Korean Americans than about any other Asian American group, let alone the other established, long-recognized minority groups, such as blacks and Hispanics.

Consequently, the impact of the 1980 census on the Korean American community both externally and internally within the community will probably be greater than that for nearly any other community, and for this reason the Census Bureau should direct particularly

well-thought-out, culturally relevant data collection procedures for this
community. Some idea of the dimensions of the social service needs that
must be met can be seen in the fact that there has been a *1,300 percent*
increase in the Korean American population from 1965 to 1976. Nationally, Korean American immigrants represent the third largest immigrating group and the second largest Asian immigrating group (see
table 1).

TABLE 1

Year*	China/ Hong Kong	Japan	Korea	Philippines	Total
1967	25,096	3,946	3,956	10,865	43,863
1968	16,434	3,613	3,811	16,731	40,589
1969	20,893	3,957	6,045	20,744	51,639
1970	17,956	4,485	9,314	31,703	63,458
1971	17,622	4,457	14,297	28,471	64,847
1972	21,730	4,757	18,876	29,376	74,739
1973	21,656	5,461	22,930	30,799	80,846
1974	22,685	4,860	28,028	32,857	88,430
1975	23,427	4,274	28,362	31,751	87,814
1976	24,589	4,258	30,803	37,281	96,931
Total	212,088	44,068	166,422	270,578	693,156

*Year ending June 30.
Source: U.S., Immigration and Naturalization Service, *Annual Report
1976*, pg. 89.

　　Korean and other Asian immigrants from China, Japan, the
Philippines, Thailand, Laos, Vietnam, Cambodia, Indonesia, Burma,
India, Pakistan, Bangladesh, Malaysia, and Sri Lanka have chosen to
come to the United States despite knowing they would have to endure a
prolonged and arduous process before reaching these shores. They have
endured this difficult process because they want to become American
citizens and want to participate fully in American life. The population
of the United States consists of a pluralistic mosaic that was created by
immigrants from a diversity of cultures, languages, and historical
backgrounds. With the exception of the Native Americans, all
Americans can trace their roots back to another country.
　　The Koreans also come from another country—a country with a
rich heritage that can contribute to the pluralistic mosaic that has made
this country so strong and an example of how diverse peoples can blend
their cultural strengths to form a flexible, pluralistic society. In view of
the history of our country, it is my hope that the Korean and other immigrants today will be welcomed as contributors to our rich history
rather than viewed as second-class citizens until they are naturalized.
　　Ninety percent of the Korean population in the San Francisco Bay
Area are essentially monolingual (Korean-speaking) immigrants who do
not comprehend American culture and society. Politically, they are

relatively powerless and tend to fall into the low- and lower-middle in-
come brackets. A report by the California Advisory Committee to the
United States Commission on Civil Rights, released in February 1975,
pointed out that, "social services had not provided for the needs of
Korean American immigrants whose knowledge of and facility in
English was limited."

In this context of the needs of the Korean American community, I
would like to say a few words about its relationship to the other Asian
American communities. While we consider ourselves part of the Asian
American community and work closely with other Asian American
organizations, it is critical to understand that while there are important
commonalities amongst these groups, there are also critically significant
differences. These differences in historical background, culture,
previous political relationships, language, immigration patterns, and
ways in which each group has responded to the culture of this country
make each group a distinct entity with distinctive patterns of social service needs.

The very term Asian American was itself, in large part, a response
to American racism which saw all Asians as yellow people to be subor-
dinated, thereby necessitating our organizing Asian Americans to meet
our common experience of American racism. However, for the Census
Bureau's and other research and social service organizations' efforts to
be successful, the heterogeneity of the Asian American groups must be
recognized. This heterogeneity is such that when you go into Asian
American communities you do not hear people referring to themselves
as Asian Americans, but as Japanese Americans or Vietnamese
Americans or Korean Americans or Chinese Americans. That is also
why I could not successfully speak for another Asian group and why
another Asian group cannot speak for Koreans. The tendency of some
to blur the differences between the long-established Chinese and
Japanese communities under the term "Asian American" is a disservice
to each of these communities when it results in a failure to recognize
their unique histories and patterns of needs. For the Korean American
community and other emerging groups, this tendency has consequences
at least as serious—for the Korean community is not only a distinct entity
but also an emerging community with all that that implies.

For example, a much larger percentage of families within the
Chinese American and Japanese American communities date back for
three or four generations.The existence of several generations within
these communities is reflected in a relative diversity of social organizations which, in many instances, function as social support systems for
new immigrants. Also, a significant portion of the population of these
communities has been somewhat successful in acculturating so that their
members can function as intermediaries between the white majority and
their communities. Consequently, while still in considerable need of
more assistance, they have internal support systems as well as partially
developed relationships with support systems outside of their communities such as municipal, state, and Federal agencies. Due to this
situation, a fair amount of research information has also been gathered
regarding these populations.

However, for the Korean American community and other emerging groups very little of the above applies. As an emerging community we are in the process of developing internal support systems. Much of the so-called Asian American research does not apply to us because much of our population is composed of recent immigrants about whom little is known. The fact that 90 percent of the Korean American population is composed of recent immigrants has numerous consequences amongst which are that our community structure is a fluid, rapidly changing one and that we have relatively few advocates for our community compared to the other Asian American communities.

Obviously, the above situation has complex ramifications for data collection. For one, a population composed largely of immigrants is likely to be considerably more suspicious of government interviewers. For another, the interviewers and collection procedures must be more carefully developed to take into consideration the characteristics of a less acculturated community compared to the more acculturated communities.[24]

NEW PERSPECTIVES ON ASIAN AMERICANS

The last two articles in this chapter update the latest findings on the Asian Americans. The conclusions of these studies attempt to correct the many misconceptions about the current status of Asian Americans.

Since the 1960s Asian Americans have become increasingly visible on the national scene. Government agencies involved in the delivery of human services now realize that Asian Americans are an integral part of America. As a result, the Division for Asian American Affairs was established within the old Department of Health, Education, and Welfare. In a study of the characteristics of Asian American population in low-income urban areas, the Asian American Field Survey represented a major effort to fill the gap in knowledge about this major ethnic group. Data were gathered in two separate surveys in the fall of 1973 of five ethnic Asian subgroups in three cities: Chinese in New York, Filipinos in San Francisco, and Japanese, Koreans, and Samoans in Los Angeles. Below is the summary statement based on the Education Agency Data of the Asian American Field Survey.

The data from the schools surveyed in each Asian consumer population area indicate that sizeable proportions of the Asian American students attending these schools had English language difficulties, 14 percent among Samoan students, 26 percent among Japanese and Korean students, 44 percent among Philipino students and 27 percent among Chinese students. . . .

Students with no or limited English language ability may require bilingual instruction in order to participate successfully in the educational process. The ratios of the total number of language-disadvantaged students in each group to the total number of bilingual teachers for each group varied by subgroup. The ratios were 10 to 1 in schools with Samoan students, 32 to 1 for the schools with Pilipino students, and 30 to 1 for schools with Chinese students. . . .

Many schools have a shortage of bilingual teachers—24 out of 34 schools surveyed in the Asian American consumer population areas of Los Angeles, New York and San Francisco indicated that they had requested that additional bilingual teachers be hired. . . .

Although the Asian American students comprised sizeable percentages of the total student body in most of the schools surveyed, few schools provided an in-service training program to familiarize staff with the ethnic backgrounds of Asian American children. Only 1 out of 6 schools in the Los Angeles Samoan sample, 1 out of 7 schools in the Los Angeles Japanese/Korean sample, 1 out of 5 schools in the San Francisco Pilipino sample, and 7 out of 16 schools in the New York Chinese sample offered training programs on Asian American students and their backgrounds. . . .

Only 4 out of 13 schools surveyed in Los Angeles (31 percent) had Asian American studies programs, while 10 out of 16 schools surveyed in New York (62 percent) and 3 out of 5 schools surveyed in San Francisco (60 percent) has such programs. Many of the schools indicated that they wanted new or additional Asian American study programs to be established in the school. Six out of 6 schools surveyed in the Samoan sample, 5 out of 7 schools surveyed in the Japanese/Korean sample, 3 out of 5 schools surveyed in the Pilipino sample, and 13 out of 16 schools surveyed in the Chinese sample wanted new or additional Asian American study programs.[25]

There is a commonly-held view that Asian Americans are economically successful, well educated, and disproportionately represented in professional and technical positions, and that they are earning salaries equal to or even higher than majority Americans.[26] This portrait of Asian Americans as a successful minority took hold in the 1960s in the United States. This is a recent perspective because throughout most of the nation's history they have been victims of discrimination. In 1979 the United States Commission on Civil Rights sponsored a consultation on civil rights issues of Asian and Pacific Americans. The stereotype of their success was examined. The following extract represents the conclusions of that official study.

The data and studies . . . do not support the assertion. . .that Asian Americans are uniformly successful. The stereotype of their success that has developed since the sixties does not convey an accurate protrayal of members of these groups for several reasons.

First, the idea that all Asian Americans have achieved a high level of economic well-being ignores vast differences among groups within the Asian communities. The data analysis shows that the groups of

Asian Americans for which data were available were extremely heterogeneous and often differed considerably on the factors of income, education, and occupation. Furthermore, there were no data at all for many Asian American groups, including people from such diverse places as Guam, Thailand, the Fiji Islands, and Cambodia. Some Asian Americans are recent immigrants; many others are from families who have lived in this country for generations. These differences should caution the reader to avoid making generalizations about "all" Asian Americans.

Second, the stereotype of success focuses on those Asian Americans who are doing well, but it ignores the large number who are not. The percentage of college graduates, for instance, is high among many groups of Asian Americans. On the other hand, the proportion of adults with fewer than 5 years of schooling is also high when compared with majority Americans. Although many Asian Americans are in high-paying occupations, a disproportionately large number are also in low-paying jobs. Moreover, many of the Asian Americans in professional and technical positions are recent immigrants. The large numbers in this occupational category at least partially reflect American immigration policy, not solely the upward mobility of second- and third-generation citizens. On the contrary, there appears to be considerable underemployment among Asian Americans; a good education has not consistently led either to a high-paying job or to an income equal to that of comparably educated majority Americans. . . .

Asian Americans as a group are not the successful minority that the prevailing stereotype suggests. Individual cases of success should not imply that the diverse peoples who make up the Asian American communities are uniformly successful. Moreover, despite their relatively high educational attainment, Asian Americans earn far less than majority Americans with comparable education and are reported to have been victims of discriminatory employment practices.[27]

1. Henry Pratt Fairchild, *Race and Nationality* (New York: Ronald Press, 1947), p. 91.

2. U.S. Bureau of the Census, *Statistical Abstract of the United States: 1978.* 99th edition. (Washington, D.C., 1978), p. 88.

3. U.S. Bureau of the Census, *Race of the Population by States: 1980,* (Washington, D.C., 1981), p. 2.

4. Betty Lee Sung, *Mountain of Gold,* (New York: Macmillan, 1967), pp. 143, 150.

5. *Civil Rights Issues of Asian and Pacific Americans: Myths and Realities* (Washington, D.C., 1979), p. 307.

6. Reprinted from Mary Roberts Collidge, *Chinese Immigration* (reprint ed., New York: Arno Press, 1969), pp. 438–439.

7. Ibid., pp. 440–443.

8. Reprinted from No-Yong Park, *An Oriental View of American Civilization* (Boston: Hale, Cushman & Flint, 1934), pp. 14–15, 28–30, 34–35, 38–40, 110–11, 114–15.

9. *1977 Annual Report: Immigration and Naturalization Service,* p. 67; *Statistical Abstract of the United States: 1978,* p. 88.

10. U.S. Bureau of the Census, *Race of the Population by States: 1980* (Washington, D.C., 1981), p. 2.

11. Yamato Ichihaski, *Japanese in the United States* (New York: Arno Press, 1969), reprint, pp. 395–96.

12. Reprinted from "A Nisei Who Said 'No'," in *War Relocation Authority,* Community Analysis Notes No. 1, January 15, 1944, pp. 1–9.

13. Reprinted from Harry H. L. Kitano, *Japanese Americans: The Evolution of a Subculture,* © 1969, p. 56. Reprinted by permission of Prentice-Hall, Inc., Englewood Cliffs, N.J.

14. Ibid., p. 97.

15. U.S. Bureau of the Census, *Race of the Population by States: 1980* (Washington, D.C., 1981), p. 2.

16. United States Immigration and Naturalization Service, *Annual Report 1976* (Washington, D.C., 1977), pp. 88–89; U.S. Bureau of the Census, *Statistical Abstract of the United States: 1978,* 99th edition (Washington, D.C., 1978), p. 88.

17. Reprinted from Bruno Lasker, *Filipino Immigration to Continental United States and to Hawaii,* pp. 333–336. Copyright © 1931 by Edward Clark Carter. By permission of the University of Chicago Press.

18. Reprinted from Iris B. Buaken, "You Can't Marry a Filipino," *Commonweal* 41 (March 16, 1945): 534–35. Reprinted by permission of Commonweal Publishing Co., Inc.

19. Stephan Thernstrom, ed., *Harvard Encyclopedia of American Ethnic Groups* (Cambridge: Harvard University Press, 1980), p. 508.

20. Tran Tuong Nhu, "The Trauma of Exile, Viet-Nam Refugees," *Civil Rights Digest* (Fall 1976), pp. 59–62.

21. U.S. Bureau of the Census, *Race of the Population by States: 1980* (Washington, D.C., 1981), p. 2.

22. Brett Melendy, *Asians in America: Filipinos, Koreans, and East Indians* (Boston: Twayne, 1977), pp. 121–31; Stephan Thernstrom, ed., *Harvard Encyclopedia of American Ethnic Groups* (Cambridge, Mass.: Harvard University Press, 1980), pp. 601–6.

23. Bok-Lim C. Kim, "An Emerging Immigrant Community, Korean Americans," *Civil Rights Digest,* Vol. 9 (Fall 1976), p. 41.

24. Tom Kim, "Statement on Census Issues—Impact and Reaction," *Civil Rights Issues of Asian and Pacific Americans: Myths and Realities*, U.S. Commission on Civil Rights (Washington, D.C.: 1979), pp. 96–99.

25. *Asian American Field Survey, Summary of Data*, Division of Asian American Affairs, Office of Special Concerns (Washington, D.C.: Government Printing Office, 1977), pp. 186–87.

26. U.S. Commission on Civil Rights, *Success of Asian Americans: Fact or Fiction?*, Clearinghouse Publication 64 (Washington, D.C.: Government Printing Office, 1980), pp. iii, 1.

27. Ibid., pp. 17, 24.

KEY QUESTIONS

1. Was there any difference between the acceptance and treatment of the Chinese and that of the Japanese when they originally entered the United States?
2. No-Yong Park stated in 1934: "Race prejudice is probably one of the ugliest scars on American civilization." Do you agree? What evidence does he provide?
3. Define the following: Issei, Nisei, Sansei.
4. Why were Japanese-American citizens placed in internment camps at the beginning of World War II? Can such action be justified militarily and constitutionally?
5. Cite the basic ethnic experiences the Filipinos encountered in the United States.
6. To what extent are the Korean Americans on the periphery of American life as compared with other Asian immigrants?
7. What has been the general attitude of Americans to the recent Vietnamese arrivals? Give specific examples.
8. Does the United States have any obligation in admitting Indochinese refugees to this country? Explain.
9. Asian Americans have been regarded as having been very successful in this country. Is this an accurate picture?
10. Cite population data on the Asian Americans. What are the trends? What conclusions can be made from these population figures?

SIX

Immigrants from the Western Hemisphere: The Canadians, Mexicans, Puerto Ricans, Cubans, and Haitians

The history of the United States leaves little doubt as to the role various ethnic peoples has played in contributing to the population growth and mix. There is little question concerning the relationship of the New World to the Old, so that although there is a distinctiveness about Americans, on the whole the European ancestry is the preponderant one. Numerically speaking, most Americans descended from European forebears. However, it is important to remember that significant influxes of people came from other continents. This chapter will focus on the ethnic impact and experiences of people from the Western Hemisphere.

Emigration was discernible from the Western Hemisphere in the pre-Civil War period with approximately a quarter of a million inhabitants from British America settling in the United States during that time. Canadian emigration accelerated in tempo in the generation following the Civil War. From 1820 to 1975, 4,048,329 people have moved from Canada to the United States, a figure exceeded by few European countries.

Immigration to the United States from the rest of the Western Hemisphere, although a more recent movement, is nevertheless sizable. A total of 8,347,615 emigrants came from the Western Hemisphere, including 4,299,286 people from Latin America. Not hampered by quota restrictions and only recently limited to an overall yearly maximum figure, Latin Americans have come to be an important ethnic minority.

According to census data, 1,911,951 Mexicans had emigrated to the United States by 1975. Also, 1,408,027 people came from the West Indies, 262,533 from Central America, 607,556 from South America, and 109,419 from other parts of the Americas not clearly identifiable.

145

Three-fifths of the population of Spanish origin lives in the five southwestern states of Arizona, California, Colorado, New Mexico, and Texas. Additionally, foreign-born persons of Spanish origin made up the largest group of foreign-born people in the United States.[1]

A recent assessment by George Hall, Associate Director for Demographic Fields, Bureau of the Census, classified the Hispanic population in the following way.

> According to the 1970 and 1980 censuses, the measured change in the population of Hispanic origin was 5.5 million, or 61 percent, from 9.1 million to 14.6 million over the 10-year period. During the same period, the total population of the country increased by 23.3 million. Thus, while the Hispanic-origin population accounted for only 4.5 percent of the population in 1970, by 1980 the Hispanic population accounted for 6.4 percent of the total.[2]

CANADIANS

The 4,048,329 people who migrated from Canada to the United States between 1820 and 1975 make the Canadians the largest group of immigrants among all people from the Western Hemisphere. Of course, the raw figures must be considered advisedly, since among other things they do not take into account the number of return immigrants, which in the case of French Canadians was considerable. Nevertheless, Canadian migration to the United States still constitutes a major phenomenon. In view of the large number of people involved, it is surprising that research concerning this group is not more extensive.

Part of the reason for the limited research may have been caused by the peculiarities of the relationship between the United States and her northern neighbor. The absence of artificial physical barriers renders it unsurprising that there has been considerable interchange between the populations of the two countries. One idea of how extensive the movement from Canada to the United States was can be gleaned from a 1930 statistic showing that over 9 percent of the foreign-born in the country at the time were Canadian immigrants. The few hundred thousand Americans to migrate to Canada did not offset the influx from Canada southward, an exodus so massive that at one point it represented 20 percent of the entire Canadian population, thereby promoting fear of depopulation.

Although the movement to the United States was discernible from the beginning of the country's history, it picked up momentum in the 1850–1900 period and continued well into the twentieth century. However, the bulk of the Canadian immigrant population in the twentieth century easily assimilated with the native population of the United States because most twentieth-century Canadian immigrants were of English stock. By contrast, the experiences of the French Canadians have been markedly different. Although the majority of immigrants were French-speaking, over a million were English Canadians.

The social and linguistic backgrounds of the English and French Canadians necessarily resulted in differing assimilation patterns. French Canadians, because of the homogeneity of language and religion, formed a compact minority. Their religion and language served to maintain ethnic identity. While these factors bound French Canadians one to another, they also constituted barriers restricting intercourse with non-French-Canadians. The heterogeneity and less definite ethnic characteristics of English Canadians posed few assimilative problems and probably explain the paucity of material about their ethnic experience in the United States.

After emigrating, the majority of newcomers from Canada settled in the northeastern states and along the Atlantic Coast, where most flocked to urban centers. A smaller number moved into the Pacific Coast region. The main cause of their migration was economic. Canada's limited financial and economic development, as contrasted with the hope or expectation of receiving good wages in the factories and industries in the United States, told the story for most.

The significance of the Canadian migration to the United States is further demonstrated in the following figures estimating the percentage of Canadian stock in various American states in 1930; Maine, 25.3 percent; New Hampshire, 29.5 percent; Vermont, 20.6 percent; Massachusetts, 17.1 percent; Rhode Island, 16.1 percent; and Michigan, 10.3 percent. In some instances they were the predominant ethnic group in cities such as in Worcester, Fall River, and Providence.

Employed upon arrival almost completely in the factory system, a considerable number also entered the commercial and professional life of their adopted country. Although not generally the recipients of prejudicial abuse, French Canadians felt a need to preserve their ethnic characteristics. Their ethnic concerns found them erecting hospitals, schools, churches, benevolent and literary institutions, and newspapers with an indelible French stamp.

Bessie Bloom Wessel, in a study entitled *An Ethnic Survey of Woonsocket, Rhode Island* (originally published in 1931), made an important effort to collect scientific data on ethnic change in one geographic region of the United States in the early 1920s. When she examined Woonsocket, Rhode Island, she found that individuals of

French-Canadian descent represented two-thirds of the community's population. The majority (three-fourths) of the population attended French-Canadian parochial schools, intermarriage outside the ethnic group was the lowest of almost all the groups in the city, and they retained language usage to a high degree, although they became bilingual as their residence in the United States lengthened. In sum, French Canadians in this community demonstrated a remarkable tenacity to their cultural values, while not remaining indifferent to the lifestyles of their new environment. The selection that follows discusses bilingualism and bicultural traits.

Bilingualism and Biculturalism

It is in its bilingualism and in its biculturalism that the French-Canadian group is peculiarly distinctive and assertive. The data on language usage as obtained from the case histories of children corroborate the impressions obtained in home visits by Mlle Bossavy, and confirm the theories asserted by leaders in brochures on the subject and in conversation.

French Canadians even when native born and English speaking assert, with pride, their French-Canadian descent. About 90 percent of all individuals who are native born can speak both languages; about half claim bilingualism in the home. They assert, most emphatically, that their tenacity for French culture is not inconsistent with loyalty to America or with full acquaintance with American institutions and the English language. They are French speaking even in the third generation. But they are English speaking, too, and become so in the very first generation. Our previous analysis of language usage indicated that with the exception of the Jews no other group in Woonsocket learns English more readily or uses it more extensively. But they differ from the Jews in one regard: Given time, the Jews drop their ancestral language; the French retain it as the familial and ancestral tongue. With the French the attachment to the French language and to French-Canadian ancestry was noted among families when even grandparents were native born. In other families one or more of the grandparents were brought here as babies, or the first member of the family came to the United States sixty, seventy, or even eighty years ago, or "too far back to remember," and yet "these families frankly and even proudly claim their French-Canadian ancestry, and still use the French language."

Mlle Bossavy offers three possible causes in explanation of this tenacity for the French language even among Old Americans. She calls attention to the extensive intramarriage between French Canadians of different generations. Numerous marriages occur between two French-Canadian persons, one of whom is native born and the other foreign born. This was noted in our own investigations, but she finds evidence of the same procedure among grandparents and even among great grandparents. Second, frequent migration back and forth to Canada keeps the contacts and the language alive. Third, internal migration in the United States from one community to another where there are centers of French-Canadian life serves to perpetuate ancestral traditions. . . .

French Canadians who came under our observation expect their children to be bilingual as a matter of course. Native-born children know English and are being taught French and French tradition.

This biculturalism is not limited to use of French as a language. There is an ardor for all things French. Nor is this devotion necessarily French Canadian. The Canadian flag is rarely exhibited, but the French flag is seen alongside the flag of the United States. To the French the former is the symbol of his culture; the latter, of his country. Loyalty to Canada as a homeland is seldom heard expressed, but loyalty to French culture and American citizenship is urged in every page of their literature. This is a conscious policy indorsed and fostered by those who represent leadership in the group. Its manifestation in Woonsocket is obviously typical of the situation in other communities.

The dependence upon language is closely related to the religious problem. Indeed, the devotion to one gathers strength from the other. To them the French Canadian church and the parochial schools are the custodians of culture values. It is here that the dominance of the Irish, and particularly the "Irish theory of Americanization"—which assumes that the use of English as the primary language is an essential characteristic in an Americanization program—evokes resentment.

The French Canadian conceives Americanization as a process which brings into harmonious relation two diverse cultures. It is a plea for diversity in American community life. In this they are not alone among foreign nationalities in this country. But they are probably unique in having promulgated, some thirty years ago, a theory of Americanization which anticipated various theories of Americanization now current, one in particular which is in practice among numerous groups in this country. . . .

Franco-Americans

In Woonsocket no other group, excepting possibly the British, can claim to represent old settlers in greater degree or can claim larger contribution to stock. In their group life here the French Canadians are true to the policies articulated in conventions, in their press, and by their leaders.

The French Canadians insist and our data would corroborate the assertion that their adherence to the French language is not inconsistent with the use of English. The indications are that we have here a people that long remains not only bilingual but bicultural. In general, this "biculturation" is uniquely American. They themselves like to describe it as Franco-American, not French Canadian, and this point is made an issue in the educational programs which they foster. "We want an American-trained French clergy," said one Rhode Island priest, "a clergy that is 'American minded.'" Looking toward the clergy for leadership, the need is expressed for leaders trained in the United States, steeped in Catholic French tradition, and cognizant of the problems arising from migration and settlement in a still new homeland. No other nationality can claim to have enunciated a theory of Americanization more clearly or to have organized its group life more consciously toward a given end than have the French Canadians. It is manifestly a theory of adjustment of Americanization, and one of frank "resistance" to certain Anglo-Saxon (and Irish) traits in American life. It is with them "a way of life" to be defended against certain encroachments which they fear, and to be harmonized with a political theory which they support.[3]

One of the most recent and most interesting examples of ethnic retention was an announcement that a group of French Canadians in Louisiana are currently attempting to implement French language courses in that state's public school system. Since French culture was imbedded in Louisiana over two centuries ago, it is revealing that this belated attempt to preserve French language and culture in Louisiana has received sanction from the state legislature.

> A committee of the Lafayette Parish School Board is looking into the possibility of implementing compulsory French language courses at the elementary level in the parish public school system.
>
> The committee was appointed by board president George Dupuis to study ways and means of funding French programs, the kinds of programs that could be implemented, and the priority French could take over other subjects already on the curriculum.
>
> The committee was created at the request of James Domengeaux, chairman of the Council for the Development of French in Louisiana (CODOFIL). He warned that the French language in this state would "die forever" unless parish school boards take the leadership in initiating French language programs at the elementary level.
>
> Domengeaux reminded board members of the 1968 legislative act which urges school boards throughout Louisiana to implement French programs in their elementary schools "as expeditiously as possible" but not later than the beginning of the 1972-73 school year.
>
> Domengeaux told the board he would see to it that hundreds of teachers from France would be sent to Louisiana to teach French in the state's public schools. The French government in cooperation with CODOFIL would send the teachers, he said.
>
> Lafayette Parish has done "very little" toward implementing French education programs in its schools, Domengeaux said, and he suggested that the school board take steps toward starting the programs.
>
> Board members applauded Domengeaux after his remarks, and they passed a resolution commending him for his leadership in the movement to preserve and expand the French language and culture in Louisiana.[4]

MEXICAN AMERICANS

Spanish-speaking people make up the largest minority in the southwest part of the United States, and of this minority Mexican Americans comprise the largest segment, over 7.2 million according to the 1970 census data. As a result of the Mexican War, the Mexicans in this region automatically became part of the United States. In the last half of the nineteenth century there was a constant flow of people between Mexico and the United States, with little regard to the border line. The numbers were not many, and there was little interest shown by either government.

Mexican migration has taken place mainly in the twentieth century because of rising regional industries: railroad construction, mining, and agriculture. Economic advancement was the major attraction drawing the Mexicans to the United States. In *North From Mexico* (originally published in 1948), Carey McWilliams estimated that about 10 percent of Mexico's adult population entered the United States from 1900 to 1930. Although the Quota Act did not apply to Mexicans, the depression caused a drop in their immigration in the 1930s. It has been difficult to maintain accurate records because of the number of Mexicans who have entered illegally and the number who have returned to their homeland. These latter were called "wetbacks" (*mojados*) because they swam the Rio Grande and entered the United States illegally.

Legal and illegal entries into the United States increased sharply during World War II because of the increase of employment opportunities. For example, both governments agreed to allow agricultural workers (braceros) to enter the United States on a temporary basis, a program ended in 1964. The Mexican-born population in the United States in 1945 was estimated at 2.5 million, with this number increasing as the wetbacks and braceros continued to arrive. The braceros were not immigrants.

As indicated, Mexicans have been concentrated geographically and economically, becoming isolated in insular communities and jobs in this country. The wetbacks have remained around the border area, and large numbers of agricultural workers have been migratory, serving as a fundamental force in the agricultural development in the southwest. Discriminated against because of their lower socioeconomic background, the color of their skin, and their lack of skills, they were further exploited by the Anglos. Thus, the Mexicans experienced serious ethnic setbacks in their attempts to integrate and adapt to the North American culture.

With the rise of the civil rights movement and a growing sensitivity concerning the treatment of ethnic minorities, attention has begun to focus on the Mexican Americans. Their problems and achievements were suddenly "discovered." Only recently do we find a growing literature on the Mexican Americans that may be able to dispel false images of this large minority.

The Mexicans who have emigrated to the United States have

come mainly from the working class with few skills and little education. The lure of economic improvement motivated their movement to the north. Dr. Manuel Gamio, who studied Mexican immigration under a grant from the Social Science Research Council in 1926-27, concluded that Mexican Americans have very little chance of vertical social mobility.

> Let us now analyze the vertical social mobility of the immigrant, or the conditions of his rise from lower social strata to higher. From the time of their arrival in the United States the great majority of Mexican immigrants are automatically and inevitably incorporated into the lowest American social strata. In these strata they will remain until conditions in Mexico make possible and desirable their repatriation. The color of their skin, more or less dark, the small pay which they find themselves obliged to accept, their traditions of slavery and servitude which weighed upon them in the colonial period and even during the nineteenth century, the fact that in their own country they occupied the lower social strata—all these and many other factors bring it about that their social situation is in various respects similar to that of the colored race, though it should be recognized nevertheless that the race prejudice which exists toward the Mexican has never been so pronounced or exaggerated as that felt toward the Negro. . . .[5]

The United States Civil Rights Commission held a series of hearings in San Antonio, Texas, in early December 1968 in order to collect data regarding the rights of Mexican Americans in the Southwest. The hearings resulted in a voluminous record of nearly 1,300 pages. The following extract contains the testimony of Dr. Jack Forbes, a research program director with the Far West Laboratory for Educational Research and Development in Berkeley, California. Dr. Forbes points out sharp distinctions between the Mexican-American population and the European immigrants. Interestingly enough, he indicates the effect of conquest on a people's behavior, specifically the Mexican American. Dr. Forbes also shows the negative impact that the Anglo-American schools have had on the culture of the Mexican Americans in the Southwest.

> Well, I would say that it's not a valid analogy to compare the Mexican American population with particularly European immigrant groups in the United States for a number of reasons. It will probably take me a couple of minutes to respond to this question, but I will try to get through various points.
> First of all, the Mexican American population is in great part a native population in the Southwest. It is not an immigrant population. Now this nativity in the Southwest stems not only from the pre-1848 period, that is, the so-called Spanish colonial and Mexican periods, but it also stems from the fact that many people who today identify as Mexican Americans or in some areas as Hispanos, are actually of local

Indian descent. That is particularly in California, a great deal of California Indian descent and New Mexico a great deal of Pueblo Indian and Plains Indian descent and quite a bit of Pima-Papago descent in Arizona and so on, so that not only do we have people who are native in the sense of coming in from what is now Mexico before 1848, prior to the Anglo, but also in the sense that these people are descended from the aboriginal groups of the area.

Now a second point is that the Mexican American population today, as always, represents a northward extension of Mexico, and this is very, very different from European immigrant populations because with the European population you have a geographical, a special, as well perhaps a cultural ideological separation from the homeland.

But in the case of the Mexican American population you have direct continuity with the homeland, and the area in question is an extension of Mexico, that is the Southwest. . . .

Now another very significant difference which is, I suspect, one of the most crucial of all for understanding present day situations is that when we talk about minority populations we have to break them down into several kinds of categories.

You have already identified one in the immigrant group, but another kind of category of minority we need to concern ourselves with here . . . is the culturally different, the racially different minority which is also a conquered population.

Now, unfortunately, the concept of conquest has very, very often been ignored, but here I can't emphasize it too much, because we're beginning to learn that the process of conquest—particularly a harsh and intensive long enduring situation of conquest—has tremendous effect upon people's behavior.

For example, a conquered population tends to exhibit certain characteristics such as apathy, apparent indifference, passivity, a lack of motivation in relation to the goals of the dominant society. Such things as alcoholism, alienation, negative self-image, inferiority complex, personalistic factionalism with the conquered population because this is a powerless group and people's bitterness and so on must be taken out within the group on each other. These things are turned inward instead of being reflected outward against a group which has in a real sense been the oppressor in relation to this population. So this process of conquest is a very significant one indeed. . . .

And if we are to do this, we would see that the U.S. conquest of the Southwest is a real case of aggression and imperialism, that it involved not only the military phase of immediate conquest, but the subsequent establishment of a colonial society—a rather complex colonial society because there was not one single colonial office to administer Mexican American people and also to enable the dominant population to acquire almost complete control of the soil and the other forms of wealth, of the social institutions, cultural insitutions, and so on.

Now this conquest and colonial period can be further understood if we think about a community such as the city of Los Angeles in California which has long had a large Mexican American population but in which no major institution of any kind is controlled even proportionally to numbers by the Spanish-speaking population.

The schools, for example, are completely controlled by Anglo-Americans, the city government, the police department, the fire department, the public library, the department of water and power, I mean, you name it, going down the public institutions that presumably serve this population, all are now and actually have been controlled essentially by Anglo-Americans.

Now at the same time, of course, the economic sector, the private sector, is largely controlled by Anglo-Americans. So that we can say that in Los Angeles as in many, many comparable communities the Mexican American population exists as a powerless population that functionally in many significant respects, although things are perhaps gradually changing, but in a very significant aspect is a colonialized population that exists in a colonial relationship to the dominant group, even though I know that we really don't like sometimes to use those terms, but I think that if we are going to understand the situation that exists in the Southwest we have to do that. . . .

You see in terms of the Southwest, which is a very distinct region of the United States, the Anglo-American is quite obviously the newcomer, and as a newcomer he had the option available to him of assimilating into the native cultures which already existed in this area.

Now, we all realize, I suspect, that the Anglo-American like most nationalities around the world is not anxious as a group . . . to give up its identity. It is not anxious to change its way of life. I mean one really finds very few people around the world who simply, all of a sudden, decide to abandon their identity and culture, especially when the group is the conqueror, especially when the group already has visions of superiority complex and messianic ideas of his role in the world and so on. But the essential point is that one cannot expect the Mexican American as a distinct people with a distinct identity and a cultural heritage to be proud of, a very beautiful and extremely useful language and so on, to do what the Anglo-American obviously would not do. . . .

We did have in the old days, around the 1850's through the 1870's in many areas some schools that were controlled by local Mexican American people and that were bilingual and bicultural schools. They did exist—primarily because in certain areas such as southern California the Anglo had not yet moved in and taken over.

However, since that time the schools that have existed in the Southwest have not been neutral, culturally speaking. Those schools have been controlled by the Anglo-American population and the curricula throughout has been Anglo in character. It doesn't take but a moment visiting a typical school to find that the history is Anglo white history, that the sewing is Anglo sewing, that the cooking is Anglo cooking, that the literature is Anglo literature, and that the music is Anglo music and so on right down the line.

Now occasionally in recent years one can find a few little changes taking place, but these are still I think more at the level of token changes bringing in a little bit of exoticism rather than significant changes. The character of the school is that of the dominant population politically and economically.

Now the school cannot be understood and changing, it cannot be understood unless we remember that the school is simply one of those institutions which the dominant population uses as a device for perpetuating a colonial relationship and as a device for transforming the heritage of the Mexican American child. In fact one can really not deal accurately with the school apart from other institutions because if the school is going to be run as an Anglo institution this is because the dominant population wants to run all institutions as Anglo ones—all that can be run in that way. And so it is perhaps unlikely to expect the school to be changed apart from wider changes that take place in the total relationship of these two groups.

Now another aspect of this that must be mentioned is that this kind of school quite obviously has not been good for Mexican American children. The same kind of school has not been good for American Indian children; it's not been good for other non-Anglo children. It tends to lead to a great deal of alienation, a great deal of hostility. It tends to lead also to a great deal of confusion where the child comes out of that school really not knowing what language he should speak other than English, being in doubt as to whether he should completely accept what Anglo people have been telling him and forget his Mexican identity, or whether he should listen to what his parents and perhaps other people have said and be proud of his Mexican identity. There is a state of great vacillation on the part of many people. And when this kind of thing happens, children drop out of school. . . .[6]

UNDOCUMENTED ALIENS

A new group of immigrants has emerged in this country, the *sin papeles*, who are here without proper documentation. Since they live on the periphery of American society, researchers have attempted to identify their status.

The seizure of larger numbers of illegal aliens in the United States has highlighted the problem. There were more deportable aliens apprehended during fiscal year 1979 than in any single year since 1954. Of the 1,076,189 deportable aliens in 1979, Mexican nationals accounted for 998,830 or 93 percent of the total, an increase of 22,189 over the previous fiscal year. The remaining 77,588 included persons from virtually every country in the world. The following figure represents this trend. The following extract, based on a study of undocumented aliens in Texas in 1978, sums up their characteristics, their origins, their reasons for coming, and their impact on employment and social services.

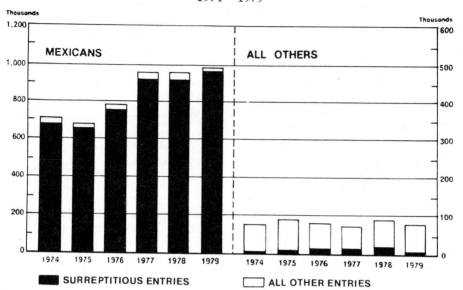

Deportable Aliens Found In The United States
1974 – 1979[7]

Most studies on undocumented aliens in Texas and elsewhere have come up with similar findings that indicate the following:
  • 1. The undocumented person is usually a young male, between the ages of 20 and 30, and unmarried.
  • 2. Of those undocumented persons interviewed, most are severely undereducated, many had not attained a sixth grade education, and a substantial portion were illiterate.
  • 3. Economic betterment or survival is the reason most frequently given by undocumented persons for coming to this country; there has been no exception to this finding in any of the literature.
  • 4. Undocumented persons are usually employed in low-status, low-skilled, and low-paid jobs.
  • 5. Undocumented workers contribute more in the way of taxes than they receive in social services.
  • 6. Undocumented persons send a significant portion of their income back to their native country to help support their families or relatives.

In the study prepared jointly by Avante Systems, Inc., and Cultural Research Associates for the Texas Advisory Committee, the above findings were, for the most part, confirmed. The study, "A Survey of the Undocumented Population in Two Border Areas," focused geographically on areas where large numbers of undocumented persons live—the region directly bordering Texas and Mexico. Two different groups of undocumented persons were examined, those in detention awaiting their return to Mexico and those unapprehended. Using these two populations, it was possible to contrast the characteristics and attitudes of undocumented persons who were being detained by the INS and those who were unapprehended.

Two areas of the border region were selected for intensive study —El Paso and the Edinburg-McAllen area located in the Lower Rio Grande Valley. In each of these areas, 300 undocumented persons were interviewed. Each sample was further broken down into three target groups of 100 persons each. The first target group—detained persons awaiting departure—as interviewed in INS Border Patrol detention and processing centers at Los Fresnos and El Paso. The second target group consisted of undocumented persons contacted through a variety of public and private agencies in each of the areas surveyed. The final group was found through a survey of residential areas known to have concentrations of undocumented persons. Persons in public places were also approached and interviewed in private. In addition, business firms known to favor and hire undocumented workers were surveyed.

Some of the key findings arising out of these 600 interviews with undocumented persons are as follows:

• A demographic profile of the cumulative sample (n=600) suggests that respondents range in age from 20 to 30 years old. Most were single males. Less than half were married and less than 40 percent had children. Most of the respondents had been in the United States less than 5 years.

• Virtually all of the respondents were from Mexico. Only about 2 percent came from other countries in Central America. Sixty-five percent of the El Paso respondents (n=300) were born and grew up in the State of Chihuahua; 5 percent were born and raised in Zacatecas. One-third of the Edinburg-McAllen sample (n=300) were raised in Mexican border states.

• Almost half of the El Paso sample arrived in the United States before 1972; 17 percent arrived in 1978. The median number of years respondents have lived in the United States was 4.8. This contrasts with the Edinburg-McAllen sample wherein 9 out of 10 (88.0 percent) have resided in the United States 5 years or less. Nearly half (48.3 percent) have lived in the United States less than 1 year.

• Of the El Paso respondents 55 percent planned to stay in the United States permanently, while the rest indicated a desire to return home. Of those individuals planning to stay, the majority (91.0 percent) indicated they would try to obtain legal residence in the United States. In contrast, only about 38 percent of the Edinburg-McAllen sample planned to remain in this country. The rest planned to stay less than 1 year.

With respect to the economic impact of undocumented persons, the interviews revealed the following:

• Of the El Paso respondents, 73 percent stated that their primary reason for entering the United States was to seek work. Approximately 57 percent (56.7 percent) of the Edinburg-McAllen sample indicated this as their primary reason for coming.

• In El Paso, construction was the major source of employment for undocumented persons. Overall, about 19 percent of the respondents were employed in construction, approximately 17 percent were working in agricultural jobs, and slightly over 12 percent were employed in service-related jobs. In the Edinburg-McAllen sample, most respondents (18.3 percent) were employed in agriculture, 17 percent were working in domestic service-type jobs, and only about 10 percent were in construction-type jobs.

• Many respondents in both survey areas worked for small business concerns employing from one to five persons. Fewer than 1 percent worked for enterprises employing more than 100 persons.

• Less than one-fifth of the respondents believed that they would be replaced by American citizens if they were to leave their jobs. Those responding affirmatively thought if American citizens were to be employed, they would receive better wages than undocumented persons. However, they said that treatment would otherwise be relatively equal.

• The mean hourly earnings for respondents was $2.75, but the mode (the answer appearing most frequently) was $2 per hour. Earnings averaged $21 a day.

Overall, the survey shows that most of the undocumented persons interviewed held jobs that required little education and little or no knowledge of English. Moreover, these jobs paid low salaries and provided few or no fringe benefits. For the most part, these workers valued their jobs more for security reasons than for advancement potential. These findings would seem to indicate that the displacement effect on American workers by undocumented workers is minimal.

Another question intimately related to economic impact is the spending pattern of undocumented persons in this country. The interviews indicated the following:

• About 22 percent of the El Paso respondents said they send money back to Mexico. Approximately 20 percent of the Edinburg-McAllen sample did likewise. On the other hand, 78 percent of the El Paso and 71 percent of the Edinburg-McAllen respondents indicated that they spend all of their money in this country.

A question frequently raised is whether the undocumented population in the United States constitutes a severe drain on public services. According to the Avante-Cultural Research Associates study, this does not appear to be the case, at least in the two areas surveyed. In fact, many respondents indicated that they have had social security taxes taken out of their pay, and many have had income tax deducted from their salaries. On the basis of 600 interviews, the following findings were derived:

• Almost 30 percent of those responding indicated they contributed to social security and slightly over 27 percent in both samples had income taxes deducted from their paychecks. Not one respondent reported that he or she received any social security benefits.

• With respect to employment, nearly 40 percent indicated they had been unemployed in the United States. However, few used governmental agencies to seek help and less than 10 percent filed for unemployment assistance. There was no indication that any of the respondents received unemployment insurance.

• In El Paso, only 8 percent of the respondents asked for help through the Texas Employment Commission, while only 1 percent of the Edinburg-McAllen sample did so. Only 4 individuals out of a total sample of 600 indicated that they had sought assistance under the Aid to Families with Dependent Children program. Fewer than 10 respondents asked for social security assistance or food stamps. Only 11 El Paso and 27 Edinburg-McAllen respondents reported that they had sought help from migrant health services.

The picture that emerged from this survey is that undocumented persons, while contributing to the local economy in the form of taxes and through the purchase of goods and services, actually use little and rarely seek out public assistance.

Another aspect of this study was to find out whether undocumented persons are treated fairly and equitably according to both the spirit and letter of immigration law. Before this question could be answered, the researchers first attempted to determine the frequency with which undocumented persons in the sample had been apprehended. According to the survey, the following pattern emerges:

• In the El Paso sample, which was comprised of one-third apprehended and two-thirds unapprehended persons, slightly over half (51.4 percent) had been apprehended since 1973 and about 48 percent had not. Approximately 31 percent of the respondents indicated that they had been apprehended only once, while 17 percent said twice. Nearly 11 percent indicated they had been caught at least three times and over 8 percent reported that they had been apprehended nine or more times.

• The Edinburg-McAllen sample, for the most part, was reluctant to respond to this question. In fact, almost half had no opinion or refused to answer this question. In the El Paso sample, only 18 respondents refused to answer this question. Still, of those who had indicated they had been caught previously in the Edinburg-McAllen sample, 41 percent reported that they had been apprehended more than once.

• The respondents' status, by definition, is outside the law, but otherwise the response indicates that they were, for the most part, lawabiding. Over 90 percent (91.6 percent) had not been arrested since 1973 for reasons other than their undocumented status. Only about 6 percent of the El Paso and 3 percent of the Edinburg-McAllen sample indicated they had been arrested for activities unrelated to their status.

• With respect to treatment by the INS, slightly over 62 percent (62.5 percent) of the El Paso sample and about 48 percent of the Edinburg-McAllen group said that they had not received bad treatment. Conversely, nearly 10 percent of both groups indicated that they had received bad treatment from officials. About 28 percent of the El Paso respondents and 42 percent of the Edinburg-McAllen sample either did not know, were unsure, or simply did not respond to the question.

• Although only about 10 percent of both the El Paso and the Edinburg-McAllen groups indicated that they had received bad treatment from officials, 26 percent of all respondents had heard about undocumented persons being abused by officials. In the El Paso sample, 35 percent of the respondents had reason to believe that undocumented persons were being abused, while 18 percent of the Edinburg-McAllen sample indicated this.[8]

Because they constituted the largest element within the Hispanic population in the United States and because of their conspicuousness as illegal entrants, Mexican Americans have become the focus of attention on the part of an American public aroused over the nation's struggling economy. It is no surprise then to find that they have received inordinate consideration from legislators and other interested parties in the latest efforts to reform the nation's basic immigration policies. In the fall of 1981, congressional hearings on the matter received testimony about Mexican Americans from many sources, one of which follows. It is the statement of Congressman Tony Coelho of California, who proposed a bill designed to enforce immigration laws against illegal entrants as well as prohibit employment of illegal aliens. It simultaneously recognized the human dilemma involved.

As the representative of a region of California in which Mexican immigrants had been prominent for many years as farmhands employed by local landowners, Coelho was cognizant of the hardship which could ensue unless some consideration were given to the needs of local growers and Mexican farm workers.

Statement by Hon. Tony Coelho, a U.S. Representative in Congress from the State of California

We are indeed a nation of immigrants. Throughout our history, newcomers have strengthened and revitalized our country. My ancestors, like yours, were immigrants. As a matter of fact, only a few short years ago my grandparents, poor by any standard, came to the United States from the Azores, to build a better life for themselves and their children. I have not come here today to suggest that while they achieved their goal, we should deny that same opportunity to others in the future.

The time has come when we must seriously entertain the idea that the United States, for all of its generosity, simply can no longer continue to accept all of the people who wish to come here. Even the words inscribed at the foot of the Statue of Liberty, which have become so much a part of the American spirit: "Give me your tired, your poor, your huddled masses yearning to breathe free," do not suggest that we accept all of the world's poor. It might also be helpful to remember that those famous lines of Emma Lazarus were not added until almost two decades after the statue was dedicated and that the real name of the Statue, is, and always has been, "Liberty Enlightening the World."

H.R. 2782 requires the Attorney General to enlarge the Border Patrol to at least 6,000 officers, and provides for the procurement and use of the most modern equipment and support available. The immigration laws passed by Congress must be enforced, and they must be enforced fairly and uniformly. Therefore, any new provisions of law designed to deter illegal immigration will be meaningless without enforcement capability.

The second large area covered by the bill is a ceiling on immigration, including refugee admissions, of 350,000 a year. The ceiling is flexible in that in an emergency, the President could authorize the borrowing of up to 350,000 from the next year. However, borrowing from the second year is not allowed: thus the integrity of the 350,000 is preserved. H.R. 2782 is the only current proposal, of which I am aware, that sets a firm ceiling on immigration, although the basic premise that limits had to be set was established when Congress reformed the law in 1962. . . .

Finally, the third major provision of H.R. 2782 would prohibit the knowing employment of illegal aliens and provide for a simple, easy to administer, three-phase system of enforcement and verification, leading to a secure social security card. In the first phase, the applicant for employment would be required to sign an affirmation that he or she is eligible to work in the United States. The affidavit could be made part of the existing W-4 withholding form, most employees must already fill out, or part of a standard application for employment. If an employer had a signed affidavit on file for an employee, he or she would enjoy a presumption of compliance with the law.

In the second phase, a verification system would be instituted. Each applicant would be required to give a social security number to the employer. The employer would then telephone a government agency, such as the Employment Security Administration of the Department of Labor, or the Social Security Administration itself, and report the number and the name of the person offering the number. When a social security was found valid, the employer would receive a transaction or authorization code, signifying that he called the number in and it was valid. If an employer had that transaction code for an employee, he or she would enjoy a complete defense against prosecution for violating the prohibition. This procedure is basically the same as that used by merchants in regard to most credit card purchases.

In the third and last phase, new secure social security cards will be issued. In order to receive one of the new cards, a person would have to provide sufficient proof that he or she was eligible to accept employment in the United States. The new cards, however, would be needed only by those who wished to change jobs, and would have unique identifying element, such as a serial number, to insure that it cannot be forged. The employers would continue telephoning the social security numbers to the government agency, but would also offer the identifying agent as well.

H.R. 2782 also offers a limited legalization program for illegal residents in the country since 1978. I am sure that the majority of people who have studied the illegal immigrant issue find themselves frustrated by the legalization or "amnesty" issue. While most would agree that we cannot realistically or humanely round up vast numbers of people whose presence has been tacitly condoned over the years by lax enforcement of our laws, they probably also feel that it is unwise, not to mention unfair, to generously reward those who have violated our laws.

H.R. 2782 attempts to balance those concerns by delaying implementation of a legalization program until efforts have been made to encourage illegal residents to depart voluntarily from the United States.

Legalization would then be open only to those who registered for the program and who met the financial and other requirements all other visa applicants must meet. . . .

My district, as you know, is located in the heart of the San Joaquin Valley of California, the most productive agricultural area of the world. Some 250 commodities are grown in that area, and although we are moving to mechanization on many crops, hand labor is still essential for the growing and harvesting of the majority of those commodities. For many crops, machine labor may never be able to replace human labor. Today, that hand labor, or human labor, is provided almost exclusively by illegal aliens. I do not like it, nor do the farmers particularly like it. I am sure you don't like it. But it is a fact of life which must be recognized and dealt with.

For a variety of reasons, not the least of which was the massive importation of Mexican workers under the Bracero program, Americans have unfortunately come to believe that farm labor is "below" them. Our sporadic, if not always lax, enforcement of immigration law since the end of the Bracero program led farmers in the Southwest to rely on the readily accessible supply of Mexican field workers.

If we completely sever that supply, without providing for some type of transition program, I fear the economy of California, indeed the entire Southwest, would be placed in grave jeopardy, and consumers throughout the nation would face skyrocketing prices.

I believe that in the final analysis, the existing H-2 program can be made to work effectively. But improvements are needed so that farmers, whose sole concern is to get that crop picked when it is ripe, can be assured that they will be able to legally employ a foreign worker when no American worker is available. During the transition period, I would suggest that we institute a temporary worker program, limited in numbers and duration, targeted to those geographic areas and industries, whose sole survival has come to depend upon a foreign, albeit, illegal labor force.

Thank you again for giving me this opportunity to be heard on this vital national issue.[9]

In a unique development, the Mexican American Legal Defense and Education Fund challenged a Texas law which prevented illegal immigrants from receiving public school education. The United States Supreme Court, 1982, in the *Plyler V. Doe* decision, settled the issue when it ruled that children who are illegal aliens have a constitutional right to a free education. For the first time the Court said that the equal protection guarantee "extends to anyone, citizen or stranger," within a state boundary, and that the state cannot cut off public funds to local districts for educating children who illegally entered the country.

Justice William J. Brennan Jr., invoking the Fourteenth Amendment, stated in the 5-to-4 majority decision that children of undocumented aliens are part of an underclass and should not bear the "onus of a parent's misconduct." He pointed out that denying these children a basic education would deny them the ability to live within the structure of our civil institutions. . . ."

Excerpts from the majority decision follow.

From Majority Opinion
By Justice Brennan

The question presented by these cases is whether, consistent with the equal protection clause of the 14th Amendment, Texas may deny to undocumented school-age children the free public education that it provides to children who are citizens of the United States or legally admitted aliens. . . .

Our conclusion that the illegal aliens who are plaintiffs in these cases may claim the benefit of the 14th Amendment's guarantee of equal protection only begins the inquiry. The more difficult question is whether the equal protection clause has been violated by the refusal of the State of Texas to reimburse local school boards for the education of children who cannot demonstrate that their presence within the United States is lawful, or by the imposition by those school boards of the burden of tuition on those children.

Sheer incapability or lax enforcement of the laws barring entry into this country, coupled with the failure to establish an effective bar to the employment of undocumented aliens, has resulted in the creation of a substantial "shadow population" of illegal migrants—numbering in the millions—within our borders. This situation raises the specter of a permanent caste of undocumented resident aliens, encouraged by some to remain here as a source of cheap labor, but nevertheless denied the benefits that our society makes available to citizens and lawful residents. The existence of such an underclass presents most difficult problems for a nation that prides itself on adherence to principles of equality under law.

The children who are plaintiffs in these cases are special members of this underclass. Persuasive arguments support the view that a state may withhold its beneficence from those whose very presence within the United States is the product of their own unlawful conduct. These arguments do not apply with the same force to classifications imposing disabilities on the minor *children* of such illegal entrants. At the least, those who elect to enter our territory by stealth and in violation of our law should be prepared to bear the consequences, including, but not limited to, deportation. But the children of those illegal entrants are not comparably situated. Even if the state found it expedient to control the conduct of adults by acting against their children, legislation directing the onus of a parent's misconduct against his children does not comport with fundamental conceptions of justice.[10]

PUERTO RICANS

Puerto Rico holds an unusual place among American possessions. Discovered by Columbus in 1493, it became a strategic stronghold for the Spanish as they used the island to protect their position in the Caribbean. Unsurprisingly, Spanish culture made an indelible impression on the island during the next few centuries. Although Indians first inhabited the island, in the course of time they became virtually extinct.

As a result of the Spanish-American War in 1898, the United States secured Puerto Rico. However, this country did not devote much of its energies to the island's development until 1941 when Rexford Tugwell became its governor. Under his leadership efforts were made to improve public education, sanitation, and social services— activities which had been sadly neglected in the prior period, during which the island was known as a "poor house." Slowly, the economic face of Puerto Rico began to change from that of a poverty-stricken land to that of a fairly healthy self-governing entity. This transformation has been attributed to several factors. First was the overwhelming support for Luis Muñoz Marin, Puerto Rico's first elected governor, whose innovative leadership proved invaluable. Second, credit is given to Operation Bootstrap, which concentrated on economic development through such steps as the attraction of new industries, breaking up large acreage holdings, and slum clearance. The result has been that per capita income has risen perceptibly, although still far below that of the United States. A third factor is the political status of the island: Its free commonwealth association with the United States was confirmed in its first constitution in 1952. This seems to have majority endorsement, although a vocal minority has demanded complete independence.

The Puerto Ricans, therefore, hold a unique place in the study of American ethnic groups. Very soon after the United States acquired the island, free access to the United States was available to its inhabitants. Together with the extension of American citizenship in 1917, this prompted 70,000 Puerto Ricans to live on the mainland prior to the beginning of World War II. It was not until after World War II that really great numbers migrated. After 1946, with the improvement of transportation, especially the airplane, hundreds of thousands relocated so that in 1971 the population figure of individuals of Puerto Rican origin is placed at 1,450,000. In the process, considerable numbers returned home, many to return again. Because of its location and its cosmopolitanism, New York City became the primary residence for most of the Puerto Ricans, especially in such areas as East Harlem, South Bronx, and other sections of Brooklyn and Queens. Nearly 70 percent of the Puerto Rican population in the United States lives in the New York City Metropolitan Statistical Area. They came for economic and social improvement. They took the unskilled jobs, and, though partially Americanized, they experienced many difficulties because of their color, religion, and lower socioeconomic background. They were also prey to exploitation. Yet the Puerto Ricans with their rich heritage have made a major impact on such places as New York City and have begun to emulate the role of the Jews and Italians who came before them.

Although most Puerto Ricans are nominally Catholic, the Church has not made as great an impact on the Puerto Rican community in New York City as it has on other ethnic groups. This can be ascribed to their experience in the homeland, the lack of Spanish-speaking priests, and the nature and size of the Catholic parish. On a smaller level, but in a more intense manner, Protestant denominations have made considerable headway in attempting to serve the religious and social needs of the New York Puerto Rican population, as indicated in the following selection.

We have already referred to the weakness of Catholicism in Puerto Rico. Roman Catholicism is not a national church, as it is in Ireland and Poland. It sets the general frame of life by baptizing (most), marrying (less) and burying, and its calendar sets the holidays and festivals, but its impact on the people, in guiding their lives and molding their ideas, and in serving as a vessel for their social life, is relatively small. It is, as elsewhere in Latin America, a church for the women. In New York the Catholic Church is engaged in an energetic program to increase the number of Spanish-speaking priests, and to widen the circle of activity among the Puerto Ricans. Since the Puerto Ricans have spread so widely through the city, the Church has for the most part carried on its Puerto Rican work in established parishes. The Puerto Ricans have not created, as others did, national parishes of their own. Thus the capacities of the Church are weak in just those areas in which the needs of the migrants are great—in creating a surrounding, supporting community to replace the extended families, broken by city life, and to supply a social setting for those who feel lost and lonely in the great city. This is a task that smaller churches, with an active lay leadership, and a ministering group that is closer to and of the people, can do better.

Most of the Puerto Ricans in the city are Catholic, but their participation in Catholic life is small. It is interesting for example that there are but 15,000 Puerto Rican children in parochial schools in the New York Archdiocese, against almost ten times as many in the public schools, a much smaller percentage than for any other Catholic group in the city. There are only 250 Spanish-speaking priests in the Archdiocese of New York for the Puerto Rican population, and most of these—as many in Puerto Rico itself—have learned Spanish to minister to the group. In 1961, in 42 Catholic parishes in New York City with Spanish-speaking priests, there was only one Puerto Rican. And the proportion of the Spanish-speaking priests to the Catholic Puerto Rican population was still one-third or one-fourth what it was for other New York Catholics.

As the problems of the first generation are overcome, as families become stabler, incomes higher, and the attachment to American middle-class culture stronger, Catholicism will probably also become stronger among the Puerto Ricans. But it does not seem likely that it will play as important a role among them as it plays in the European Catholic ethnic groups. For there is already well established a strong rival to Catholicism among the Puerto Ricans, and if we were to reckon religious strength not by mild affiliation but by real commitment, it would be likely that there are not many less committed Protestants among the Puerto Ricans than there are committed Catholics.

Protestantism's history on the island dates from the American occupation, when some major denominations divided up the island and began work there. A 1947–1948 study of the island showed that about 82 per cent called themselves Catholic, that 6 per cent of the population belonged to the major Protestant denominations, 2 per cent to Protestant sects, and 2 or 3 per cent were Spiritualists. The Mills-Senior-Goldsen 1948 study of New York Puerto Ricans showed about 83 per cent Catholic and slightly higher proportions of Protestants in the major denominations—9 per cent—and in the sects—5 per cent. But the fervor of the Protestants seems greater than that of the Catholics; and the fervor of the members of the Pentecostalist and similar sects of the hundreds of the storefront churches that dot the Puerto Rican neighborhoods is even greater.

There are about 70 Spanish-language Protestant churches of major denominations in the city, and close to another 50 that have both English and Spanish services. Another 70 have some Spanish members. All told, there are about 14,000 Spanish-speaking members of major Protestant denominations in the city, about 10,000 in their own all-Spanish churches. Attendance in the Spanish churches is high, evangelical zeal puts most Anglo-Saxon Protestantism to shame, and the willingness to spend money to support the church is also great. . . .

But the most vigorous and intense religious movements among the Puerto Ricans are the Pentecostal and independent Pentecostal-type churches. The 1960 study of the Protestant Council of New York located 240 such churches—there are certainly more than this. Their membership was conservatively estimated at about 25,000. These tiny churches generally run services every day of the week. They demand of their members that they give up smoking and alcohol and fornication. They are completely supported by their memberships, and often a church of 100 members will suport a fulltime minister. The Pentecostal movement, which began in America, has for reasons that are not clear been successful in penetrating a number of Catholic areas, for example, Italy and Chile. Two Catholic sociologists who have studied the Pentecostal churches in New York suggest that they derive their strength from Catholicism's weakness. Many migrants feel lost in the city; many search for a community within the Church, and the integrated Catholic parish, whose base is another ethnic group and whose priests are not Spanish, cannot give this. The preachers and ministers of the Pentecostal Church in New York are almost all Puerto Ricans. Though it was initially spread to the island by English-speaking evangelists. working through translators, the requirements for preaching and ministering make it possible for devout members to rise rapidly to such positions. "In the Catholic Church," one member told the investigators, "no one knew me." Here, if a stranger comes in, he is warmly greeted; if a member falls sick, he is visited; the tight congregation is one of the most important expressions of a community that is found among Puerto Ricans in New York.

Protestantism is an interesting if minority phenomenon among the Puerto Ricans; and there exists here a real field for competition between Catholicism and Protestantism in the city. It is impossible now to predict how things will come out.[11]

In any discussion of Puerto Rican culture, a seminal question is the one that asks about Americanization of the Caribbean island. For nearly three-quarters of a century, American influence has continued to penetrate the island, and the question remains whether it will result in drab uniformity of culture or in the persistency of cultural diversity. Gordon K. Lewis, in *Puerto Rico, Freedom and Power in the Caribbean*, discusses the problem and concludes that the process of Americanization of Puerto Rican society goes on relentlessly and that this becomes more significant as it proceeds largely in the absence of contact with other Latin cultures. If this continues, he concludes, the Puerto Ricans will lose their virtues, and intellectualism becomes sterile.

The American record in Puerto Rico since 1900—whatever the future may hold—does not warrant any more optimistic conclusions about the Puerto Rican place in the national picture. The Puerto Rican child, from the beginning, has been taught American rather than Puerto Rican history. His attributes have been built up in a colonial atmosphere, where the mass media have portrayed to the populace a culture that is not their own and to which they have been taught to attribute everything that is worthwhile in their experience. The very linguistic symbols of merit and authority become those of the dominant power; thus the Puerto Rican student still manages, only too frequently, to address his teacher as "Mister," rather than maestro or professor, as if the teacher were an American. Nor is this applicable to the past only for, as Rene Marques has pointed out, the ancestral sense of helplessness in the individual Puerto Rican is still psychologically worked upon through modern methods of education that are only somewhat more subtle than those used previously. Since the burden of taking on the inconvenient aspects of communications between the ruled and the rulers has always been the compulsory lot, in colonial situations, of the ruled, Puerto Ricans have been compelled to learn English rather than Americans Spanish. The depreciation of the local culture has encouraged a corresponding self-depreciation in individuals. For some it has taken the form of a blind submission to the American style, expressing an urgent drive, frequently only half understood by its victims, for identification and incorporation with the elite of the governing power; and the guilt feelings thereby engendered have frequently been covered up by the device of identifying Puerto Rico with "Western civilization" rather than with the United States, so that terms like this and others— "the crisis of the West," "Western culture," the free world," and so on—play a therapeutic role in the psychology of that type of Puerto Rican. For others again the response to a situation so basically intolerable to sensitive spirits and so powerfully buttressed by all the institutions of the society, private and public, political and economic, has been a retreat into feelings of bitterness, inferiority, chauvinism; and the life of a spirit like Pedro Albizu Campos is a tragic monument to those elements in Puerto Rican politics.

Even when the individual American in the picture has been genuinely liberal, the liberalism has only too often blandly assumed the natural superiority of American values (just as, in the case of the British Caribbean, even the sympathy of British Fabian Socialists with local aspirations has been grounded on the assumption that West Indian nationalism ought to perpetuate English modes and manners). The matter of race is an apt illustration. Americans liberal on everything else have drawn the line (with some individual exceptions) at accepting the Latin principle of race mixing. It has been a widespread, and quite unscientific, belief among them that the mixing engenders a decline in mental and physical capacities, . . .

There is not much more truth in the second assumption that Puerto Rico can be viewed as an overseas crucible of Hispanic culture. The Spanish legacy, as already noted, did not transplant to the island any of the outstanding features of Spanish life—a ceremonial urban culture, a complex bureaucracy (except in the military government), a sophisticated agricultural economy. Nor did it introduce any of its imposing civil and ecclesiastical hierarchies, as it did in its Mexican and Peruvian viceroyalties: the missions of the religious orders, the great peninsular universities, the tradition of splendid architecture, both civil and religious. There was nothing like the strong institutional fabric of the continental colonial societies to form a foundation for later emancipation from peninsular suzerainty. The psychological consequences of all this have been momentous, not least of all the continuing dependency of the Puerto Rican spirit upon external deliverance and the comparable failure to look inwards for national salvation. So, if there are unique Puerto Rican characteristics, it is profoundly misleading to expect them to be Caribbean echoes of the original Hispanic. Indeed the expectation is grossly unfair, for it presupposes a sort of tribal ancestor worship of merely snobbish utility. The American critic who compares the twentieth-century Puerto Rican with the sixteenth conquistadores, to the disadvantage of the former, rarely pauses to reflect upon the conclusions that might be derived from comparing his own type with the independent American farmer we read of in the pages of Crevecoeur. The modern Puerto Rican must be judged by what he is, not by what his ancestors were: the warning applies to both the Puerto Rican and American cultivators of the myth of Puerto Rico as a bridgehead between two world cultures. Consequently the attempt to explain the island culture and institutions as a crossing between two growths of pre-established national entities, the one Spanish, the other American, unavoidably results in shallow analysis. The metaphor has too easily seduced even critical observers, so that the cultural reality—that Puerto Rico exists as a local Creole culture in its own right, not merely as a tropical mirror of metropolitan Europeans or American societies—is too readily lost sight of. For what has really taken place in the last sixty years is not the growth of an ideal common life shared on equal terms by both Puerto Ricans and Americans—the ideal was typically expressed in a book like Juan Bautista Soto's volume of 1928, *Puerto Rico ante el Derecho de Gentes*—but the relentless imposition of American standards upon a dependent society helpless to resist the process. . . .

For the truth of the matter is that as the Americanization of the society proceeds apace its isolation from other cultural influences becomes more and more pronounced. Apart from the odd trip, the insular artists and intellectuals are starved of any fruitful contact with the Latin American world. The fact that the general output of the Institute of Puerto Rican Culture is weak in the field of painting, so powerfully resurgent elsewhere in the Caribbean in Mexico and Haiti, and strong in those fields that are not Pan-Caribbean in character—mural decoration, wood sculpture, lithography, and poster art—suggests a regrettable separation from what is going on elsewhere. Everything, increasingly, is seen through the American perspective. The strident tones in which so many Puerto Ricans congratulate themselves upon enjoying political "stability"—which really means the protection afforded by the virtual protectorate of the United States military power—shows how deeply they have removed themselves from a sympathetic identification with the Latin-American peoples. The humiliation, frequently self-imposed, of that situation is no better exhibited than in the spectacle of the Puerto Rican statehood fan pleading with the American people to take on an assimilation policy which would mean the erosion of all the social and cultural characteristics which distinguish his people from those of the United States. In such a context, people come to despise their own virtues. So, there are private hospitals in San Juan where all signs are in English despite the fact that the staff are overwhelmingly Spanish-speaking. The man in the street will convert himself into a pathetic comedy as he tries to parade the little store of mangled English phrases he has somewhere picked up. The comic strips in the newspapers are all of them American, with Spanish titles, even although some of them, "Blondie," for example, or "Bringing up Father," portray the type of abject American husband so far removed from the Puerto Rican male's image of himself.[12]

CUBANS

Cubans had little influence on the ethnic mix of American society until the 1960s. In fact, there is a direct relation between the success of Fidel Castro's revolution, beginning in 1959, and the increase of Cuban immigration to the United States. Cuba, long a possession of Spain, received her nominal independence in 1898. During the major portion of the intervening years, the United States exercised significant control on the island through the Platt Amendment and economic investments. The Good Neighbor Policy of the 1930s attempted to promote a new era of friendship and equality with Cuba. Though World War II alerted the United States to the strategic value of the entire Caribbean area, the United States funneled most of her energies and resources to Europe and Asia after the war. The Alliance for Progress and other programs are the recent responses to the needs of Latin-American neighbors.

In the immigration statistics recorded by the U.S. Bureau of the Census, Cuba is included with the West Indies from 1820 to 1950. During this period a total of 496,696 migrated here from the West Indies.

When it became clear that the Cuban revolution under Fidel Castro would go much further than many had assumed, the exodus from Cuba escalated to immense proportions. It accelerated after the Bay of Pigs invasion in 1961 and the missile crisis in 1962. When Castro announced in September 1965 that he would permit Cubans to leave the country, it is believed that the waiting list ranged from 50,000 to 700,000. By 1977 the census estimated the American Cuban population at 681,000.

It soon became obvious that the original intention of many Cubans to return to the homeland had to evaporate overnight and the Cubans had to adjust to making the United States their permanent residence, since little chance remained of overthrowing the Castro regime. Thus, since 1959 over 635,000 Cubans have emigrated here. The remarkable thing about the Cuban immigrants is their rapid adaptability to American society and life. In fact, because they are so well educated and skilled, they have been referred to as the "golden exile." In many ways the United States has gained from their knowledge and expertise.

The Cuban immigration in the 1960s made a great impact on the city of Miami. At first, relations between the Cubans and Miamians were strained, but eventually adjustments were made to the benefit of each group. Both private and public aid hastened the transitional period of adjustment. The Cuban success actually resulted from their own private initiative and their advanced backgrounds. The following selection concentrates on the Cuban ethnic experience in Miami.

A Plus for Miami

Virtually all the Cubans who come directly to the U.S., rather than by way of some other country, come first to Miami for processing. There they are screened by immigration and naturalization authorities who, among other things, investigate the possibility that Cuban Government agents are included among the arrivals. Once cleared, however, the immigrants are technically free to do what they please. What would please most of them would be to settle in Miami, where the climate is agreeable and where previous immigrants have virtually created a little bit of old Havana. Something over a quarter of the 300,000 refugees are now living in Miami.

For some time this concentration was viewed as a social problem that might get out of control. Ripples of dread have passed through Miami as each of the successive waves of refugees hit town. In the early 1960s there was, indeed, a plausible case for being worried about the immigrants. Miami's was a depressed economy. Nearly 100,000 Cubans had recently been dumped into the metropolitan area, raising its total population by over 10 percent. Over two-thirds of the refugees were then on public assistance. The area's total unemployment rate hung around the 10 percent mark, and loud, anguished cries came from the Negro community and some labor unions because Cubans were going to work for half the prevailing wages. Miami schools had trouble accommodating the 18,000 refugee children, most of whom spoke only Spanish. Furthermore, preoccupied with overthrowing Castro and returning to their homeland, many of the refugees were devoting a lot of their energies and spare capital to roiling agitation and sometimes even to harassing raids on the Cuban mainland.

Most of the refugees have long since given up any ideas about freeing Cuba by their own efforts and are now devoting their talents to getting along in their adopted home. . . .

"Send Us a Thousand More"

Most Cubans would almost certainly still be in Miami but for some pressures exerted on them by the Cuban Refugee Center, which has charge of financing and coordinating most of the government and voluntary agencies' aid to refugees. Registration with the center is voluntary, but anyone who fails to register forgoes a wide range of benefits: temporary financial assistance (up to $100 a month per family), medical care, food, hospitalization, and education loans for Cuban college students, plus a variety of adult-education programs that include English and vocational courses, teacher training, and refresher courses for physicians. At the same time, it is made clear to the refugees that those who register must agree to resettlement as soon as suitable jobs are found for them.

Most of the resettlement work is handled through the center's contracts with four voluntary agencies: the National Catholic Welfare Conference, the Church World Service (a Protestant agency), United HIAS (Hebrew Immigrant Aid Society), and the nonsectarian International Rescue Committee. The refugee is free to choose any one of these agencies and it then helps him find a job outside Miami. Within twenty-four to forty-eight hours of their arrival in the city, most Cubans are on their way to somewhere else. John Thomas, who directs the program from Washington, is convinced that the worst thing that can happen to refugees is to be detained for long periods while they are being "processed." Says Thomas: "Only two weeks in a refugee camp is enough to destroy a person."

Wherever Cubans have settled, they have elicited remarkably consistent praise for their energy, ability, and exemplary conduct. Many of the firms that have employed a few send back to Miami for more. And one company in Texas, which had taken on a lot of Cuban construction workers, later sent a wire to the refugee center, "Send us a thousand more."

Like Miami, most other cities have found that some widespread fears and prejudices about Cubans are groundless. In Miami, where Cubans make up between 10 percent and 15 percent of the population, they account for only 2.9 percent of the arrests, with most of these being for traffic violations—Cubans seem not to be very good drivers, for some reason. In most communities where Cubans have settled, welfare officials have noted with astonishment their powerful urge to stay off relief rolls whenever jobs are available—and, with even more astonishment, have noted the effort that some Cubans make to pay back any welfare money they may have received. Of New York's 30,000-odd Cubans, only about 500 are on relief. Robert Frutkoff, a management expert with the New York State Employment Service, testified in Senate hearings on refugee problems this past spring that Cubans are "a highly motivated group. We found, for example, that they would prefer to take any type of job than apply for welfare."[13]

By the beginning of the 1980s, the presence of Cubans in America was so pronounced that they were recognized as important social, economic, and political forces in a number of communities: Newark and New York, for instance. Although heavily respresented in Florida, it was in Miami and surrounding suburbs such as Hialeah and Coral Gables that they really emerged as an ethnic force. Hispanics constitute well over half of Miami's population (207,000 out of 370,000), with the majority of Hispanics being Cuban. They were part of the largely middle-class exodus of 700,000 Cubans who left their native island after Fidel Castro came to power and before the Mariel boatlift of 1980. A five-square-mile area known as "Little Havana" has become a neighborhood where the fragrance of *pasteles* (pastry) and *café cubana* wafts from hundreds of neighborhood coffee stands.

Cubans are conspicuous, moreover, for the degree of success

they have achieved in their adopted land. Their enterprise has transformed the economy of Miami and its environs. Hundreds of Cuban restaurants and dozens of factories ranging from furniture production to shoe manufacturing are their understandable boast. They are prominent in land development, construction, banking, and numerous small enterprises. Clearly, although their stay has been brief, it has already resulted in significant impact. A Hispanic, Maurice Frere, was elected mayor of Miami.

Lest this seem a panegyric for Cuban-style "Horatio Alger" stories, it should be remembered that success and upward mobility have come after years of hard work.

The following extract illustrates the response of the United States to the Cuban refugees of the 1960s and 1970s.

Cuban refugee program

The Cuban refugee program is administered by the Department of Health, Education, and Welfare under the authority of the Migration and Refugee Assistance Act of 1962. Fiscal year 1979 is the second year of a 6-year phaseout of the Cuban refugee program which was initiated by the fiscal year 1978 Labor-HEW Appropriations Act.

Federal assistance has been provided for Cuban refugees since 1960, and the Cuban refugee program has been part of HEW since 1961. The Migration and Refugee Assistance Act authorizes assistance to or on behalf of needy Cuban refugees, including financial assistance to State and local public agencies providing health and educational services, and special employment training services, to Cuban refugees; funding for the transportation and resettlement of refugees within the United States; and funding for employment training or refresher professional training projects.

Cuban refugees in the United States are concentrated in Florida, particularly in the Miami (Dade County) area. One of the primary reasons for the establishment of the Cuban refugee program was to offset the financial impact of the sudden arrival of a large number of refugees on the relatively limited resources of any single jurisdiction.

While funding has been available for employment training and other activities designed to promote refugee self-sufficiency, by far the greatest emphasis has been on the reimbursement of State and local agencies for 100 percent of the cost of welfare assistance and services provided to Cuban refugees. Refugee welfare assistance, including medical assistance, accounted for 82 percent of the Cuban refugee program budget for 1977. Under the phaseout, Cuban refugees who are eligible for cash assistance under the aid to families with dependent children (AFDC) program, and medical assistance under the medicaid program, will be served by those programs, with Federal reimbursement provided for a decreasing portion of what is normally the non-Federal share. Federal reimbursement is also being phased out for assistance provided to refugees under State and local general assistance programs.

Federal assistance for refugee education has consisted primarily of aid to the Dade County, Fla., public school system. Aid to Dade County public schools accounted for 15 percent of the Cuban refugee program budget for fiscal year 1977.

As the Cuban refugee population became more prosperous, and as Cuban refugees began to make substantial tax contributions to the communities where they lived, there was thought to be less need for special Federal assistance. Although HEW attempted to initiate a phaseout of the Cuban refugee program in 1973, and again in 1974, it was not until 1978 that an agreement was reached by Congress on a phaseout scheme. The long duration of the Cuban refugee program is an indication of the difficulty of determining when refugees can and should be regarded as successfully resettled and when Federal refugee assistance can and should be terminated.[14]

The Cuban experience is marked by the trauma of uprootedness from familiar settings and the requirement to adjust to markedly different mores and cultural patterns. Thus even as Cubans climb the ladder of success and achieve degrees of assimilation, they cannot easily forget their past. These sentiments and observations run through the testimony of Ramon Fernandez who came from Cuba as a young boy in 1961 and was raised in the Cuban environment of Miami. Fernandez recounts a tale of family members who at first supported Castro, but then became disillusioned and left their native country.

. . . And then, of course, when Castro took over, everything was different. They began taking over certain companies—big companies and socializing them. You could see the trend. And my father used to argue with some folks about the way communism worked when it came into a country and the first things they started doing. Right away he started smelling a rat. One day there was a big hassle in the Catholic school. The guys came in with guns and started threatening the nuns. Things like that. A couple of priests got beaten up. They were trying to stop all kinds of religion. So my father decided it was time to leave the country. . . .

We flew to Miami. Miami was full of Cubans then. And my father started working and we moved into this little house—a one-bedroom house; a bedroom—it was more like a big closet—like a beach house, where you don't want to live. It was pretty bad. The government gave us a hundred a month for a family and gave us food—Spam, lard, rice, beans, things like that, and a big piece of cheese. I said, "I get tired of eating the same things over and over again." Of course, we expected everything. The beginning was really tough.

My father started working at the Americana Hotel in Miami. His job was to *help* a busboy. He used to work mostly nights. My mother started working in a factory where they made purses and handbags. My father was very proud. He didn't want to go downtown to get the food that we were given. To him it was humiliating to have to go through that, after feeling that you were financially well-off and you didn't have to have anybody to help you. That's the way he's always been. My mother had the good luck to go downtown and get the food that we were given. But he wasn't too proud that he couldn't do this menial job just to get food on the table, which he did. He was willing to go around picking up dirty dishes, and taking them down to be washed, and having to sit down eating in the corner surrounded by dirty plates. Kind of a shock to have your own business for a while and then have to go back to something like that.

I started to go to school and there were maybe another ten Cubans in the whole school, so at first, of course, they didn't have anything planned. Those few months I was in school they didn't have any special classes. I was just thrown into a class with people I'd never seen before, who didn't speak my language. I couldn't understand them. They couldn't understand me. They had us Cubans do a lot of copywork from dictionaries and definitions and things like that. We were like a flock of lost sheep. We couldn't go to any other classes except gym because we didn't have to talk there. Personally, I feel I learned more English from watching TV than I learned in school. I spent all summer in front of the TV set, and by the time I got to eighth grade I didn't have any problems at all. It was different then. There was a lot of friction in the school between Cubans and, shall we say, Americans—I don't know what other word to use. There was a leader of one gang and the leader of the other gang, and the two fighting. Big crowds around, but only the two throwing punches until the cops would come in and settle everything. It was mild compared to what went on afterward with the blacks and things like that. Really, it wasn't much.

Of course, from my personal standpoint there's no difference in color. I never even heard of racism until I got to the United States. In Cuba, you know, a person is black and you have mulattoes and things like that, but you go to the same restaurant that they go to and you pray in the same church they pray in; you never even think about it.

I started asking questions. Of course, not even my father could answer them, because he wasn't even adjusted to the situation. So I started asking at school, "How come all the blacks ride in the back?" No one seemed to know why. "That's just the way it happens," they said, "because they're black." "Why? What's wrong with that? They don't have leprosy; why should they be separated?" I didn't understand. Of course, now everything is reversed. You have one extreme or the other. Now everything is black-oriented. You have one extreme or you have the other. There's no happy medium.

It wasn't easy for my family. My father coming home all tired out after fourteen hours of work. Couldn't play with me or couldn't take me out someplace because he had to sleep sometime; and my mother coming home with her hands all full of glue and dirt all over the place. That's when reality came along and I started helping out and getting a job. It wasn't bad. I'm not going to say it's bad. It was an experience.

After I finished high school, I got a job with this big company, and I took some training in computering. I started as a stockboy, and then I went to the engineering department and then to the receiving department and then into the transportation department, and I was promoted to supervisor three years ago and everything's been coming out right since. I'm manager of the order-entry and, of course, my computer training came in handy, because last year we went to a computerized system. And the only guy that knows anything about computering in the area is me. I'm no expert, but I know more than anybody else, so I'm running the whole department now. I came in at the right time and I guess I was lucky. . . .

Sometimes I have dreams, and I see myself walking into my grandparents' house in Cuba and I see them sitting there. She's just sewing like she's always doing at night, and my grandfather's smoking a cigar and watching TV. It brings back a lot of memories. The States is home. I have no qualms about it, but I'm still attracted to that little island, no matter how small it is. It's home. It's your people. You feel, if it's ever possible again, you'd like to reconstruct what was there. You want to be a part of it.

When the Bay of Pigs happened I was just a little boy, but I heard other people talking about it and I knew some guys that were there and were jailed. You become kind of angry about that, but there's nothing you can do about it. But you think "If only they'd given air support," then things would have turned differently. I wouldn't be here talking to you now. I just hope another time it will happen, and I feel, myself, that if the time comes and they try to do something and they say to me, "Do you want to go?" I'd be very glad to go in there and try to recover it.[15]

The United States government announced on September 26, 1980, that Cuba had officially ended the boat lift of Cubans from Mariel Harbor, Cuba. About 125,000 Cubans had migrated in shrimp boats, pleasure boats, yachts, and other craft to Key West, Florida. The boat lift had started April 21 and lasted five months. During this period the United States Coast Guard and the Navy assisted the migration in keeping the loss of life down to twenty-six persons. More than twenty-five government and private voluntary agencies contributed time and money in the resettlement of the Cuban refugees.

However, this movement of Cuban immigrants lacked order. Floridians felt besieged by Caribbean poor at a time of increasing domestic economic problems and anti-immigration sentiment, because at the same time a similar but longer running flow of 16,000 Haitians was arriving in the United States. The Cubans were characterized as "social dregs and undesirables," as compared to the "golden exile" of the 1960s when professional people, businessmen, and the educated had arrived. However, data collected by the Immigration Service at the two processing centers in Miami and Eglin Air Base revealed that the refugees did not come from either extreme of Cuban society but possessed educational and skill levels above the average of those remaining in the homeland.

The Cuban-American community in Florida greatly facilitated the adaptation of the boatlift people. The ethnic enclave there possesses a solid vitality to the extent that Cubans in Miami "can be born, or die and be buried, Cuban Style."[16]

HAITIANS

During the twentieth century large numbers of immigrants have arrived from the West Indies. Through the period of the Great Depression it has been estimated that over 300,000 entered the United States from Haiti, Cuba, the British West Indies, and the French West Indies. They brought with them varied backgrounds and settled in cities along the eastern seaboard, such as New York and Boston. Many were professional people, some entered the garment industry, and most took lower paying jobs. They kept to themselves because of American racial patterns and the friction between themselves and American blacks.

The British West Indians, the largest of this group, were permitted to use the unfilled British immigrant quota up until 1952, when the McCarran-Walter Act provided a maximum quota of 100 per unit: 100 for Trinidad, 100 for Jamaica, etc. The new Immigration Act of 1965 established more generous provisions: effective July 1, 1968, a ceiling of 120,000 was set for immigrants from the Western Hemisphere countries on a first-come, first-served basis with no limit on the number from any one country. By the end of the 1970s it was estimated that over 300,000 lived in the United States.

The recent wave of Haitians arriving on Florida's shores has led to allegations that a double standard exists in the treatment of the Haitians and the Cubans. Not having a major lobby group to defend them, large numbers of Haitian boat people have been labeled undesirable illegals and denied political asylum. The following extract analyzes the plight of the Haitian boat people.

> The Haitian boat people, like the most recent flow of Cubans to this country represents the lowest socioeconomic sector of the population of their country to have come to the United States so far. Most come from rural rather than urban areas of Haiti; a large percentage of them suffer from malnutrtion; and the overwhelming majority is illiterate. One Haitian community leader in Miami estimates that 90 percent of those she sees are illiterate. A mental health expert working with Haitians in Little Haiti determined that 40 percent of those who have been served by the mental health clinic are totally illiterate, that 20 percent can sign their names but are functionally illiterate, and that about 40

percent have had the equivalent of two to three years of schooling. Like the Cubans, most of the Haitian boat people are young men between the ages of 18 and 35 anxious for employment even in the unskilled sectors of the American labor force. In southern Florida, many have moved into unskilled low-paying agricultural jobs, into the unskilled sectors of the construction and marine industries, and into the growing garment industry. But adaptation is slow because they are unaccustomed to urban life, often unfamiliar with electricity, and unable to speak anything besides Haitian Creole.

Their numbers are small. The highest estimate I have yet encountered is 35,000, and more reasonable estimates are probably 18,000 to 25,000. By comparison to the millions of Mexicans who reside in the United States at any given point without proper documentation, this flow is totally insignificant. Even if it is compared to the number of Haitians who reside in the New York metropolitan area illegally (and I estimate well over 100,000 in New York), the entry of Haitian boat people is insignificant. But the significance of the Haitian boatlift is in the nature of the flow and the treatment of the migrants once they have arrived.

It is this treatment of the Haitians by our immigration officials implementing official U.S. immigration policy that concerns me greatly. The U.S. government has been less than willing over the years to grant many Haitians refugee status. Richard Gullage of the INS testified last summer in a Miami court case that "as of today there are less than 100 Haitians who have been recognized by the Government as refugees." Yet clearly the government is unsure of its own conviction that these Haitian migrants are not suffering political persecution or that they do not have well-founded fears of political persecution. Periodically we send factfinding teams to Haiti to explore allegations of torture and political persecution. Throughout the late sixties and most of the 1970s, immigration judges in the New York area refused to deport most of the Haitians caught by the Immigration and Naturalization Service and brought in for deportation hearings. In the 15 years of heavy Haitian migration to the United States, a very small proportion of Haitians have been deported or required to depart from this country. Instead, most Haitians have been given permission to work in the United States though few have obtained permanent residence. Between November 1977 and July 1978, the immigration service in Miami freely issues work permits to all Haitians who applied for them.

On the other hand, Haitians have frequently been treated as undesirable illegals. Gullage testified on April 18 of this year that "at one point we were incarcerating all Haitian males," that he received orders from Washington late in 1978 to detain up to 1,000 Haitians for as long as 90 days for health examinations, and that to his knowledge, "that has never been done [before] with Haitians or any other [immigrant] group." He added that when INS was ordered to "expedite" processing of Haitians in 1978, changes in immigration policy were being issued "almost daily" by INS headquarters. Immigration judges were ordered to triple their hearing schedules. Up to 50 Haitians a day were being ordered deported from South Florida. Many of the Haitians were denied political asylum by form letter, something to his knowledge done by no other INS district. Moreover, the absence of a legal, sizeable and vocal Haitian community in the United States means that there is no political interest group to defend them. Too many of the Haitians in New York live here without immigrant papers, and too few have become U.S. citizens. While they are black and have repeatedly gained the support of black leaders in this country, most Afro-Americans sense only a remote tie to these Haitian migrants. In times of worsening recession, fear of competition from new immigrants (whatever their color) tends to supersede any sense of social or racial solidarity. The masses of Afto-Americans have yet to demonstrate on behalf of the Haitian boat people. . . .[17]

By 1982 the pressure of 50,000 Haitian refugees in Florida had led to complaints that they could not be easily absorbed into society. The Reagan Administration had already instituted a tough policy in 1981 of detaining undocumented aliens at federal prisons and military bases. One of these, the Krome Avenue Processing Center in Miami, held 437 Haitians, most of whom had been picked up along the Florida coast attempting to enter the country. The Krome Center was an austere prison surrounded by double cyclone fences topped by barbed wire and high watchtowers. Human rights advocates challenged this tough policy. In 1982 a U.S. District Court ordered 1,910 Haitians released from detention camps from Texas to Puerto Rico. The Court of Appeals in Atlanta upheld the decision.[18]

Long periods of confinement resulted in many cases of psychological depression and physical illness. The following letter, written by a Haitian detained at Fort Allen, Puerto Rico, describes the personal feelings and reactions to the confinement.

Haitians:
We'll Kill Ourselves

Dear Readers, Gentlemen, Civilian, and Military Authorities,
For the last few months we have been imprisoned without knowing what outcome our fates would have.

You can imagine that if we risked our lives by leaving our country on sailboats and planes it was in order to find a haven on the soil of America, which we thought was capable of receiving us, since it is a large power in the world.

Since 1957, we have endured atrocious suffering due to the lack of a good government. But now it is worse, and we cannot stand it. This is why we are forced to emigrate in larger numbers. At home if we manage to get work, we cannot collect our salary. If we claim our rights, our life would be, in danger. Not only one's own, but also that of the entire family, which would be implicated by the authorities.

To our great surprise, upon arriving to the Immigration Center in Miami, we were made to wait for several hours during which time we were interrogated on one single topic, to wit, "Why did you come to the United States?" Since our answer is positive and always the same, we were finally accepted although we were told that we would have to spend a few days in the Krome [detention center] for formalities.

Upon arriving, our eyes widened with fear and surprise at the conditions of life. We thought we were throwing ourselves into a stable. One thousand persons are jammed into one and the same cell. It reminds us of black slavery. But alas, after shedding many tears and imploring God to come help us, we finally resigned ourselves to accepting this sufferance for a few days. Because we did not want to go back. Each day that would go by was one day less for us. We hoped that maybe in 8, 10, or 15 days we would be called to be freed.

One day around 4 p.m., we [women] were all gathered at the sound of whistles. We spent a day and a night awaiting our fate, after having been tagged with a plastic ID bracelet. After that we were made to parade in the nude in front of men and women. We were splashed, badly dressed. Stripped of our own clothes and belongings, we were made to sit in a room where we were to spend the night. In this distress, the room was like a wake, where sad songs were being sung. At that moment an enormous chill would run down the spine. Around 5 a.m., we were jammed into a bus which was to drive us to the airport. This is how we left Miami for Puerto Rico.

If sometimes a few of us misbehave, it is not their fault. You must understand that all of us don't have the strength, the same understanding, nor the same degree of education, and that we all suffer a lot from the behavior of others. Life at Fort Allen has been very hard for us.

When we left Miami, we were led to believe that we were only going to Puerto Rico for a few days. And until now we have been suffering for eight months without knowing why. Each day we hear only one thing: those who wish to return to Haiti can come give their names.

Since we arrived on American soil, we have been mistreated. We have been made to suffer and we have accepted it all, we have endured it. We have left at home relatives who are relying on our help. How can we return to Haiti now, empty handed and stripped of everything? Oh no, it would be the greatest injustice. If the Americans did not want to take us in, they should have sent us back the very same day. And now, instead of making us suffer, why not send us to other countries like Russia, Cuba, France or Canada, who are willing to take us in with open arms?

We are Christians. We have blood in our veins and thoughts like all the other people who are free. We want our freedom because we have been suffering for five months, because we left our relatives in order to help others get out of the lion's mouth in Haiti.

Our situation is pitiful. We have been locked up behind barbed wire from Miami to Puerto Rico. The days are always the same for us. We don't know what the date is. Sometimes we are hungry and cannot eat.

We have needs and cannot satisfy them. Is this the better life we are seeking? We took refuge in the United States in the hopes of filling our voids. Can we not fill them? Where are we going?

Now we cannot stand it any more. It is too much. If we have not been freed by the end of November, a good number of us are going to commit suicide. Because we have sworn to die in the United States.

We are asking why you treat us this way. Is it because we are Negroes? Why are you letting us suffer this way, America? Don't you have a father's heart? Haven't you thought we were humans, that we had a heart to suffer with and a soul that could be wounded? Give us back our freedom. Why among all the nations that emigrate to the United States have only the Haitians known such suffering?[19]

1. Immigration and Naturalization Service, *1975 Annual Report* (Washington, D.C., 1976), pp. 62–64 and U.S. Bureau of the Census, "Selected Characteristics of Persons and Families of Mexican, Puerto Rican, and Other Spanish Origins: March 1971," *Current Population Reports*, Series P-20, No. 224, p. 3.

2. U.S. Congress, House Committee on Post Office & Civil Service, *Hispanic Immigration & Select Commission on Immigration's Final Report*, 97th Congress, 1st Session (Washington, D.C., 1981), p. 9.

3. Reprinted from Bessie Bloom Wessel, *An Ethnic Survey of Woonsocket, Rhode Island* (reprint ed., New York: Arno Press, Inc., 1970), pp. 242–246.

4. *Times Picayune* (New Orleans), 10 April 1971.

5. Reprinted from Manuel Gamio, *Mexican Immigration to the United States*, pp. 156–158. Copyright © 1930 by University of Chicago Press. By permission of the University of Chicago Press.

6. Reprinted from U.S., Commission on Civil Rights, *Extract from Hearing Before the United States Commission on Civil Rights*, 9–14 December 1968 (Washington, D.C.: Government Printing Office, 1969), pp. 25–31.

7. *1979 Annual Report of the Immigration and Naturalization Service*, p. 3.

8. Texas Advisory Committee to the United States Commission on Civil Rights, *Sin Papeles: The Undocumented in Texas* (Washington, D.C.: Government Printing Office, 1980), pp. 40–43.

9. *Immigration Reform, Hearings Before the Subcommittee On Immigration, Refugees, and International Law of the Committee on the Judiciary*, Ninety-Seventh Cong., Serial No. 30 (Washington, D.C., 1981).

10. *New York Times*, 16 June 1982, p. A1; p. D22.

11. Reprinted from *Beyond the Melting Pot* by Nathan Glazer and Daniel P. Moynihan by permission of The MIT Press, Cambridge, MA, pp. 103–7.

12. Reprinted from Gordon K. Lewis, *Puerto Rico, Freedom and Power in the Caribbean* (New York: Harper and Row, 1963), pp. 244–46, 258–60.

13. Reprinted from Tom Alexander, "Those Amazing Cuban Emigres, *Fortune Magazine*, vol. 74 (October, 1966), pp. 144–49. By permission of the editors.

14. Committee on the Judiciary, U.S. Senate, 96th Congress, 1st Session *Review of U.S. Refugee Resettlement Programs and Policies*, (Washington, D.C.: Government Printing Office, 1979), pp. 20–22.

15. Joan Morrison, and Charlotte Fox Zabusky, *American Mosaic, The Immigrant Experience in the Words of Those Who Lived It*, E. P. Dutton, New York, 1980, pp. 324–27.

16. U.S. Congress, House Judiciary Committee, *Caribbean Migration, Oversight Hearings*, 96th Congress, 2nd Session (Washington, D.C., 1980), pp. 289–304; Robert L. Bach, "The New Cuban Immigrants: Their Background and Prospects," *Monthly Labor Review* (October 1980).

17. U.S. Congress, House Judiciary Committee, "Prepared Statement of Virginia Dominguez," *Caribbean Migration, Oversight Hearings*, 96th Congress, 2nd Session (Washington, D.C., 1980), pp. 132–33.

18. "For 1800 Haitians--Freedom," *Time* (July 26, 1982), p. 14; "Florida's Haitian Refugee Scare," *U.S. News & World Report* (July 12, 1982), p. 10.

19. *New York Times*, 19 November 1981, p. E19, Section 4.

KEY QUESTIONS

1. What is meant by terms "bilingualism" and "biculturism"?

2. Why are large numbers of Mexicans migrating to the United States? What is their status in the United States?

3. "The Puerto Ricans are not so much immigrants as they are migrants." Explain the meaning of this statement. Has this made a difference in their treatment and status on the mainland?

4. What has been the influence of Catholicism and Protestantism on the Puerto Ricans in the United States?

5. Explain why the Cubans who migrated immediately after 1959 to the United States were called the "golden exile."

6. Is there any evidence that the Haitians want to become assimilated into American society? What role has their color played in New York City?

7. Contrast the experiences of the Latin and the Anglo-Saxon immigrants in the United States. Explain any similarities.

8. Analyze the experiences of the Latin Americans and Asians as recently arrived immigrants.

SEVEN
The American Indians and Blacks

Included in this chapter are images of the experiences of American Indians and American blacks. Long exploited, these two ethnic minorities in recent years have achieved a renewed sense of ethnic pride and identity. They have withstood, though at great cost, the severe oppression imposed upon them by the material and numerical superiority of the white man's civilization. In seeking to return to their roots, the more conscious blacks wish to be known as Afro-Americans; similarly, the more militant Indians wish to be identified as Native Americans, terms that reflect subtle but profound ethnic considerations. Certainly the history and traditions of these two groups exemplify the archetypical peripheral Americans.

THE AMERICAN INDIANS

To describe the Indians as an ethnic group might at first glance seem to be gratuitous, since they do not fall into the traditional image of immigrant groups. With the exception of the American Indians, America is entirely populated by immigrants and their descendants. Moreover, even the American Indians were at one time immigrants to the American shores. Of a certainty they have been one of the groups most victimized by the distinctions that separate one ethnic group from another. In any case American Indians constitute a unique segment of a nation composed of a variety of cultural, linguistic, racial, and religious strains. As such they can be viewed as an ethnic minority in America's midst.

The author of the following extract, taken from a guide to the West for immigrants, presents a negative description of the Indians living in the rapidly developing area of the Mississippi Valley. As he details the characteristics of the Indians, he inevitably draws ethnocentric conclusions about the Indians.

As to moral habits, they are unquestionably indolent as it regards such labour as we are accustomed to perform. —This might be expected.

Their mode of life from time immemorial has been wholly diverse. They need the exciting circumstances of the chase or war, and then they will travel further, and perform more incredible exploits of activity and daring, than those who are unacquainted with them would imagine to be possible. But steady, unremitting industry is intolerable to them. Excepting the Cherokees and some of the Choctaws, very few of the Indians have made much progress in the knowledge of the arts of civilized life. But the truth is, that very few, and these inadequate, efforts have been made in other tribes to induce them to live a civilized life. The great and only hope of their civilization is with the children, through intellectual and religious education. . . .

They manifestly have not the acute sensibility which civilization imparts, or rather increases.—That they have affections is certain, but not generally of an ardent, tender kind. Born amidst forests, and perpetual gloom; from their childhood conversant with rocks, woods, deserts, and the dreariness and solitude of the wilderness; having only a precarious, and often a scanty, subsistence; subject to constant and deep alternations of hope and fear; enjoying but little the present life, and having no certain hopes of a life to come, it is no wonder that cheerfulness and joy should seldom be depicted in their countenances. It is not surprising that they should have little fear of death. They scarcely regard it in any other light than as the end of a life void of attractions, and even of existence, which few of them *firmly* believe to be prolonged beyond the present stage of being. Their fortitude in the endurance of suffering results from a physical insensibility, to which is added the effect of constant inculcation of it as a chief or only virtue. No ordinary stimulus can move them. But when they are excited, they have no moderation. Their rage, their fury in battle, their alternations of hope and despair exhibited in gaming, their brutal exhiliration in drunkenness, are truly horrible.

It is interesting to observe how manifestly the Indians, degraded and ignorant as they are, show the traces of the moral law written on the hearts of all men. There are certain virtues which they hold as being of universal obligation, such as honour, constancy, generosity, forbearance, and regard for truth. They generally admit, under some form of modification, the being of a God, and the immortality of the soul. Many of the tribes have forms of prayer which they use on extraordinary occasions, such as when starting on expeditions of hunting or war. They are exceedingly superstitious, and greatly under the influence of their prophets or "medicine men." Every thing with them which is inexplicable is a "medicine." Their prophets and jugglers have almost as much influence as their chiefs and warriors. Their ideas of a future world are of course dark and confused. Their Elysium is a great and beautiful country of prairie and forest, filled with wild beasts, which are hunted by the happy and good, that is, those who were brave on earth, and killed many of their enemies: whilst the cowardly and undistinguished sink into oblivion, not being able to pass with fearless hearts, the "narrow bridge."

As to matrimony, it is well known that every man may marry as many wives as he can maintain. All the evils which naturally flow from polygamy are of course experienced. Jealousy among the wives, their quarrels and their brawls, are frequent occurrences in the harem of an Indian chief. Marriage is generally managed by the parents.

The vices of the Indians are such as might be expected among an uncivilized people, who are destitute of the power of Christianity. And it is greatly to be regretted, that their intercourse with the whites has been generally, any thing else than beneficial to their morals. The most shameless abominations are committed by men, whom the Indians, in their ignorance, call Christians, only because they have a white complexion, and belong to a nation which professes to be Christian.

The more civilized Indians dress after the fashion of the white people. This is the case with the Cherokees, some of the Choctaws, and of the small tribes in Ohio and Indiana. Their clothes are coarse, but decent. The Cherokees, having made considerable progresss in the arts—having farms on which they raise grain and cotton, and possessing looms and mills, and blacksmith's shops, and horses and cattle, &c. not only dress comfortably, but many of them have respectable cottages and houses. But the uncivilized tribes wear a calico jacket, and over that a blanket or buffalo skin wrapped around them, and have moccasins and leggings. But in summer, their youth especially, go without the last named garments. When they can afford it, the squaws of the partially civilized tribes, wear blue broad cloth petticoats.

Their laws have the nature of universal custom, and are like a spell in their influence over the Indians; so much so, that if any Indian knows that he has committed an offence for which he must die, (according to their custom), he seldom embraces the opportunity of escape, but will return home to die, and dies as if there was an irresistible fatality which prevented him from doing otherwise. This is an inexplicable circumstance, excepting upon the principle that public opinion is every thing; and an Indian considers that he might as well die, as live under the conviction that he deserves, in the opinion of all, to die. This consciousness is intolerable. This fact, of itself, demonstrates how low their conceptions of death are!

I think that no man who has any correct moral sentiments, or any just idea of what constitutes true human happiness, can avoid feeling a deep sympathy for these poor benighted 'children of the wood.' Is not their condition a miserable one? Are they not, in some degree, intelligent, and of course accountable beings? And what can be done to raise them from their degradation and misery? The answer, to my mind, is plain—that is, instruct them in the principles of Christianity, and the arts of civilized life. Especially begin with the young. Almost all the tribes are willing to have their children thus instructed. And our government, as well as the Christian community, ought to arise, and give to every tribe these great blessings. They can be made Christians, and civilized men. They have minds, and vigorous ones too. They are not more barbarous than our ancestors once were. The Gospel of Jesus Christ can influence their hearts, and raise their thoughts, and their despairing eyes, towards heaven.[1]

Though white men displaced Indians across the length of the country, it was not without thought or shame. George Catlin, painter and student of American Indians, displayed a sensitivity about Indian life and lamented the inexorable expansion of white culture at the expense of Indian traditions. He also demonstrated the problems encountered when ethnic cultures confront each other, as in the following excerpt.

For the purpose of placing the Indian in a proper light before the world, as I hope to do in many respects, it is of importance to me—it is but justice to the savage—and justice to my readers also, that such points should be cleared up as I proceed; and for the world who enquire for correct and just information, they must take my words for the truth, or else come to this country and look for themselves, into these grotesque circles of never-ending laughter and fun, instead of going to Washington City to gaze on the poor embarrassed Indian who is called there by his "Great Father," to contend with the sophistry of the learned and acquisitive world in bartering away his lands with the graves and the hunting grounds of his ancestors. There is not the proper place to study the Indian character; yet it is the place where the sycophant and the scribbler go to gaze and frown upon him—to learn his character, and write his history! and because he does not speak, and quaffs the delicious beverage which he receives from white mens' hands, "he's a speechless brute and a drunkard."An Indian is a beggar in Washington City, and a white man is almost equally so in the Mandan village. An Indian in Washington is mute, is dumb and embarrassed; and so is a white man (and for the very same reasons) in this place—he has nobody to talk to.

A wild Indian, to reach the civilized world, must needs travel some thousands of miles in vehicles of conveyance, to which he is unaccustomed—through latitudes and longitudes which are new to him—living on food that he is unused to—stared and gazed at by the thousands and tens of thousands whom he cannot talk to—his heart grieving and his body sickening at the exhibition of white men's wealth and luxuries, which are enjoyed on the land, and over the bones of his ancestors. And at the end of his journey he stands (like a caged animal) to be scanned—to be criticised—to be pitied—and heralded to the world as a mute—as a brute, and a beggar.

A white man, to reach this village, must travel by steamboat—by canoes—on horseback and on foot; swim rivers—wade quagmires—fight mosquitoes—patch his moccasins, and patch them again and again, and his breeches; live on meat alone—sleep on the ground the whole way, and think and dream of his friends he has left behind; and when he gets here, half-starved, and half-naked, and more than half sick, he finds himself a beggar for a place to sleep, and for something to eat; a mute amongst thousands who flock about him, to look and to criticise, and to laugh at him for his jaded appearance, and to speak of him as they do of all white men (without distinction) as liars. These people are in the habit of seeing no white men in their country but

Traders, and know of no other; deeming us all alike, and receiving us all under the presumption that we come to trade or barter; applying to us all, indiscriminately, the epithet of "liars" or Traders.

The reader will therefore see, that we mutually suffer in each other's estimation from the unfortunate ignorance, which distance has chained us in; and (as I can vouch, and the Indian also, who has visited the civilized world) that the historian who would record justly and correctly the character and customs of a people, must go and live among them. . . .

The civilized world look upon a group of Indians, in their classic dress, with their few and simple oddities, all of which have their moral or meaning, and laugh at them excessively, because they are not like ourselves—we ask, "why do the silly creatures wear such great bunches of quills on their heads?—Such loads and streaks of paint upon their bodies—and bear's grease? abominable!" and a thousand other equally silly questions, without ever stopping to think that Nature taught them to do so—and that they all have some definite importance or meaning which an Indian could explain to us at once, if he were asked and felt disposed to do so—that each quill in his head stood, in the eyes of his whole tribe, as the symbols of an enemy who had fallen by his hand—that every streak of the paint covered a wound which he had got in honourable combat—and that the bear's grease with which he carefully anoints his body every morning, from head to foot, cleanses and purifies the body, and protects his skin from the bite of mosquitoes, and at the same time preserves him from colds and coughs which are usually taken through the pores of the skin.

At the same time, an Indian looks among the civilized world, no doubt, with equal, if not much greater, astonishment, at our apparently, as well as really, ridiculous customs and fashions; but he laughts not, nor ridicules, nor questions,—for his natural good sense and good manners forbid him,—until he is reclining about the fireside of his wigwam companions, when he vents forth his just criticisms upon the learned world, who are a rich and just theme for Indian criticism and Indian gossip.[2]

While a full account of this people's history is not going to be attempted, some highlights of this history will be mentioned so as to illumine aspects of white man-Indian relations. In point of fact, the record of this relationship is a dismal story acknowledged by virtually all quarters. Thus President Rutherford B. Hayes said in 1877:

The Indians were the original occupants of the land we now possess. They have been driven from place to place. The purchase money paid to them, in some cases for what they called their own, has still left them poor. In many instances, when they had settled upon lands assigned to them by compact and begun to support themselves by their own labor, they were rudely jostled off and thrust into the wilderness again. Many, if not most, of our Indian wars have had their origin in broken promises and acts of injustices on our part.[3]

Much of the problem centered around the Indian's desire above all to continue his own way of life, and the white man's denial of that wish. Indians were pressured to "settle down" and engage in agricultural pursuits like the rest of American citizens. This pressure was accompanied by invasion of hunting grounds, wanton destruction of buffalo, and disregard for Indian rights. American legislative policy attempted to persuade Indians to abandon tribal identification in preference to individual land ownership or live on government rations on a reservation. The Dawes Severalty Act of 1887 provided for the dissolution of Indian tribes as legal entities and the division of their tribal lands among individual members. Rights of disposal were withheld for twenty-five years. For the most part, the latter policy was a failure as the lot of the Indian continued to deteriorate. By an act of Congress in 1924 all Indians born in the United States were admitted to full citizenship. In 1934 the Indian Reorganization Act ended land allotments in severalty and provided for reinvestment to tribal ownership of surplus lands hitherto open to all.

In recent years it has become apparent that the national Indian scene is undergoing an extraordinary stirring. This stirring is undergirded by the phenomenon of population growth which shows the Indian population increasing from 269,388 in 1901 to 523,591 in 1960 to 791,839 in 1970 to 1,361,869 in 1980. It is estimated that these figures include only half of the Indian population in the United States, namely those on reservations. Moreover, Indian ethnic consciousness gathers momentum as individual Indians rejoin their tribes and speak increasingly about Indian tribal sovereignity. Thus the contemporary scene once again seems to confirm the tenacity of ethnicity within a social order.

Indian leaders throughout the second half of the nineteenth century were consistent in their assertions that the white man exploited them and left them with little hope. Typical is the lament of a Comanche chief when he said his people had

> . . . never first drawn a bow or fired a gun against the whites. . . . The blue-dressed soldiers. . . killed my braves. . . and made sorrow come to our camps. . . . The white man has the country which we loved, and we only wish to wander on the prairie until we die.[4]

One of the most famous Indians was the Apache Geronimo. Proud, bellicose and durable, he spent the last twenty years of his life as a prisoner of the United States in the late 1800s, during which time he wrote a remarkable autobiography in which he "told it like it was." In his story he reveals some of the problems encompassed by the victor-to-vanquished relationship between white man and Indian.

These problems were encountered despite the trust the Indians had in the white man, particularly in the person of General Miles who was to administer a mutually-agreed-to treaty backed by the President of the United States. Impressed by General Miles's exhortation that by entering into a treaty with each other they would be acknowledging a fraternal relationship, the emissary of the United States government also promised that the material needs of the Indians would be met, i.e., horses, cattle, houses, farm implements, water, and grass land. With some misgivings Geronimo agreed to sign the treaty. In later years he came to believe that he never violated this treaty, although General Miles failed to live up to its provisions.

In the following extract, Geronimo confesses his feelings near the close of his life as he reviewed the ethnic difficulties encountered and the prospects for the future.

There is a great question between the Apaches and the Government. For twenty years we have been held prisoners of war under a treaty which was made with General Miles, on the part of the United States Government, and myself as the representative of the Apaches. That treaty has not at all times been properly observed by the Government, although at the present time it is being more nearly fulfilled on their part than heretofore. In the treaty with General Miles we agreed to go to a place outside of Arizona and learn to live as the white people do. I think that my people are now capable of living in accordance with the laws of the United States, and we would, of course, like to have the liberty to return to that land which is ours by divine right. We are reduced in numbers, and having learned how to cultivate the soil would not require so much ground as was formerly necessary. We do not ask all of the land which the Almighty gave us in the beginning, but that we may have sufficient lands there to cultivate. What we do not need we are glad for the white men to cultivate.

We are now held on Comanche and Kiowa lands, which are not suited to our needs—these lands and this climate are suited to the Indians who originally inhabited this country, of course, but our people are decreasing in numbers here, and will continue to decrease unless they are allowed to return to their native land. Such a result is inevitable.

There is no climate or soil which, to my mind, is equal to that of Arizona. We could have plenty of good cultivating land, plenty of grass, plenty of timber and plenty of minerals in that land which the Almighty created for the Apaches. It is my land, my home, my fathers' land, to which I now ask to be allowed to return. I want to spend my last days there, and be buried among those mountains. If this could be I might die in peace, feeling that my people, placed in their native homes, would increase in numbers, rather than diminish as at present, and that our name would not become extinct.

I know that if my people were placed in that mountainous region lying around the headwaters of the Gila River they would live in peace

and act according to the will of the President. They would be prosperous and happy in tilling the soil and learning the civilization of the
white men, whom they now respect. Could I but see this accomplished,
I think I could forget all the wrongs that I have ever received, and die a
contented and happy old man. But we can do nothing in this matter
ourselves—we must wait until those in authority choose to act. If this
cannot be done during my lifetime—if I must die in bondage—I hope
that the remnant of the Apache tribe may, when I am gone, be granted
the one privilege which they request—to return to Arizona.[6]

When the United States government acknowledged the
failure of the Dawes Act in attempting to assimilate the
American Indians, President Franklin D. Roosevelt, with the
support of Secretary of Interior Harold L. Ickes and Indian Affairs Commissioner John Collier, now encouraged the tribes to
maintain their own institutions. The Indian Reorganization Act
of 1934 ended the land allotment program, provided financial
aid, aided tribal self-government, and encouraged the revival of
Indian culture and tradition.

Under the Eisenhower Administration, however, legislation in 1953–54 was adopted to terminate federal responsibility
for the Indians by ending all services to the Indians while
dispensing tribal lands among the members. This policy proved
to be disastrous and was thus rejected in the 1960s. President
Richard M. Nixon, in a message to Congress on July 8, 1970,
suggested,

. . . This, then must be the goal of any new national policy toward the
Indian people: to strengthen the Indian's sense of autonomy without
threatening his sense of community. We must assure the Indian that he
can assume control of his own life without being separated involuntarily
from the tribal group. And we must make it clear that Indians can
become independent of Federal concern and Federal support.[7]

This verbal commitment implicit in the presidential statement is,
of course, welcome, but time will tell whether appropriate deeds will
follow. In the meantime, Indian people continue to struggle with the
challenges and demands of trying to straddle two cultures. They are
desirous of inculcating their culture to their children, while recognizing the practical necessity of coming to grips with an English society.
At best they aim to achieve a kind of delicate balance which is captured in the statement of a Miccosukee Indian leader before a U.S.
Senate Subcommittee.

. . . We try to teach our Indian children, do not be ashamed, even
though you are Indians. You are Indians, therefore you should realize
you are Indians, nothing else but Indians. Think like Indians, but learn

English, learn how to write, be educated. You are Indian, you have other ideas. Be educated and you can work with both. You can have three languages, or two. . . .

We do not want to lose out on being Indians.[8]

The American Indian Population[9]

The 1980 census revealed that the American Indian population reached 1,361,869, an increase of about 569,000 persons or 72 percent over 1970. This was the first time it exceeded a million since the Indian population was first counted in 1890. The latest count was the result of natural increase and the overall improvement in census procedures. One-half of the Indian population lived in five states: California, Oklahoma, Arizona, New Mexico, and North Carolina. California had the largest population with 198,095. The following figures represent the official counts:

1890	-	248,253
1900	-	237,196
1910	-	265,683
1920	-	244,437
1930	-	332,397
1940	-	333,929
1950	-	343,410
1960	-	523,591
1970	-	791,839
1980	-	1,361,869

THE BLACKS

The entry of blacks into what is now the United States was different from that of every other ethnic group. They were involuntary immigrants; they came in chains. Even before the establishment of the first English colony, blacks were performing as slaves in what is now Florida. Then came the establishment of the English colonies and the planting of slavery in those settlements. It began in Virginia in 1619 and was formally recognized by that colony in 1661. Maryland recognized the institution three years later. Indeed, slavery took hold in all the southern colonies, although Georgia forbade it in the early years of its history. The middle colonies soon succumbed to the practice, although their number of slaves was never great. Nevertheless, even Quaker Pennsylvania recognized slavery in 1700. In New England the system met with little success, although it did exist there.

Despite the gains made by blacks during the Civil War era through the Thirteenth, Fourteenth and Fifteenth Amendments, American society remained essentially segregationist and racist. However, World War II proved to be a pivotal event in the fight for equal rights. In the battle against the racist regime of Adolph Hitler's Nazi Germany, blacks and many whites brought to the attention of Americans the irony of institutional racism at home.

The shift of power to the federal government signalled important strategic considerations for Afro-Americans, as many blacks now wished to be identified. The increased power of the Supreme Court as a force for social change was significant, as was the effect of the mass media. The widespread impact of instant news via television in part made this one nation. Its use by civil rights demonstrators was extensive. The increasing necessity of education in a technological society was to make it a major battleground. The political independence gained by many African nations served as an impetus to the civil rights movement.

From 1945 to the present one sees not only strategic shifts in the blacks' struggle to attain full equality but also a constantly shifting and changing America and world. From 1945 to 1956, the major emphasis of blacks, led by the National Association for the Advancement of Colored People, was the repeal of laws which enforced and legitimatized their caste status. From 1956 to 1966, the major emphasis was on a largely nonviolent confrontation with racist institutions in order to change their practices. The most charismatic leader of this period was Dr. Martin Luther King, president of the Southern Christian Leadership Conference. The next period, 1966 to the present, witnessed a shift from the legal to the economic and the political. "Black Power" became its rallying cry. The political leadership was represented by such individuals as former Congresswoman Shirley Chisholm, Atlanta Mayor Andrew Young, Los Angeles Mayor Tom Bradley, Newark Mayor Kenneth Gibson, Detroit Mayor Coleman Young, Samuel Pierce, Secretary of Housing, Georgia Legislator Julian Bond, and New York Congressman Charles Rangel.

The primary black experience in early America, was one of a slave population. From this peripheral position the black has been viewed and has viewed American society and culture, with the inevitable consequence that black ethnicity has been reinforced. This ethnic identity often manifested itself in slave revolts despite the desperate odds against them. Unsuccessful in these attempts blacks developed a culture within the slave experience. The selections that follow depict aspects of that culture as well as demonstrate distinguishing features between the blacks and other ethnic groups.

Skin color has played a prominent and degrading role in American history. In November 1787, in Philadelphia, the Right Reverend Richard Allen described how this condition led to the forcible expulsion of free blacks from St. George's Church and how the ousted black men formed the African Methodist Episcopal Church. Clearly, skin color differences resulted in distinctive ethnic grouping.

Negroes of Philadelphia Stage a "Kneel In," and Start Their Own Church

(The Right Reverend Richard Allen tells of the incidents leading up to the establishment of the African Methodist Episcopal Church of Philadelphia. The date was a Sunday in November, 1787—only a month after the Constitutional Convention ended.)

A number of us usually attended St. George's Church in Fourth street; and when the colored people began to get numerous in attending the church, they moved us from the seats we usually sat on, and placed us around the wall, and on Sabbath mornings we went to church and the sexton stood at the door, and told us to go in the gallery. He told us to go, and we would see where to sit. We expected to take the seats over the ones we formerly occupied below, not knowing any better. We took those seats. Meeting had begun, and they were nearly done singing, and just as we got to the seats, the elder said, "Let us pray." We had not been long upon our knees before I heard considerable scuffling and low talking. I raised my head up and saw one of the trustees, H_____ M_____, having hold of the Rev. Absalom Jones, pulling him off his knees, and saying, "You must get up—you must not kneel here." Mr. Jones replied, "Wait until prayer is over." Mr. H_____ M_____ said, "No, you must get up now, or I will call for aid and force you away." Mr. Jones said, "Wait until prayer is over, and I will get up and trouble you no more." With that he (Mr. H_____ M_____) beckoned to one of the other trustees, Mr. L_____ S_____ to come to his assistance. He came, and went to William White to pull him up. By this time prayer was over and we all went out of the church in a body, and they were no more plagued with us in the church.[10]

The following brief but poignant protest against slavery by a black emphasizes the paradox of American democracy in 1788.

(In 1788 there apperared the first known Negro protest against slavery to be published. Its author, "Othello," has left no history.)

In you (whites) the superiority of power produces nothing but a superiority of brutality and barbarism. Weakness, which calls for protection, appears to provoke your inhumanity. Your fine political systems are sullied by the outrages committed against human nature and the divine majesty.

When America opposed the pretensions of England, she declared that all men have the same rights. After having manifested her hatred against tyrants, ought she to have abandoned her principles?[11]

Solomon Northup, an upstate New York resident, was an educated freeman, married, and father of three children. At the age of thirty-two years he was enslaved. He was forcibly sold to a slave trader in the District of Columbia, then shipped to New Orleans, where he spent a dozen years in bondage. In 1853 he was rescued from a cotton plantation in Louisiana. Northup vividly described his experiences, which offer a valuable comment on the institution of slavery.

> The existence of Slavery in its most cruel form among them has a tendency to brutalize the humane and finer feelings of their nature. Daily witnesses of human suffering—listening to the agonizing screeches of the slave—beholding him writhing beneath the merciless lash—bitten and torn by dogs—dying without attention, and buried without shroud or coffin—it cannot otherwise be expected, than that they should become brutified and reckless of human life. It is true there are many kind-hearted and good men in the parish of Avoyelles—such men as William Ford—who can look with pity upon the sufferings of a slave, just as they are, over all the world, sensitive and sympathetic spirits, who cannot look with indifference upon the sufferings of any creature which the Almighty has endowed with life. It is not the fault of the slaveholder that he is cruel, so much as it is the fault of the system under which he lives. He cannot withstand the influence of habit and associations that surround him. Taught from earliest childhood, by all that he sees and hears, that the rod is for the slave's back, he will not be apt to change his opinions in maturer years.
>
> There may be humane masters, as there certainly are inhuman ones—there may be slaves well-clothed, well-fed, and happy as there are surely those half-clad, half-starved and miserable; nevertheless, the institution that tolerates such wrong and inhumanity as I have witnessed, is a cruel, unjust and barbarous one. Men may write fictions portraying lowly life as it is, or as it is not—may expatiate with owlish gravity upon the bliss of ignorance—discourse flippantly from arm chairs of the pleasures of slave life; but let them toil with him in the field—sleep with him in the cabin—feed with him on husks; let them behold him scourged, hunted, trampled on, and they will come back with another story in their mouths. Let them know the *heart* of the poor slave—learn his secret thoughts—thoughts he dare not utter in the hearing of the white man; let them sit by him in the silent watches of the night—converse with him in trustful confidence, of "life, liberty, and the pursuit of happiness," and they will find that ninety-nine out of every hundred are intelligent enough to understand their situation, and to cherish in their bosoms the love of freedom, as passionately as themselves.[12]

The career of Mifflin Wistar Gibbs is as remarkable as it is fascinating. Born a freeman in 1823 in Philadelphia, he witnessed and participated in the events attending the antislavery agitation. He assisted the Underground Railroad and was an associate of Frederick Douglass and later, Booker T. Washington. He was a carpenter, contractor, antislavey lecturer, merchant, railroad builder, graduate of Oberlin Law School, attorney at law, country attorney, register of

United States lands, receiver of public monies, and United States Consul to Madagascar. As an eyewitness to the post-Civil War events, he assumed a leadership role in the struggle for black peoples' rights. He was a Republican Elector from Arkansas in 1876 and he had close contacts with Presidents Grant and McKinley and other public officials.

As a child Gibbs vividly recalled the impact the Nat Turner Rebellion had on him. He describes the event in his autobiography. Also, a few years later at the age of twelve, he worked for a prominent Philadelphia lawyer who took the young boy to his plantation in Maryland. This experience forms an important part of his autobiography.

At eight years of age, as already stated, two events occurred which had much to do in giving direction to my after life. The one the death of my father, as formerly mentioned: the other the insurrection of Nat Turner, of South Hampton, Virginia, in August, 1831, which fell upon the startled sense of the slaveholding South like a meteor from a clear sky, causing widespread commotion. Nat Turner was a Baptist preacher, who with four others, in a lonely place in the woods, concocted plans for an uprising of the slaves to secure their liberty.Employed in the woods during the week, a prey to his broodings over the wrongs and cruelties, the branding and whipping to death of neighboring slaves, he would come out to meetings of his people on Sunday and preach, impressing much of his spirit of unrest. Finally he selected a large number of confederates, who were to secretly acquire arms of their masters. The attack concocted in February was not made until August 20, when the assault, dealing death and destruction, was made.

All that night they marched, carrying consternation and dread on account of the suddenness, determination and boldness of the attack. The whole State was aroused, and soldiers sent from every part. The blacks fought hand to hand with the whites, but were soon overpowered by numbers and superior implements of warfare. Turner and a few of his followers took refuge in the "Dismal Swamp," almost impenetrable, where they remained two or three months, till hunger or despair compelled them to surrender. Chained together, they were taken to the South Hampton Court House and arraigned. Turner, it is recorded, without a tremor, pleaded not guilty, believing that he was justified in the attempt to liberate his people, however drastic the means. His act, which would have been heralded as the noblest heroism if perpetrated by a white man, was called religious fanatacism and fiendish brutality.

Turner called but few into his confidence, and foolhardy and unpromising as the attempt may have been, it had the ring of an heroic purpose that gave a Bossarius to Greece, and a Washington to America. A purpose "not born to die," but to live on in every age and clime, stimulating endeavors to attain the blessings of civil liberty.

It was an incident as unexpected in its advent as startling in its terrors. Slavery, ever the preponderance of force, had hitherto reveled in a luxury heightened by a sense of security. Now, in the moaning of the wind, the rustling of the leaves or the shadows of the moon, was heard or seen a liberator. Nor was this uneasiness confined to the South, for in the border free States there were many that in whole or in part owned plantations stocked with slaves.

In Philadelphia, so near the line, excitement ran high. The intense interest depicted in the face of my mother and her colored neighbors; the guarded whisperings, the denunciations of slavery, the hope defeated of a successful revolution keenly affected my juvenile mind, and stamped my soul with hatred to slavery.

At 12 years of age I was employed at the residence of Sydney Fisher, a prominent Philadelphia lawyer, who was one of the class above mentioned, living north and owning a plantation in the State of Maryland. Over a good road of 30 miles one summer's day, he took me to his plantation. I had never before been that distance from home and had anticipated my long ride with childish interest and pleasure. After crossing the line and entering "the land of cotton and the corn," a new and strange panorama began to open, and continued to enfold the vast fields bedecked in the snowy whiteness of their fruitage. While over gangs of slaves in row and furrough were drivers with their scourging whip in hand. I looked upon the scene with curious wonder. Three score of years and more have passed, but I still see that sad and humbled throng, working close to the roadway, no head daring to uplift, no eye to enquiringly gaze. During all those miles of drive that bordered on plantations, as machines they acted, as machines they looked. My curiosity and youthful impulse ignoring that reticence becoming a servant, I said: "Mr. Fisher, who are these people?" He said, "They are slaves." I was startled but made no reply. I had not associated the exhilaration of the drive with a depressing view of slavery, but his reply caused a tumult of feeling in my youthful breast. The Turner episode of which I had heard so much, the narratives of whippings received by fugitives, slaves that had come to my mother's house, the sundering of family ties on the auction block, were vividly presented to my mind. I remained silent as to speech, as to feelings belligerent. A few moments elapsed and Mr. Fisher broke the silence by saying, "Mifflin, how would you like to be a slave?" My answer was quick and conformed to feeling. "I would not be a slave! I would kill anybody that would make me a slave!" Fitly spoken. No grander declaration I have ever made. But from whom did it come—from almost childish lips with no power to execute. I little thought of or knew the magnitude of that utterance, nor did I notice then the effect of its force. Quickly and quite sternly came the reply: "You must not talk that way down here." I was kept during our stay in what was known during slavery as the "great house," the master's residence, and my meals were eaten at the table he had quit, slept in the same house, and had, if desired, little or no opportunity to talk or mingle with the slaves during the week's visit. I did not understand at that time the philosophy of espionage, but in after years it became quite apparent that from my youthful lips had came the "open sesame to the door of liberty," "resistance to oppression," the slogan that has ever heralded the advent of freedom.

earnings. The success of their efforts in that important direction is attested by the fact that when the regiment was mustered out nearly $90,000 stood to their credit in savings institutions in Baltimore and Washington.

Not only were the men remarkable for their temperate habits, cases of drunkenness being very rare, but they were quiet and orderly as well, and their freedom from the use of profane and obscene language was remarkable.

For these reasons, it seems the negro soldier must be admitted to be fully equal, in all respects, to soldiers of other races and colors, particularly if it can be shown that he has stood the supreme test of battle by taking and maintaining his position side by side and shoulder to shoulder with his fellow white soldiers—facing the same enemy, with the same dogged persistence; storming the same fortifications, with the same undaunted heroism, and resisting the assaults of the common enemy with equal courage and efficiency.[14]

In the celebration of the seventy-fifth anniversary of the proclamation of the Thirteenth Amendment to the United State Constitution, a series of exhibits and concerts was held at the Library of Congress in Washington, D.C., to honor the contributions made by the Negro to American culture. The event took place December 18 through 21, 1940. The concerts featured outstanding Negro compositions performed by leading Negro artists. The art exhibit included works by contemporary painters from various American cities. An exhibit of books and manuscripts included the Emancipation Proclamation and many other documents relating to Negro achievements.

In the selection below, Dr. Alain Locke comments on the importance of spirituals.

Spirituals

Nothing so subtly or so characteristically expresses a people's group characters as its folk music. And so we turn to that music to discover if we can grasp the essence of what is Negro or, if we cannot do that, at least to try to sample the best of the Negro's racial experience . . . .

Certainly, in terms of the historic occasion which this festival thoughtfully and reverently commemorates, the slave songs have a particular place and significance. It is that dark but rich and worthy side of our people's past which gives us at once and the same time the most illuminating background of our present race accomplishment, the true perspective of our future hopes and ambitions and, most important of all for us at this moment, the sampling of the mother soil of our creative genius. For the musical talent that has grown up and flowered so distinctively, to the extent that it is original, has its basic rootage there. It is that soil of folk experience which gives the special taste and tang, the form and flavor to what we are proud to claim as typically Negro in art

and I might even be said to possess a mind. I am invisible, understand, simply because people refuse to see me. Like the bodiless heads you see sometimes in circus sideshows, it is as though I have been surrounded by mirrors of hard, distorting glass. When they approach me they see only my surroundings, themselves, or figments of their imagination— indeed, everything and anything except me.

Nor is my invisibility exactly a matter of a bio-chemical accident to my epidermis. That invisibility to which I refer occurs because of a peculiar disposition of the eyes of those with whom I come in contact. A matter of the construction of their inner eyes, those eyes with which they look through their physical eyes upon reality. I am not complaining, nor am I protesting either. It is sometimes advantageous to be unseen, although it is most often rather wearing on the nerves. Then too, you're constantly being bumped against by those of poor vision. Or again, you often doubt if you really exist. You wonder whether you aren't simply a phantom in other people's minds. Say a figure in a nightmare which the sleeper tries with all his strength to destroy. It's when you feel like this that, out of resentment, you begin to bump people back. And, let me confess, you feel that way most of the time. You ache with the need to convince yourself that you do exist in the real world, that you're a part of all the sound and anguish, and you strike out with your fists, you curse and you swear, to make them recognize you, and, alas, it's seldom successful.[16]

A. Philip Randolph, organizer and president of the Brotherhood of Sleeping Car Porters, planned a mass march on Washington when industry in 1941 refused to hire blacks for defense jobs. President Franklin D. Roosevelt forestalled the march by issuing a fair employment practices executive order. As a leader in the civil rights movement, Randolph demanded full equality and singled out the black problem as economic. He looked to the "complete integration of the Negro workers into the organized labor movement. . . . The March on Washington Movement rejects the economic discrimination of the Negro worker and call for the abolition of the racial blind alley job."[17]

The pivotal event for blacks in the post-World War II era was the *Brown v. Board of Education,* 1954, Supreme Court decision whereby the Court unanimously declared that "separate educational facilities are inherently unequal" and that segregated schools deprived blacks of their "equal protection of the laws guaranteed by the Fourteenth Amendment" of the United States Constitution.

Nevertheless, progress in achieving full equal rights was slow, and civil rights leaders had to use such pressure tactics as sit-ins, boycotts, demonstrations, picketing, rallies, etc., to make their point. One civil rights approach was led by Dr. Martin Luther King, Jr., of the Southern Christian Leadership Conference. King applied his direct nonviolent campaign against Birmingham, Alabama, in April 1963. Placed in jail for protesting Birmingham's notorious racist policies, he

was criticized by white religious leaders. Dr. King responded with his "letter from Birmingham Jail" in which he appealed for justice, love, understanding and nonviolence. Though he was an "outsider," injustice had brought him to Birmingham and he recognized the "interrelatedness of all communities and states." His nonviolent campaign included four steps: "collection of the facts to determine whether injustices exist; negotiation; self-purification; and direct action." He warned that black nationalist groups, filled with bitterness and hatred were developing across the nation and threatening the stability of society. The best known of these was the Black Muslim sect.

Malcolm X (1925-1965) was the brilliant leader of the Black Muslims. Violent and enigmatic, he occupied a special niche in the recent history of the Afro-Americans. A self-educated man, he experienced a religious conversion to the Black Muslim faith which was later followed by a break with that group, although he remained a Muslim. He assumed the role of leader of black nationalism until his assassination. During a press conference in New York, March 12, 1964, he stated the political philosophy of black nationalism.

> The political philosophy of black nationalism means: we must control the politics and the politicians of our community. They must no longer take orders from outside forces. We will organize, and sweep out of office all Negro politicians who are puppets for the outside forces. . . .
>
> . . . Whites can help us, but they can't join us. There can be no black-white unity until there is first black unity. There can be no workers' solidarity until there is first some racial solidarity. We cannot think of uniting with others, until after we have first united among ourselves . . . .
>
> Concerning nonviolence: it is criminal to teach a man not to defend himself when he is the constant victim of brutal attacks. It is legal and lawful to own a shotgun or a rifle. We believe in obeying the law.
>
> In areas where our people are the constant victims of brutality, and the government seems unable or unwilling to protect them, we should form rifle clubs that can be used to defend our lives and our property in times of emergency. . . . When our people are being bitten by dogs, they are within their rights to kill those dogs.
>
> We should be peaceful, law-abiding—but the time has come for the American Negro to fight back in self-defense whenever and wherever he is being unjustly and unlawfully attacked.
>
> If the government thinks I am wrong for saying this, then let the government start doing its job.[18]

The Black Population[19]

The black population totaled 26,488,218 in 1980, an increase of 17 percent over 1970. The proportion of the total black population living in the South was 53 percent, the same as in 1970. The West had the

smallest proportion of blacks, although it was the only region to experience an increase of blacks. New York State ranked first in the number of blacks, as it had in the last four decades. The census counts represent recent trends:

Year	Total	Black	Percent Black
1900	76.0	8.8	12
1940	131.7	12.9	10
1950	150.7	15.0	10
1960	179.3	18.9	11
1970	203.2	22.6	11
1980	226.5	26.4	12

1. Robert Baird, *View of the Valley of the Mississippi* [Philadelphia: H.S. Towner, 1834], pp. 92-95.

2. Reprinted from George Catlin, *Letters and Notes of the Manners, Customs, and Conditions of the North American Indians* [London: 1841], vol. 1, pp. 85, 86, 102, 103.

3. From *Messages and Papers of the Presidents*, Vol. X, edited by James B. Richardson [New York: The Bureau of National Literature, Inc., 1897], p. 4427.

4. U.S. Bureau of the Census, *Race of the Population by States: 1980* [Washington, D.C., 1981], p. 6.

5. Dee Brown, *Bury My Heart at Wounded Knee* [New York: Holt, Rinehart and Winston, 1970], pp. 241-42.

6. From the book *Geronimo: His Own Story.* Ed. by S.M. Barrett Newly with an Intro. and Notes by Frederick W. Turner III. Intro. and Notes Copyright © 1970 by Frederick W. Turner III. Published by E.P. Dutton & Co., Inc. and used with their permission. pp. 172-73.

7. Vincent N. Parrillo, *Strangers to These Shores* [Boston: Houghton Mifflin, 1980], pp. 242-246.

8. Virginia Irving Armstrong, *I Have Spoken, American History Through the Voices of the Indians* [Chicago: Swallow Press, 1971], p. 156. Statement of Buffalo Tiger of the Tribal Council of the Miccosukee Indians of Florida, testified December 14, 1967, before U.S. Senate Subcommittee studying the education of Indian children.

9. Official Census Reports, 1890-1980; U.S. Bureau of the Census, *Race of the Population by States: 1980* [Washington, D.C., 1981], pp. 1-2.

10. Reprinted from William L. Katz, *Eyewitness: The Negro in American History* [New York: Pitman Publishing Corporation, 1967], pp. 58-59.

11. Ibid., p. 35.

12. Reprinted from Solomon Northup, *Twelve Years a Slave*, ed. Sue Eakin and Joseph Logsdon [Baton Rouge: Louisiana State University Press, 1968], pp. 157-158.

13. Mifflin Wistar Gibbs, *Shadow and Light, An Autobiography* [Washington, D.C., 1902], pp. 15-19.

14. George B. Sherman, "The Negro as a Soldier," *Personal Narratives of Events of the War of the Rebellion* [Providence: Rhode Island Soldiers and Sailors Historical Society, 1913], pp. 16-19.

15. Alain Locke, "Spirituals" *75 Years of Freedom* [Washington, D.C.: Library of Congress, 1940], pp. 7-11.

16. Reprinted from Ralph Ellison, *The Invisible Man* [New York: New American Library, 1952], pp. 2-3, Copyright © 1947, 1948, and 1952 by Ralph Ellison. By permission of Random House, Inc.

17. A. Philip Randolph, "March on Washington Movement Present Program for the Negro," in *What the Negro Wants*, ed. by Rayford W. Logan [Chapel Hill: University of North Carolina Press, 1964], pp. 133-47.

18. N.Y. Daily News March 12, 1966.

19. Official Census Reports, 1900, 1940, 1950, 1960, 1970; U.S. Bureau of the Census, *Race of the Population by States: 1980* [Washington, D.C., 1981], p. 6.

KEY QUESTIONS

1. Did the white man and the Indian suffer in their estimation of each other? Discuss this by reference to the selection on Indians.

2. In the selections dealing with the Indians in this chapter, what are the recurring themes?

3. To what extent are the black man's ethnic experiences similar or dissimilar to the experiences of the European immigrants?

4. Compare the contributions made by Solomon Northup and Mifflin Wistar Gibbs.

5. Explain the blacks' participation in the Civil War?

6. What was the special relationship of spirituals to the blacks?

7. Ralph Ellison's book, *The Invisible Man,* is one of the most important in the understanding of race relations. Why did he use this title?

8. Trace the impact each of the following men had on rise of Afro-American rights? A. Philip Randolph, Martin Luther King, Jr., and Malcolm X.

9. State-imposed racial segregation was declared unconstitutional in the case of *Brown v. Board of Education of Topeka,* 1954. Explain the importance of the case. How did it impact on black Americans?

10. Explain the status of black Americans in regard to their full participation in American society.

EIGHT
Immigration Policy and Ethnicity

The story of American immigration is unique and one of the most fascinating of all the sagas of this country's past. It is the story of one of modern history's greatest mass movements of population. The familiar epic is found in traditional texts in American history and society as they narrate the odyssey of one group of sojourners after another who came to this land, some of their own free will, others in bondage, some to escape religious, economic, or political persecution, and others to seek happiness. And yet there is a paradox in this picture of the United States as a country welcoming all, rich and poor, mighty and weak, black and white, Jew and gentile.

It is a picture best epitomized by the poem written by the Jewish immigrant, Emma Lazarus, and inscribed on the base of the Statue of Liberty, part of which reads: "Give me your tired, your poor, your huddled masses yearning to breathe free, The wretched refuse of your teeming shore. Send these, the homeless, tempest-tossed to me, I lift up my lamp beside the golden door." Thus, on the one hand, immigration truly has been America's *raison d'être*. It has been the most persistent and pervasive influence in her development. On the other hand, the history of immigration, both before and after the Civil War, has been marked by racism and discrimination. This has produced a picture that could very well have changed Lazarus' description to read "Give me your energetic and solvent, your educated and healthy, The cream of the crop of your teeming shore. Exclude the undesirable, the illiterate, the poor, the uneducated, the sick to whom is closed the golden door."

It is this divergence between romanticism and reality that pervades the succession of laws that established United States immigration policy, which will now be explored.

When President Lyndon B. Johnson signed the immigration bill of 1965, he stated it, "Corrects a cruel and enduring wrong in the conduct of the American nation. . . . Yet the fact is that for over four decades the immigration policy of the United States has been twisted and distorted by the harsh injustice of the National Origins Quota

System." This chapter will examine the ethnic concern of the generation that brought about the policies that were applicable in these decades alluded to by President Johnson. Particular attention will be placed on the quota system of the 1920s, the demand for total restriction, the more progressive legislation of 1965, and the reaction to these policies.

Since the immigration law of 1965 represented a pivotal development in American immigration policy, this chapter will also examine its recent impact on ethnic population trends. In attempting to adjust to the changing ethnic patterns of the nation, the policymakers have been striving to maintain a fair immigration program compatible with the interests of the nation.

United States restrictive policies were fashioned out of a matrix of ethnocentrism, which encompasses the powerful human desire for acquiescence to one's own ways and the simultaneous fear that the indigenous population will be overwhelmed by hordes of inferior alien peoples. The need for uniformity was not in and of itself a new phenomenon. From the beginnings there were indications of its strength as a basic social force. This strength would exact a heavy price from the newcomers of the "new immigration" period. Since a painless and a rapid transition from one culture to another is not common, the more the immigrant group differed from the old stock, the more it excited the wrath of the dominant group, and the more the dominant group demanded the annihilation of all that was peculiarly ethnic among the newcomers. This was what was referred to as the "Americanization" process, and because it did not seem to be progressing swiftly enough, the old immigrant stock sought refuge in restrictive immigration policies against the spectre of ethnic mongrelization.

The first general immigration law was passed in 1882. It established a head tax on immigrants, excluded convicts, lunatics, idiots, and others liable to become public charges. That same year also saw ethnic discrimination, as Chinese were excluded from lawful immigration to the United States. Likewise, the "Gentlemen's Agreement" of 1907 had the same effect on Japanese immigrants. Efforts to establish qualitive ethnic distinctions among European immigrants was attempted by means of literacy test legislation. The issue was, as Prescott F. Hall, a Boston Brahmin and guiding spirit of the Immigration Restriction League, put it, whether this country wanted "to be peopled by British, German, and Scandinavian stock, historically free, energetic, progressive, or by Slav, Latin and Asiatic races, historically down-trodden, atavistic and stagnant." Negative value

judgments were at the core of the drive for restrictive legislation. Proponents of the literacy test were not immediately successful, as presidential vetoes stymied the drive during the years of and between the administrations of Cleveland and Wilson. Nevertheless, in 1917, Congress overrode Wilson's veto, and the literacy test became law.

The first selection in this chapter is an appeal by Senator Henry Cabot Lodge, Sr., for immigration restriction through literacy tests. Lodge was joined by pressure groups from organized labor, racists, and superpatriots who feared a radical impact on American society. Next, Woodrow Wilson, writing as a professional historian before becoming President, revealed a strong nativist tendency in an extract from his college textbook. In part, official substantiation for the anti-"new immigration" prejudice came from the report of the Dillingham Commission Report of 1911, an extract of which is the third article. This is followed by Oscar Handlin's criticism of the Dillingham Commission philosophy. The fifth extract is from a United States Senator's defense of the "new immigration" and rebuke of American ethnocentrism, followed by a brief statement on immigration policy and the ethnic composition of the nation. An Asian-American scholar then critically analyzes the history of anti-Asian immigration policy. Two extracts from the research of the Select Commission on Immigration and Refugee Policy deal with an item-by-item listing of American immigration policy and its first semi-annual report. The final selections include a figure showing the trend in naturalization in the 1970s and a table comparing 1977 immigration with that of 1965. In addition, there are two contrasting reactions to the proposal to change the nation's basic immigration law.

One of the most vigorous voices urging immigration restrictions was that of Senator Henry Cabot Lodge, Sr., of Massachusetts. In the extract that follows, he suggests that because increasing immigration is deteriorating in quality and producing many serious domestic problems, illiterate immigrants should be barred. In 1917, after more than two decades of debate on the issue, the literacy test provision was enacted into law, although it did not significantly reduce immigration.

> Thus it is proved, first, immigration to this country is increasing and, second, that it is making its greatest relative increase from races most alien to the body of the American people and from the lowest and most illiterate classes among those races. In other words, it is apparent that, while our immigration is increasing, it is showing at the same time a marked tendency to deteriorate in character. . . .
>
> In an word, the continued introduction into the labor market of four hundred thousand persons annually, half of whom have no occupation and most of whom represent the rudest form of labor, has a

very great effect in reducing the rates of wages and disturbing the labor market. This, of course, is too obvious to need comment. Moreover, the shifting of the sources of the immigration is unfavorable, and is bringing to the country people whom it is very difficult to assimilate and who do not promise well for the standard of civilization in the United States—a matter as serious as the effect on the labor market.

The question, therefore, arises,—and there is no more important question before the American people,—What shall be done to protect our labor against this undue competition, and to guard our citizenship against an infusion which seems to threaten deterioration? We have the power, of course, to prohibit all immigration, or to limit the number of persons to be admitted to the country annually, or—which would have the same effect—to impose upon immigrants a heavy capitation tax. Such rough and stringent measures are certainly neither necessary nor desirable if we can overcome the difficulties and dangers of the situation by more moderate legislation. These methods, moreover, are indiscriminate; and what is to be desired, if possible, is restriction which shall at the same time discriminate. We demand now that immigrants shall not be paupers or diseased or criminals, but these and all other existing requirements are vague, and the methods provided for the enforcement are still more indefinite and are perfectly ineffective. Any law, to be of use, must require, in the first place, that immigrants shall bring from their native country, from the United States consul or other diplomatic representatives, an effective certificate that they are not obnoxious to any of the existing laws of the United States. We ought, in addition, to make our test still more definite by requiring a medical certificate in order to exclude unsound and diseased persons. . . .

We ought also to insist that the consular certificate be given only after careful inquiry and due proof, and we must make a further definite test which will discriminate against illiteracy if we desire any intelligent restriction or sifting of the total mass of immigration. It is a truism to say that one of the greatest dangers to our free government is ignorance. Every one knows this to be the case, and that the danger can be overcome only by constant effort and vigilance. We spend millions annually in educating our children that they may be fit to be citizens and rulers of the Republic. We are ready to educate also the children who come to us from other countries; but it is not right to ask us to take annually a large body of persons who are totally illiterate and who are for the most part beyond the age at which education can be imparted. We have the right to exclude illiterate persons from our immigration and this test, combined with the others of a more general character, would in all probability shut out a large part of the undesirable portion of the present immigration. It would reduce in a discriminating manner the total of immigrants and would thereby greatly benefit the labor market and help to maintain the rate of American wages. At the same time it would sift the immigrants who come to this country, and would shut out in a very large measure those elements which tend to lower the quality of American citzenship, and which now in many cases gather in dangerous masses in the slums of our great cities.[1]

Historian Woodrow Wilson, in his American history textbook, written at the turn of the twentieth century, clearly demonstrated a typically nativist attitude toward the newly arrived immigrants. He contrasted the older Europeans with the newer southern-eastern European immigrants. Wilson even considered the Chinese "were more to be desired . . . than most of the coarse crew" that congested the Eastern ports.

> The census of 1890 showed the population of the country increased to 62,622,250, an addition of 12,466,467 within the decade. Immigrants poured steadily in as before, but with an alteration of stock which students of affairs marked with uneasiness. Throughout the century men of the sturdy stocks of the north of Europe had made of the main strain of foreign blood which was every year added to the vital working force of the country, or else men of the Latin-Gallic stocks of France and northern Italy; but now there came multitudes of men of the lowest class from the south of Italy and men of the meaner sort out of Hungary and Poland, men out of the ranks where there was neither skill nor energy nor any initiative of quick intelligence; and they came in numbers which increased from year to year, as if the countries of the south of Europe were disburdening themselves of the more sordid and hapless elements of their population, the men whose standards of life and of work were such as American workmen had never dreamed of hitherto. The people of the Pacific coast had clamored these many years against the admission of immigrants out of China, and in May, 1892, got at last what they wanted, a federal statute which practically excluded from the United States all Chinese who had not already acquired the right of residence; and yet the Chinese were more to be desired, as workmen if not as citizens, than most of the coarse crew that came crowding in every year at the eastern ports. They had, no doubt, many an unsavory habit, bred unwholesome squalor in the crowded quarters where they most abounded in the western seaports, and seemed separated by their very nature from the people among whom they had come to live; but it was rather their skill, their intelligence, their hardy power of labor, their knack at succeeding and driving duller rivals out, rather than their alien habits, that made them feared and hated and led to their exclusion at the prayer of the men they were likely to displace should they multiply. The unlikely fellows who came in at the eastern ports were tolerated because they usurped no place but the very lowest in the scale of labor.[2]

The arguments for restrictive immigration laws appeared to be validated by two government investigations: The Dillingham Commission Report of 1910 and the Report of the House Immigration Committee in 1922, both of which were instrumental in fostering the belief that the new immigration was socially inferior to the older immigration. The earlier report served as the foundation for the Quota

Acts of the 1920s. The following selection includes an explanation about the scope of the Congressional inquiry and the Commission's conclusion that basic qualitative differences existed between the ethnic groups that made up "old immigration" and "new immigration."

Plan and Scope of the Inquiry

Briefly stated, the plan of work adopted by the Commission included a study of the sources of recent immigration in Europe, the general character of incoming immigrants, the methods employed here and abroad to prevent the immigration of persons classed as undesirable in the United States immigration law, and finally a thorough investigation into the general status of the more recent immigrants as residents of the United States, and the effect of such immigration upon the institutions, industries, and people of this country. As above suggested, the chief basis of the Commission's work was the changed character of the immigration movement to the United States during the past twenty-five years.

During the fiscal year 1907 in which the Commission was created, a total of 1,285,349 immigrants were admitted to the United States. Of this number 1,207,619 were from Europe, including Turkey in Asia, and of these 979,661, or 81 percent, came from the southern and eastern countries, comprising Austria-Hungary, Bulgaria, Greece, Italy, Montenegro, Poland, Portugal, Roumania, Russia, Servia, Spain, Turkey in Europe, and Turkey in Asia.

Twenty five years earlier, in the fiscal year 1882 648,186 European immigrants came to the United States, and of these only 84,973, or 13.1 per cent, came from the countries above enumerated, while 563,213, or 86.9 per cent, were from Belgium, Great Britian and Ireland, France, Germany, the Netherlands, Scandinavia, and Switzerland, which countries furnished about 95 per cent of the immigration movement from Europe to the United States between 1819 and 1883.

During the entire period for which statistics are available—July 1, 1819, to June 30, 1910—a total of 25,528,410 European immigrants, including 106,481 from Turkey in Asia were admitted to the United States. Of these, 16,052,900 or 62.9 per cent came from the northern and western countries enumerated, and 9,475,510, or 37.1 per cent, from southern and eastern Europe and Turkey in Asia. For convenience, the former movement will be referred to in the Commission's reports as the "old immigration" and the latter as the "new immigration," The old and the new immigration differ in many essentials. The former was from the beginning, largely a movement of settlers who came from the most progressive sections of Europe for the purpose of making for themselves homes in the New World. They entered practically every line of activity in nearly every part of the country. Coming during a period of agricultural development, many of them entered agricultural pursuits, sometimes as independent farmers, but more often as farm laborers, who, nevertheless, as a rule soon became landowners. They formed an important part of the great movement toward the West during the last century, and as pioneers were most potent factors in the development of

and poetry and music. We must remember, too, that it lends its substance, by a spiritual chemistry which men cannot curb or control, to those other precious and representative cultural products which we are proud to call "American." The spirituals are the tap-root of our folk music, stemming generations down from the core of the group experience in the body and soul suffering of slavery, and expressing for the race or the nation—for the world, indeed—the spiritual fruitage of that hard ordeal.

But the spirituals are not merely slave songs or even Negro folk songs. The very elements that make them spiritually expressive of the Negro make them at the same time deeply representative of the soil that produced them. They constitute a great and now increasingly appreciated body of regional American folk song and music. As unique spiritual products of American life, they become nationally, as well as racially, characteristic. They also promise to be one of the profitable well-springs of native idiom in serious American music. In that sense, they belong to a common heritage and, with proper appreciation and use, become a part of the cultural "tie that binds."

While this is true to a degree of all folk music, it is eminently true of the spirituals. For just before and immediately after the Civil War they were the first American folk songs to be discovered and collected. Again in 1871, through the Fisk Jubilee Singers, they were the first to gain serious musical attention, nationally and then internationally. Still again about 1894, through Dvořák and others, they were the first native folk idioms proposed as the base for a nationally representative American music. We still hear the beautiful echoes of the Dvořák *Quartet on American Themes*, which, more convincingly even that the *Symphony from the New World*, brought them that musical tribute and vindication.

Finally, the spirituals, in these glorious times of Roland Hayes, Paul Robeson, Marian Anderson, Dorothy Maynor and others have brought our interpretive artists a welcome opportunity, after mastery of the great universal language, to pay their racial homage to the native source of their artistic skill and spiritual strength, to express artistic indebtedness to the singing generations behind them and to the genius of the anonymous peasants who were, in James Weldon Johnson's apt phrase, "the black and unknown bards of long ago." . . .

For the spirituals are, even when lively in rhythm and folkish in imagination, always religiously serious in mood and conception. That does not exclude humor of a sort, but the true spiritual is always the voice of a naive, unshaken faith, for which the things of the spirit are as real as the things of the flesh.

This naïve and spirit-saving acceptance of Christianity is the hallmark of the true spiritual. To be sure, other factors have entered in; otherwise we should have merely dialect versions of evangelical Protestant hymns. First and foremost, there is the primary ingredient of a strong peasant soul, with its naïve faith, a literal-believing and soul-saving faith which preserved the emotional sanity of the Negro and kept his spirit somewhat above the fate of his body.

Then there was, even out of the Negro's mass illiteracy, some

great intuitive understanding of his own experience, stated in terms of a grand and inspired analogy with the bible narratives, from which came all those vivid parables which kept hope and faith alive in even the humblest Negro souls and formed the basis of the dramatic heart of the spirituals. The backbone of the spirituals' narrative tradition is just such Bible parables, selected on the basis of their closeness to the slave's experience—his own spiritual experience.

There was, too, born out of the emotional fire of the group, a folk imagination, the transport that turned the already glowing King James texts into real folk poetry. This has given us—and I wish I had more time to illustrate the poetic sides of the spiritual—gems like—

I lay in the grave and stretch out my arms
When I Lay this body down
I go to the judgment in the evening of the day
When I lay this body down,
When I lay this body down.
And my soul and your soul meet the day
I lay this body down

Or, again things like that spiritual which Roland Hayes sings so beautifully,

My Lord is so high, you can't get over him,
My Lord is so low, you can't get under him,
You must come in and through the Lamb.

And, finally, there is the music itself, that great literacy of musical speech towering up over the dialect and the broken, sometimes feeble words to make an instinctive welding of all the text into an amalgam of music that shades every measure and evokes a meaning almost independently of the words.

Such is that blend of factors which constitutes the Negro spiritual and make it unique. The purest of them, the oldest of them, must have been pure prayer songs, definitely coming out of the context of a worshipping band with a leader. And orginally, of course, there must have been somebody acting as a leader, improvising a lead-line and a lead-idea, with that spreading from some kind of contagion that became instinctive as the tradition grew into a choral song, in which finally the lead-line and the burden of the refrain merged with the whole body to make a great choral improvisation . . . . [15]

The uniqueness of the black's ethnic experience is acknowledged by numerous observers of society. To most Americans, one black was indistinguishable from another, leading to the "they-all-look-alike" syndrome. There was an incongruous irony about the situation. The nation's most visible ethnic group left its people as invisible men. It is this aspect of Afro-American life that is explored in the excerpt that follows from Ralph Ellison's *The Invisible Man*.

I am an invisible man. No, I am not a spook like those who haunted Edgar Allan Poe; nor am I one of your Hollywood-movie ectoplasms. I am a man of substance, of flesh and bone, fiber and liquids—

As I passed to manhood the object lesson encountered on the Maryland plantation did much to intensify my hatred of slavery and to strengthen my resolution to ally myself with any effort for its abolition.[13]

Blacks have fought in all the wars in which Americans have fought, from the Revolution to the Vietnam struggle. Their participation in the Civil War contributed to the Union victory. There were some, however, who opposed the Negroes' right to fight, but by the end of the Civil War the Negroes as soldiers were universally accepted, especially after displaying their bravery and discipline. In all, 179,000 Negroes were enrolled in the Union Army.

The following firsthand account, written by a captain of the Seventh U.S. Colored Infantry, relates the success and progress of the Negro soldiers resulting from the opportunities afforded them in the war.

The enlisted men of my regiment were mostly slaves from the plantations of those counties of Maryland and Virginia which lie east of the Chesapeake Bay. These recruits came to us ignorant of books, without interest in anything outside their own plantation world; they were ignorant of everything except to obey. Very few could read a word, and excepting only a few free born men, scarcely one could write his name. To compensate for these disadvantages, there was at once manifested by them great eagerness to learn their duties, and an interest in them that could not be excelled. They gave themselves up to the work before them, wholly and without reserve, while the officers of the regiment seemed imbued with an earnest determination and a common ambition to make the regiment second to none. To this end the latter labored unceasingly, not in matters of drill and discipline only, but also to remedy, as far as possible, their almost total lack of education. Classes were organized in each company for the non-commissioned officers, and they would go out among the men to teach them the A,B,C; and except when military duty prevented, these classes were kept up almost to the day of discharge. It was an interesting sight, that might have been witnessed almost every day during the first year, to see groups of five or six men gathered around a primer or spelling book, learning the alphabet, and as time passed on, to see those men writing letters to their friends, or reading a book or paper.

When the regiment was disbanded, after a full three years' service, nearly all of them could read, a large percentage could write fairly well, and many had acquired considerable knowledge of the elementary branches, and, what was of even greater importance, all had learned self-reliance and self-respect, and went back to their homes with views enlarged, ambition aroused, and their interest in the outside world thoroughly awakened.

After the regiment was in fair working order, the officers sought to teach their men the value of money and induce them to save their

the territory between the Allegheny Mountains and the Pacific coast. They mingled freely with the native Americans and were quickly assimilated, although a large proportion of them, particularly in later years, belonged to non-English-speaking races. This natural bar to assimilation, however, was soon overcome by them, while the racial identity of their children was almost entirely lost and forgotten.

On the other hand, the new immigration has been largely a movement of unskilled laboring men who have come in large part temporarily, from the less progressive and advanced countries of Europe in response to the call for industrial workers in the eastern and middle western States. They have almost entirely avoided agricultural pursuits, and in cities and industrial communities have congregated together in sections apart from native Americans and the older immigrants to such an extent that assimilation has been slow as compared to that of the earlier non-English speaking races.

The new immigration as a class is far less intelligent than the old, approximately one-third of all those over 14 years of age when admitted being illiterate. Racially they are for the most part essentially unlike the British, German, and other peoples who came during the period prior to 1880, and generally speaking they actuated in coming by different ideals for the old immigration came to be a part of the country while the new, in a large measure, comes with the intention of profiting in a pecuniary way, by the superior advantages of the new world and then returning to the old country.

The old immigration movement, which in earlier days was the subject of much discussion and the cause of no little apprehension among the people of the country, long ago became thoroughly merged into the population, and the old sources have contributed a comparatively small part of the recent immigrant tide. Consequently the Commission paid but little attention to the foreign-born element of the old immigrant class and directed its efforts almost entirely to an inquiry relative to the general status of the newer immigrants as residents of the United States.

Assimilation of Immigrants

It is difficult to define and still more difficult to correctly measure the tendency of newer immigrant races toward Americanization, or assimilation into the body of the American people. If, however, the tendency to acquire citizenship, to learn the English language, and to abandon native customs and standards of living may be considered as factors, it is found that many of the more recent immigrants are backward in this regard, while some others have made excellent progress. The absence of family life, which is so conspicuous among many southern and eastern Europeans in the United States, is undoubtedly the influence which most effectively retards assimilation. The great majority of some of these races are represented in the United States by single men or men whose wives and families are in their native country. It is a common practice for men of this class in industrial communities to live in boarding or rooming groups, and as they are also usually associated with each other in their work they do not come in contact with Americans, and consquently have little or no incentive to learn the English language, become acquainted with American institutions, or adopt American standards. In the case of families, however, the process of assimilation is usually much more rapid. The families as a rule live in much more wholesome surroundings, and are reached by more of the agencies which promote assimilation. The most potent influence in promoting the assimilation of the family is the children, who, through contact with American life in the schools, almost invariably act as the unconscious agents in the uplift of their parents. Moreover, as the children grow older and become wage earners, they usually enter some higher occupation than that of their fathers, and in such cases the Americanizing influence upon their parents continues until frequently the whole family is gradually led away from the old surroundings and old standards into those more nearly American. This influence of the children is potent among immigrants in the great cities, as well as in the smaller industrial centers.

Among the new immigration as a whole the tendency to become naturalized citizens, even among those who have been here five years or more is not great, although much more pronounced in some races than in others. This result is influenced by language considerations and by the fact that naturalization is accomplished with greater difficulty than formerly, as the requirements are higher and expense greater, and that adequate facilities are not in all cases provided. Another reason is that many do not regard their stay here as permanent.

In recent years the work of promoting the welfare and assisting in the assimilation of recent immigrants has been inaugurated on a large scale by various religious and civic organizations. Until recently a great part of the efforts of this nature was carried on by organizations of the various races or peoples, but now the movement has been joined by organizations composed of all classes of citizens. In general this propaganda is in the main divorced from any semblance of proselytizing and is confined to practical efforts calculated to promote the well-being and advancement of the immigrant. Most of the societies lay particular stress upon influencing the immigrant to become acquainted with the duties and privileges of American citzenship and civilization. Teaching the English language and the primary branches of learning is a prominent feature in most of this work. It does not appear that the Federal Government can directly assist in this work, but where possible effort should be made to promote the activities of these organizations.[3]

The following extract is from a book written by Oscar Handlin, a foremost student of American immigration. In his study, *Race and Nationality in American Life*, Handlin expands on the rationale (philosophy) underlying the Dillingham Commission report. The historical setting is vital to an understanding of the climate. Restrictionist intentions intensified in the 1917-1924 period, culminating in the end of unrestricted immigration. This was the result of multiple historical factors: the misgivings with which Yankee families of New

England viewed the foreign-born, the concern for job security on the part of the organized labor, and the unfavorable attitude toward immigration by substantial blocs of Southerners, Populists, and Progressives. But a basic motivation behind restriction was the ethnic one: the desire to limit the influx of undesireable ethnic peoples.

> One fundamental premise lay behind the immigration legislation of 1917-1924 and animated also the McCarran-Walter Act of 1952. Embodied in the quota system, this premise held that the national origin of an immigrant was a reliable indication of his capacity for Americanization. It was averred, and science seemed to show, that some people, because of their racial or national constitution, were more capable of becoming Americans than others. Furthermore, is was argued that the "old immigrants," who came to the United States before 1880, were drawn from the superior stocks of northern and western Europe, while those who came after that date were drawn from the inferior breeds of southern and eastern Europe.
>
> There was a demonstrable connection between the diffusion of this assumption and the course of immigration legislation in the first quarter of the century. Those who argued in favor of a restrictionist policy did so not merely, perhaps not primarily, because they wished to reduce the total volume of immigration, but, more important, because they wished to eliminate the "new" while perpetuating the "old" immigration.[4]

Nativism accelerated during and after World War I as the fear of cheap labor was augmented by the fear of radicalism and communism, the growing awareness of the changing character of immigration, and the hostility of nativistic groups expressed in anti-Semitic, anti-Catholic, and anti-new ethnic group drives. The political, intellectual, and social climate was, therefore, conducive to the triumph of Anglo-American supremacy, as it culminated in the most restrictive immigration policy in United States history—the quota systems. The most important of these laws was the National Origins Act of 1924, clearly an example of ethnic-motivated legislation. The act's provisions gave decided preference to northwestern European ethnic groups, while discriminating heavily against southern and eastern European nationalities. Asians and Africans were subject to virtual total exclusion. Thus of the maximum allowance of 165,000 immigrants annually (the Western Hemisphere was excluded), northwestern European peoples received 80 percent of the quota.

The fact that the act placed an end to unrestricted immigration was less important than the fact that the nation had by law adopted a policy of ethnic preference. Moreover, this policy would be adhered to for the next four decades.

The discriminatory intent of the act under the guise of immigration limitation is attacked in the excerpt below by Senator David I. Walsh of Massachusetts, the first United States senator of Irish immigrant parents.

Mr. President, the proposal to make the census of 1890, instead of that of 1910, the basis for the quota hereafter to be admitted, as advocated by many, is objectionable on many grounds.

A few facts regarding the population census of 1890, as compared with the census of 1910, give practical assurance that a great American principle would be violated by the change proposed.

Two per cent of the alien inhabitants in 1890 would total about 160,000, whereas the same percentage in 1910 would number about 238,000. This represents a material reduction in the number of aliens to be admitted and indicates a tendency to further restrict the number of admissible immigrants.

The most important aspect of this question, however, is that such a change would inject into the law a very apparent discrimination against immigrants of certain nationalities. The census of 1890 shows that a large majority of our alien inhabitants were then natives of northern and western Europe, while the census of 1910 shows more nearly equal proportions from southern and eastern Europe. In 1890 about 87 per cent of our alien population were people from northern and western Europe, as compared with 56 per cent in 1910. Who can say that it would be fair to abandon a basis of calculation that is very close to an equal division between the races of northern and western Europe and the races of southern and eastern Europe and adopt a basis that will give the people of northern and western Europe 87 per cent of our immigration during the coming years?

Since we have said to the people of all nations, "We are going to admit only a certain percentages of your future immigrants," can we go further and add that to certain nationalities we shall extend preference? That is what the suggestion of the 1890 census basis means. It simply amounts to reducing and practically eliminating all emigration from southern and eastern Europe.

Whatever may be the surface for the change in data, it must be insisted that the true reason is social discrimination. An attempt is being made to slip by this proposal, which is aimed clearly and mercilessly at the Slav, the Latin, and the Jew, under the harmless guise of a change in the data of the census.

Mr. President, if I were convinced that the admission of immigrants to this country, however it might ease conditions abroad, could in the slightest degree imperil not merely the safety of our institutions, but the prospect of employment for our own laborers or of prosperity of the American people, I would advocate not lessening but preventing it. But because I believe the immigrants who cultivate the soil, such as those who have of recent years taken possession of the abandoned farms of New England, contribute to the welfare of the country as much as they derive from it, I am opposed to too rigidly restricting a source of benefit so important and valuable.

To everything that has been said concerning the admission of insane, diseased, depraved persons—persons against whom any objection
can be made on the score of their capacity for citizenship—I most emphatically subscribe and support. We have set up stringent requirements
to keep out the weak and incapacitated. We very properly require that
the immigrant must possess an established good character, be of sound
body, and that his political opinions must not be in conflict with those
principles which underlie the stability of our Government. More than
that we require—what is not imposed on an American citizen—the immigrant be able to read a language. What more desirable addition to our
citizenship can be demanded than a man or woman meet all these requirements? If we do not rigidly and effectively enforce these
requirements, it is our own not the immigrants' fault.

Mr. President, what is the real driving force behind the movement
of basing the quota on the census of 1890? The peoples of the world will
attribute it to our belief that the "Nordic" is a superior race. The world
will assume that our Government considers the Italians, Greeks, Jews,
Poles, and the Slavs inferior to the Nordics congenitally as well as
culturally. It is a dangerous assumption. Millions of people here in
America will resent this slur upon their racial character. The vilification
of whole races does not produce a very pleasant mental state in that part
of our population who happen to be foreign born. Do we not realize
that we are making for ourselves a greater national problem than ever
before? Does the agitation provoked by the proposed law conduce to
the early assimilation of the immigrant which you claim is your
desideratum? . . .

Men and women, Mr. President, do not come 3,000 or 5,000
miles, suffering the utmost hardships of a trans-Atlantic voyage, parting
oftentimes with the last penny in order to obtain passage, by a desire
that is not worthy and commendable. Can there be a higher proof of
devotion to the benefits and blessings of our country than that men and
women to come under its blessings will take all the discomforts and risks
of journeying to a country of whose language they are ignorant, to
whose customs they are strangers, leaving their house and their fireside,
often their most loved ones, and the associations of all the generations
that preceded them?

Leave your places of comfort and visit the places where the immigrants are found in American life before you condemn them. Whose
faces are those going up and down in the shafts that bring to the surface
of the earth our mineral deposits? They are those of our immigrants.
Stand at the mill gates and the exits of the sweatshops, where those commodities are manufactured that require the most exacting labor. Our
immigrants are the "factory hands." Watch at the entrance of a savings
bank in our industrial centers. The depositors most numerous in the
lines are our immigrants. Whose children are those running in and out
among the vehicles of the city streets, with no playground but the
crowded and littered roadway in the midst of the cities marts? They are
our immigrants. Whose weary and careworn faces—mothers'
faces—are leaning out over the fire escapes in the tenement rows trying
to catch a breath of fresh air? They are our immigrants. Look in at the

winter sessions of our evening schools. Who are the men and women, simply clad with drawn countenances and calloused hands, seeking a knowledge of our language and the history of our country? They, too, are our imigrants.

The records, Mr. President, show that immigrants must seek employment where they can find it, and as they are without funds to travel any great distance, they are obliged to enter the mines and mills near the places of their arrival. We have made them the slaves of our industrial system. Our greed and not their self-seeking has directed them and sent them and their families into the factories, sweatshops, down into the depths of the earth and on the docks of our waterways, wherever there is lowly and fatiguing work.

In 1918, 58 per cent of the steel and iron workers were foreign born, 61 per cent of our packers' labor, 62 per cent of the bitumious miners and wool weavers, 69 per cent of the cotton-mill operators, 72 per cent of clothing shopmen, and 65 per cent of the sugar refiners' help came from abroad.

Mr. President, we have, I fear, often been the means of causing them to substitute the material for the spiritual. It is toil, toil, ceaseless toil, which we have offered them. The industrial master is their first and often their only teacher of Americanism. They soon learn his interest is not entirely altruistic.

Look about and observe more closely the conditions prevailing in the immigrant settlements, especially in the crowded districts of our large cities. What are the conditions in these areas? Over crowded dark tenements, lack of sanitation, sunless and airless narrow streets. Does anyone for a minute believe that the immigrants choose to reside in these unattractive surroundings? They have no choice. It is true that they find there a kindred acquaintance willing to sympathize with them and if possible assist them, but they are there because they are forced into these districts.

With this knowledge of our neglect, of our indifference to the immigrant and his opportunities for assimilation and Americanization, how unfair, how injurious is the opprobrious language used in the references to him in the pages of the *Congressional Record* and the public discussion of this measure! They have been called mongrels, garbage, riffraff, anarchists, socialists, and Bolshevists. Every conceivable name that could be thought of has been used in describing these immigrants and their families whom we have forced into most unsatisfactory living and working conditions. Men and women who have come from the open fields of Europe, farmers and peasants who have lived in the sunshine and amid the song and laughter of their native surroundings, overnight have been forced into the conditions of living of which complaint is very properly made. Well you know we have done this, and we have done it regardless of their souls, regardless of their spiritual welfare. Let us be humane and just to the immigrant, and if we are we will in the future concern ourselves more about the living conditions of these foreigners rather than condemn and abuse them and close our ports to them. Let us think of them as human beings and less as undesirables.

Mr. President, our slight work of assimilation, let us frankly admit, has been haphazard and often misguided, yet the war proved, to the credit of our immigrants, that we were as closely united a country as many of the more homogeneous State of Europe; we attained without conscious effort rresults in assimilation that Germany with all her systematic efforts failed to attain. . . .

The theories of superior race value and selection that have accompanied the discussion of this question are humilating and insulting. Do we fancy that the peoples and Governments of Italy, Poland, Hungary, Austria, Greece, or Rumania have no national pride?

What are the nationalities whose coming to America is chiefly curtailed by this arbitrary resort to the 1890 censes? The Greeks, to whom civilization owes so much in the fields of literature, science, art, and government. The Italians, who from the day of early Roman history have contributed immensely to civilization along the lines of government, literature, art, music, and navigation, including the gift of the discoverer of America. The Liberty-loving Poles, whose sacrifices and struggles for freedom have arrested the admiration of mankind and who saved all Europe from the Turks at Vienna scarcely two centuries ago, and who were once in the van of culture. The Jews, who contributed to the world literature, religion, standards of righteous conduct that can not be overvalued. . . .

Have we learned nothing from the earlier generations' mistaken notions about the Dutch, the French. the Irish, the Germans, and the Scandinavians, now an essential element in our assumed racial superiority? They were condemned and criticized by the earlier settlers, just as we are now undertaking to condemn the races from southern Europe. Have we forgotten that at the time of the Revolution one-fifth of the population of America could not speak the English language? Have we forgotten that more than one-half of the population of America at the time of the Revolution was not Anglo-Saxon?

Factors of all sorts enter into play in determining race values, and often an alien most desirable from one point of view is least so from another. But is not the whole concept in variance with fundamental American principles and policies?

The whole idea of relative values is objectionable, unreasonable, and grossly offensive. Ever since Edmund Burke's famous saying it has been generally recognized that you can not draw an indictment against a whole nation.

Illiteracy and poverty may be high among the races from southern and eastern Europe, but these are not crimes. In the statistics of alcoholism, insanity, and disease, their racial inferiority does not hold. Considering their opportunities, these immigrants have done about as well as any other nationalities that have been here for the same length of time. All these races have brought with them a rich cargo of values, a keen sense of good workmanship, tireless industry, a remarkably sane and intelligent outlook upon life, a family solidarity, a simplicity of life, and a depth of spirituality that is most commendable.

Attempt to grade our aliens! Which race is to be rated "100 per cent American"? It is a shortsighted view which measures the desirability or undersirability of any group of aliens only by the rapidity or tardiness with which they forget their past spiritual connections and allow themselves to be rapidly molded into an undeterminate type which is vagued termed a "100 per cent American." . . .

Mr. President, what group of aliens failed to respond willingly and serve bravely when our country needed them? On the outskirts of this city, in the National Cemetery, within a few months we buried the body of an American soldier, born in Greece, who was acclaimed as one of the bravest of the brave, whose heroism in death was one of the thrilling and inspiring episodes of the recent war. And we are now, after such an illustration of patriotism—and it could be multiplied many times—to inform the Americans of Hellenic descent that they are among the undesirables.

Read the names upon the crosses in the American military cemeteries in France. Go there, you who are saying that certain races are undesirable, and read the names upon the graves of the poor lads who had neither father nor mother nor any other loved one to request that their bodies be interred in Arlington Cemetery. Read the names of these dead; read the names of those over whom the poppies now grow, practically all of them foreign born—Poles, Italians, Greeks, and Slavs—scarcely an Anglo-Saxon name among America's brave dead now sleeping in France. . . . [5]

There is a close correlation between American immigration policy and the ethnic composition of the nation. Immigration laws, especially the quota acts, are among the most complicated and difficult to understand. Nevertheless, their discriminatory effects are obvious. In the following selection, Helen F. Eckerson states the purposes of the national origins plan.

The national-origins plan was to accomplish two purposes: (1) to reduce the volume of immigration by establishing a numerical limit for all countries except the designated countries in the Western Hemisphere and (2) to make automatic the selection of immigrants by nationalities by providing a fixed number of each nationality. It was said to be non-discriminatory since all nationalities were treated the same way. At the same time the underlying intention of the law—that is, to preserve the ethnic composition of the population of the United States through the selection of immigrants whose tradition, languages, and political systems were akin to those in this country—would be accomplished. . . .

When the national-origins quotas were finally proclaimed, it seemed that here was a scheme that would control immigration both in volume and in selectivity. It was held that most of those who would come would be those easily assimilable, and in the tradition of the American Dream. [6]

In her examination of United States immigration policy, Professor Shirley Hune of the University of the District of Columbia concluded that this immigration policy had always been based on the preference of family stock, race, labor skill, or educational background. Conscious of her own ethnic roots she asserts that the

American attitude "toward immigration has been one of ambivalence [and] . . . it has been racist and exclusionary."[7] In the following extract she presents evidence of anti-Asian immigration legislation.

1. The first victims of immigration discrimination, as a group, were the Chinese who were also the first Asians to migrate to the U.S. in significant numbers. There has been an historic policy of Chinese exclusion in America. The first bill to limit Chinese immigrants to the U.S. was passed in 1882 restricting the entry of Chinese laborers for a period of 10 years. It is the only American immigration bill to specifically restrict the migration of foreign peoples by race. It also denied the Chinese in America the right to U.S. citizenship through the process of naturalization. Over a period of time additional legislation was passed extending Chinese restriction for 80 years and broadening the application of restriction to include other categories of Chinese such as Chinese laborers' wives. Chinese restriction was not fully repealed until the Immigration and Naturalization Act of 1965; there had been a modest lift in the exclusion policy in 1943 when an annual quota of 105 Chinese was introduced.

This policy of Chinese exclusion in particular is viewed by Asian Americans as not only a policy of racism and discrimination, but a policy of genocide. A policy which prevented Chinese women from joining their husbands or fiances in America in conjunction with State regulations against intermarriage of Chinese and Caucasian denied Chinese males the human right to form families in America. Such a policy could only be designed to eliminate the Chinese population in America. Thus, the glowing remarks that Americans make about the tradition of the Chinese family are crude and horrible jokes. The Chinese family *in America* did not exist except for a few in the late 19th and early 20th centuries. These remarks are met with not joy put pain, with the knowledge of those thousands of Chinese men who spent their lives away from family members in China and died alone in America never knowing their children and grandchildren and of the thousands of parents, women, and children who were never permitted to share their lives with their menfolk.

2. The Chinese were not the only Asian group to face hostility. Opposition to Japanese, Korean, "Hindu" (East Indian), and Pilipino immigrants also appeared in the late 19th and early 20th centuries. Thus, in 1908, in the face of anti-Japanese opinion and violence, the U.S. Government negotiated a Gentlemen's Agreement with the Government of Japan whereby Japan was to limit the number of Japanese immigrants to America.

3. In 1917 the policy of Asian restriction was further extended with the introduction of the barred zone act. Asians in the geographic triangle in the Asia/Pacific region defined by degrees of latitude and longitude to include India, Southeast Asia, the Indonesian Islands, New Guinea, and parts of Arabia, Afghanistan, and Siberia were barred from admission to the U.S. by this act. Only Japan was exempted.

4. Then in 1922, the U.S. Supreme Court declared "Orientals," in general, ineligible for citizenship. Based on this decision, an act was passed in 1924 declaring all aliens ineligible for citizenship. In this man-

ner, a policy of Japanese exclusion was finally introduced. This act was part of a series of restrictive immigration legislation in the 1920s that established the national origins quota system and limited the entry of Southern and Eastern Europeans to America.

5. Pilipino Americans, who had escaped earlier attempts at restriction because of their colonial relationship with the U.S. and their status as U.S. nationals, were also affected by this general policy of immigration restriction. Part of the drive to achieve independence for the Philippines was coupled with attempts by opponents of Asians to restrict the entry of Pilipinos to America. With the acquisition of political independence in 1934, an annual quota of 50 was given to the Philippines.

This policy of Asian exclusion or restriction to an annual quota of 100 or 50 was carried out in the same period that approximately 35 million Europeans were permitted to enter the U.S. and in which European countries (after 1920) were given annual quotas for their immigrants numbering in the thousands. Thus, the policy of restriction and exclusion was aimed primarily at limiting the entry of Asians; a policy that was based upon race and, therefore, part of the system of institutionalized racism in America.

In addition to limiting the numbers of Asian immigrants, U.S. immigration policy has been discriminatory on the basis of the right to citizenship. Asians were declared ineligible for citizenship through naturalization on the basis of their race. It was argued that "Orientals" were inferior and incapable of understanding American institutions. This policy was not changed for the Chinese until 1943 and for the Pilipinos not until 1946 when they were granted the right to citizenship through naturalization. The immigration law was finally repealed in 1952, thus permitting all other Asian groups access to citizenship. But for those first-generation immigrants, many of whom lived in the U.S. for several decades, life in America meant institutionalized second-class citizenship.

The Immigration and Naturalization Act of 1965—eliminating quotas based on race and national origin—has finally ended Asian restriction. The act facilated family reunification; however, it is still selective on the basis of the socioeconomic background of the immigrant. As a consequence, the total number of Asians entering the U.S. has increased dramatically in the past decade and Asian immigration now constitutes almost one-third of the total annual quota. In addition, the new Asian immigrants come from a broad socioeconomic background and many are part of the so-called "third world brain drain." They are highly skilled and educated, such as doctors; others are relatively unskilled and do not speak English.

However, the 1965 act does not eliminate opposition to Asian immigration. Hostility and racism still persist as the mixed response to the arrival of Indochinese refugees and the famous "baby lift" out of Vietnam in 1975 attests. The reluctance of Federal and State officials to receive the Indochinese, statements in the popular media alluding to the "yellow hordes," socially communicable diseases, and the untrustworthiness of the most recent Asian immigrant group to America is a repetition of the reception given to other Asian immigrant groups of an earlier period and recalls for us the long history of the Asian immigrant experience in the United States.

A second factor in the development of U.S. immigration policy relating to Asians is the effect of American foreign policy in Asia on U.S. immigration policy. This interrelationship of foreign policy and immigration policy has had a serious impact on the lives of Asian Americans. The formulation of a U.S. policy towards immigration is complex and involves not only Federal legislation but also court cases, administrative decisions and even the personal intervention of Congressmen. Immigration is generally viewed as a domestic matter and immigration policy as a reflection of internal political, social, and economic needs and interests. But, in reality, like all other domestic policies, immigration policy is also influenced by American international relations and interests. It is, therefore, not solely a domestic policy.[8]

The Immigration and Nationality Act of 1952 (McCarran-Walter Act) is the law that governs American immigration policy. It has been amended several times since 1952 and its provisions are extensive and complex. An immigrant is defined as a noncitizen who is allowed to settle permanently in the United States. In recent years about 500,000 immigrants and refugees have entered this country annually. The fixed numerical annual limit is 290,000, but many are exempt from this limit, including the husbands, wives, and minor children of U.S. citizens, the parents of adult U.S. citizens, and refugees admitted under the parole authority of the Attorney General. Those immigrants who come under the annual ceiling of 290,000 are limited to 20,000 per year from any one nation. The following represents the development of United States immigration policy.

U.S. Immigration Policy

Changing emphases in U.S. immigration policy are reflected in the history of our laws and programs.

1783 George Washington proclaims that the "bosom of America is open to receive not only the opulent and respectable stranger, but the oppressed and persecuted of all nations and religions, whom we shall welcome to a participation of all our rights and privileges. . . ."

1819 For the first time, the U.S. government begins to count immigrants.

1864 Congress passes law making it easier to import contract laborers.

1875 The first federal restriction on immigration prohibits prostitutes and convicts.

1882 Congress curbs Chinese immigration.

1882 Congress excludes convicts, lunatics, idiots, and persons likely to become a public charge, and places a head tax on each immigrant.

1885 Legislation prohibits the admission of contract laborers.

1903 List of excluded immigrants expands to include polygamists and political radicals such as anarchists.

1907 Head tax on immigrants is increased; added to the excluded list are those with physical or mental defects that may affect their ability to earn a living, those with tuberculosis, and children unaccompanied by parents.

1907 Gentleman's agreement between U.S. and Japan restricts Japanese immigration.

1917 Congress requires literacy in some language for those immigrants over sixteen years of age, except in cases of religious persecution, and bans virtually all immigration from Asia.

1921 Quotas are established; each nation is allowed three percent of the foreign-born persons of that nationality living in the United States in 1910. Limit on European immigration set at about 350,000.

1924 National Origins Law (Johnson-Reed Act) sets annual quotas at two percent of a nationality's U.S. population as determined in 1890 census.

1929 Quotas of 1924 now to be based on a nationality's proportion of U.S. population in 1920 census.

1939 Congress defeats refugee bill to rescue 20,000 children from Nazi Germany, despite willingness of American families to sponsor them, on the grounds that the children would exceed the German quota.

1942 United States and Mexico adopt bracero program, allowing temporary foreign laborers to work in the United States.

1943 Ban on Chinese immigration repealed.

1946 Congress passes War Brides act, facilitating immigration of foreign-born wives, husbands, and children of U.S. armed forces personnel.

1948 Congress passes Displaced Persons Act (amended in 1950), enabling 400,000 refugees to enter the United States.

1952 Immigration and Nationality Act of 1952 (McCarran-Walter Act):
—reaffirms national origins system, giving each nation a quota equal to its proportion of the American population in 1920;
—limits immigration from Eastern Hemisphere to about 150,000; immigration from the Western Hemisphere remains unrestricted;
—establishes preferences for skilled workers and relatives of U.S. citizens; and
—tightens security and screening standards and procedures for immigrants.

1953 Refugee Relief Act admits over 200,000 refugees.

1960 Cuban refugees paroled into United States.

1964 United States ends bracero program.

1965 Immigration and Nationality Act Amendments of 1965:
—abolish the national origins system;
—establish an annual ceiling of 170,000 for the Eastern Hemisphere with a 20,000 per-country limit; immigrant visas distributed on a first-come, first-served basis according to a seven-category preference system, favoring close relatives of U.S. citizens and permanent resident aliens, those with needed occupational skills, and refugees; and
—establish an annual ceiling of 120,000 for the Western Hemisphere with no preference system or per-country limit.

1976 Immigration and Nationality Act Amendments of 1976:
—extend the 20,000 per-country limit and the seven-category preference system to the Western Hemisphere; and
—maintain the separate annual ceilings of 170,000 for the Eastern Hemisphere and 120,000 for the Western Hemisphere.
1978 Immigration and Nationality Act Amendments of 1978 combine the ceilings for both hemispheres into a worldwide total of 290,000, with the same seven-category preference system and 20,000 per-country limit uniformly applied.
1978 Congress establishes the Select Commission on Immigration and Refugee Policy.[9]

The Select Commission on Immigration and Refugee Policy, created by Public Law 95-412, 1978, constituted the first major effort by a joint Presidential-Congressional commission to examine and overhaul the immigration laws of the United States since 1911. The Select Commission was ordered to "study and evaluate . . . existing laws, policies, and procedures governing the admission of immigrants and refugees to the United States and to make such administrative and legislative recommendations to the President and to the Congress as are appropriate." In its first semiannual report the Commission submitted significant findings in its section, "What Have We Learned?"

III. What Have We Learned?

From past research:
There are probably no more than 6 million illegal migrants in the United States at any one time and considerably fewer most of the time.
There are probably no more than 3 million illegal Mexican migrants in the United States at any one time and probably many fewer most of the time.
The research on the economic impact of illegal migrants does not enable us to generalize about the characteristics and impact of illegal migrants as a whole.
Very little comprehensive research on the impact of recent immigrants and refugees exists.
Such research as does exist indicates fairly rapid participation in and adaptation to American life by most of the immigrants and refugees who have come to this country and have acquired the status of either resident alien or citizen.
The rate of population growth in the United States is much more affected by slight changes in fertility rates than by substantial changes in the rate of immigration.
If the present fertility rate of 1.8 remains constant (an assumption and *not* a certainty), net immigration from all legal sources of 750,000—immigration over emigration—would result in population stabilization by the year 2030. (Remainder: This does not take into account illegal migration, which we assume must be reduced to a much smaller level.)
Research on emigration is badly needed. Estimates of annual

emigration from the United States vary widely.

On the basis of what we have heard at our public hearings and from other aspects of our public information analysis, the following generalizations can be made:

The racism and xenophobia which once characterized strong opposition to immigration in the United States have not surfaced in the media or in our public hearings to a considerable extent.

There is great public sympathy for refugees, but considerable concern over the impact of refugees on social services and the economy, as reflected in recent public opinion polls.

There is a strong feeling on the part of religious and humanitarian groups in the country for immigrants as well as refugees, partly connected to our concern for human rights and our tradition as a nation of immigrants.

There is debate over the relationship of immigration to resource conservation.

While there is much sympathy for a policy based on family reunification, there is widespread opinion that the present system of labor certification does not work well.

One body of opinion believes that the United States should inaugurate some kind of temporary worker program; this opinion is usually opposed by representatives of organized labor and many others.

There are many who believe any system of numerical ceiling should give preference to border neighbors, although the idea meets considerable opposition.

There is a strong popular belief held by many that illegal migrants have an overall negative impact on the economy, but there is a large body of expert opinion—not without opposition from other experts—which contradicts the more popular view.

There is widespread belief that the presence of a substantial number of illegal aliens in the United States is bad for society apart from its controversial effect on the economy. The reasons given: They are vulnerable to economic exploitation; they are preyed upon easily by criminals; they do not report health problems; many of their children are not in school; and their presence corrodes confidence in a government which presumes to apply laws consistently and equitably.

Many believe that legalization of the present population of illegal aliens is necessary to eliminate many of the problems described above.

There is interest in a system of flexible immigration levels with periodic target goals to adjust to changes in fertility and changes in demand resulting from economic changes and refugee upheavals.

There is growing support for discouraging the movement of illegal entry into the United States for purposes of work through the development of a noncounterfeitable work authorization card which could be administered for *all* equitably, easily, and inexpensively and which only properly documented aliens and citizens could possess.

There is concern over the lack of effective civic education, employment counseling, and English-language training for refugees and immigrants.

There is strong criticism of various aspects of the Immigration and

Naturalization Service as underfunded, unprofessional, inefficient, and occasionally corrupt.

There is a strong opinion that much more must be done to crack down on smugglers of illegal aliens.

There is a nearly universal belief that our present criteria for excluding immigrants and nonimmigrants are arbitrary, capricious, and much too long.[10]

There has been considerable rise in the number of applications for naturalization. Applications have increased from 147,954 in fiscal year 1971 to 238,586 in 1978, a 61 percent increase. Moreover, the actual increase in becoming a citizen through naturalization rose from 120,740 in 1973 to 173,535 in 1978, a dramatic 69 percent increase, as the following figure indicates. Note and compare the origins of those who were naturalized.

Table 8.1 Persons Naturalized[11]
1973 – 1978

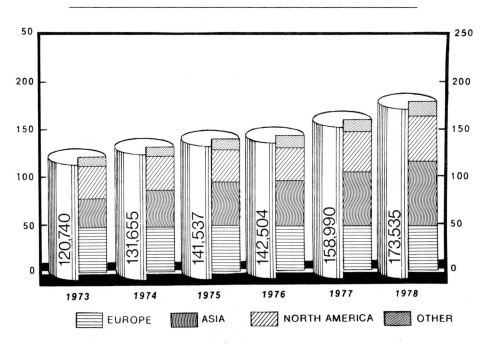

The impact of the 1965 immigration law is clearly evident for the first twelve years by the following report of the Immigration and Naturalization Service. Note the dramatic increases in immigration to the United States from Greece, Portugal, the Soviet Union, and from the regions of Asia, the Caribbean, and Africa.

Table 8.2

Immigrants Admitted by Country or Region of Birth[12]

Fiscal Years Ended September 30, 1977 and June 30, 1965

	Number		
Country of birth	1977	1965	Percent change
All countries	462,315	296,697	+55.8
Europe	70,010	113,424	−38.3
Austria	400	1,680	−76.2
Belgium	377	1,005	−62.5
Czechoslovakia	575	1,894	−69.6
Denmark	433	1,384	−68.7
France	1,618	4,039	−59.9
Germany	6,372	24,045	−73.5
Greece	7,838	3,002	+161.9
Hungary	853	1,574	−45.8
Ireland	1,238	5,463	−77.3
Italy	7,510	10,821	−30.6
Netherlands	1,014	3,085	−67.1
Norway	334	2,256	−85.2
Poland	4,010	8,465	−52.6
Portugal	9,657	2,005	+381.6
Romania	2,015	1,644	+22.6
Spain	2,487	2,200	+13.0
Sweden	571	2,411	−76.3
Switzerland	610	1,984	−69.3
U.S.S.R.	5,742	1,853	+209.9
United Kingdom	12,477	27,358	−119.3
Yugoslavia	2,791	2,818	−.96
Other Europe	1,088	2,438	−55.4
Asia	157,759	20,683	+662.7
China and Taiwan	19,764	4,057	+387.2
Hong Kong	5,632	712	+691.0
India	18,613	582	+3,098.1
Iran	4,261	804	+430.0
Japan	4,178	3,180	+31.4
Korea	30,917	2,165	+1,328.0
Pakistan	3,183	187	+1,602.1
Philippines	39,111	3,130	+1,149.6
Thailand	3,945	214	+1,743.5
Vietnam	4,629	226	+1,948.2
Other Asia	23,526	5,426	+333.6
North America	187,345	126,729	+47.8

Country of birth	Number		Percent change
	1977	*1965*	
Canada	12,688	38,327	−66.9
Mexico	44,079	37,969	−16.1
West Indies	114,011	37,583	+203.4
Cuba	69,708	19,760	+252.8
Dominican Republic	11,655	9,504	+22.6
Haiti	5,441	3,609	+50.8
Jamaica	11,501	1,837	+526.1
Trinidad and Tobago	6,106	485	+1,159.0
Other West Indies	9,600	2,388	+302.0
Other North America	16,567	12,850	+28.9
South America	32,954	30,962	+6.4
Argentina	2,787	6,124	−54.5
Brazil	1,513	2,869	−47.3
Colombia	8,272	10,885	−24.0
Other South America	20,382	11,084	+83.9
Africa	10,155	3,383	+200.2
Oceania	4,092	1,512	+170.6
Other Countries	....	4	....

A clamor for a revision of the nation's basic immigration laws surfaced within a few years of the passage of the 1965 immigration policy. Critics charged that the present law was unrealistic and even harmful and that therefore a complete overhaul was necessary. They were especially exercised over governmental failure in dealing with the undocumented aliens, a subject which elicited spirited controversy. Critics maintained that this lack of government supervision served to undermine the nation's laws because it encouraged large numbers to evade laws. They also stated that these illegal newcomers took jobs away from Americans, exploited community social services—while refraining from paying taxes—and introduced other asocial practices and traditions which were harmful to the social fabric.

Another point of view was held by a smaller but dedicated group of defenders of the rights of newcomers, legal and otherwise. Sensitive to the human needs of the undocumented aliens they called for enactment of unvindictive immigration policies which would protect the rights and welfare of people whose only crime was trying to improve their condition, just as had been the case of millions of immigrants to America in the earlier periods of history.

The Refugee Act of 1980 established a permanent statute revising United States refugee admissions policy and authorizing uniform settlement assistance for all refugees arriving in this country. The act defined a refugee as

> . . .any person who is outside any country of his nationality or, in the case of a person having no nationality, is outside any country in which he has habitually resided, and who is unable or unwilling to return to, and is unable and unwilling to avail himself of the protection of, that country because of persecution or a well-founded fear of persecution on account of race, religion, nationality, membership of a particular social group or political opinion.[13]

By 1982 Congress was prepared to consider proposals which would deal with the serious questions posed by the nation's basic immigration laws and their partial noncompliance. The result was H. R. 5872, a bill designed to revise and reform the Immigration and Naturalization Act.

What follows are excerpts from the testimony of numerous witnesses called by the committee. The first is the narrowly framed view of Donald Mann of the organization Negative Population Growth, Inc., who was unsympathetic to amnesty for illegal aliens.

Testimony of Donald Mann, President, Negative Population Growth, Inc.

Mr. Mann. Thank you, Mr. Chairman, for the opportunity to testify before you today.

I am Donald Mann, president of Negative Population Growth, Inc., known as NPG.

Mr. Mazzoli. As distinct from ZPG.

Mr. Mann. Yes.

Mr. Mazzoli. I have not read your statement, but what are the different goals? ZPG has testified before us before.

Mr. Mann. We seek a level of population size in this country of roughly half of present levels, whereas ZPG, I believe would like to stabilize population at present levels or more.

Mr. Mazzoli. You really want to reduce the population?

Mr. Mann. Yes.

Mr. Mazzoli. I just was not sure of the demographics here.

Mr. Mann. We are a national membership organization founded in 1973.

We do believe that the population size of this country already far exceeds the long-term carrying capacity of our resources and the capacity of our environment to absorb pollution.

For this reason, we advocate a national population policy aimed at a very gradual reduction in our numbers to about half our present size.

We oppose proposals to grant legal status to illegal aliens now residing in this country. The primary reason for this is the impact that amnesty would have on the population size of this country.

Estimates of the number of illegal aliens now residing here vary. The most commonly cited figures range between 3 and 10 million.

It has been estimated that the average illegal alien has as many as six to seven close relatives in his or her country of origin.

At some time in the future, these close relatives would have the right to legally enter this country under a family reunification program.

In other words, if we try to assess the impact on U.S. population size that an amnesty program would have, it is clear that we must take into account not only those aliens residing here now but also their close relatives who will eventually join them.

To halt the degradation of our environment and reduce our alarming dependence on imports for the vital resources we need, we need to halt—and NPG believes that we eventually need to reverse—U.S. population growth.

We believe that the question of amnesty for illegal aliens must be seen within the context of our overall immigration policy which, in turn, should be, we believe, an integral part of a national population policy aimed at halting U.S. population growth.

We feel that as a guiding principle, annual immigration should not exceed the number of American citizens leaving this country permanently by emigrating. In this way, migration would not contribute, on balance, to U.S. population growth.

What solution then does NPG recommend in order to resolve the problem of vast numbers of illegal aliens now living in this country?

We recommend that the Government put into effect a secure worker identification system, coupled with sanctions for employers who hire illegal aliens. In our view, sanctions should include criminal penalties and apply to all employers of whatever size.

Under such a program, illegal aliens now here would be unable to work and would be obliged to leave the country of their own volition.[14]

A more compassionate view of the proposed revision of the Immigration and Naturalization Act was presented by Reverend Joseph A. Cogo, executive secretary of the American Committee on Italian Migration, a nonprofit, voluntary agency whose primary purpose is to implement a fair immigration policy. Pointing out the need for a constant updating of immigration policy, Reverend Cogo's attention focused on a program that favored family reunion, benefited the economy, and alleviated refugee problems. Family reunion, then, ranked highest in priority because it was "the basic human right of any American citizen to have his immediate family members join him in the United States."

The passage of the Immigration Reform Act of October 3, 1965 marked a milestone in the history of our immigration legislation. It abolished the discriminatory national origins quota system and established a fair and equitable immigration policy. The present law reaffirmed and sanctioned our traditions in favoring family reunion; but provided as well for the admission of professionals and skilled workers in the interest of our national economy, and set aside a permanent number of visas to be used for the relief of refugee problems. We believe these criteria are sound, humane and fair.

The Act of 1965, therefore, was a good start; it was, in my opinion, the best product that could have been conceived at that time, and we are proud of having had the opportunity to make it come into being the way it did. However, the experience of 16 years of its operation has amply shown serious deficiencies that must now be corrected in order to make that law responsive to the present needs and to the needs of the foreseeable future. It is generally agreed that the phenomenon of immigraiton is a constantly changing phenomenon; no law, therefore, can ever expect to rigidly regulate it for an indefinite number of years. That is why we feel that a revision of the 1965 Act is now necessary.

The principles, however, of the 1965 Act remain sound and should be firmly preserved, and in fact strengthened in any new legislation. They are: First, family reunion; second, the good of our economy; third, the alleviation of refugee problems.

These principles are each so important that no one should be sacrificed for the sake of the others. And this is one deficiency that can be detected in the present law, where we have third preferences intermingled with family reunion. We noted with satisfaction that in the area of refugees, the new law of 1980 did set aside a fixed, yet flexible number to respond to this situation in a much better way than the 1965 Law provided.

We believe that the law should be structured in such a way as to deal with these three principles separately: a set number for family reunion with its own preference categories and percentages; a set number for workers with its own preference categories and percentages; and a set, yet flexible, number for refugees. . .

The family reunion concept should have, as it now does, a definite priority in our immigration policy. It is the basic human right of any American citizen to have his immediate family members join him in the United States. This right should not be in any way curbed or restricted in our immigration laws. Therefore, it is our recommendation that immediate relatives, as defined in the present law, not be subject to numerical limitations. . .

For Italians, and for many other ethnic groups, brothers and sisters, whether or not they are married, are an integral part of the family reunion concept. Elimination of this preference category would violate a sacrosanct human right of an American citizen to live with his family according to his own tradition and lifestyle.

Furthermore, this category of immigrants is the easiest to resettle for the obvious reasons that they have the support of their families here. There is practically no potential for need of public assistance: and these immigrants would, generally speaking, take jobs our citizens are not anxious to have.[15]

Identifying the actual numbers of persons within the ethnic constellation has posed a problem to demographers, especially since the Census Bureau counted only nonwhites and foreign-stock whites. Responding to the pressure emanating from the new ethnic movement, the census has attempted to measure accurately Americans of single ancestry and multiple ancestry in this 1979 special study.

Table 8.3 Reported Single and Multiple Ancestries: November 1979[16]

(Numbers in thousands. Civilian noninstitutional population)

Ancestry	Total	Percent of total	Persons reported single ancestry		Persons reported multiple ancestry	Percent of persons by kind of ancestry response		
			Number	Percent		Total	Single ancestry	Multiple ancestry
Reported at least one specific ancestry	179,078[1]	100.0[1]	96,496	100.0	82,582[1]	100.0	53.9	46.1
Afro-American, African	16,193	9.0	15,057	15.6	1,136	100.0	93.0	7.0
American Indian	9,900	5.3	2,053	2.1	7,847	100.0	20.7	79.3
Asian Indian	182	0.1	156	0.2	26	100.0	85.7	14.3
Austrian	1,070	0.6	385	0.4	685	100.0	36.0	64.0
Belgian	448	0.3	113	0.1	335	100.0	25.2	74.8
Canadian	609	0.3	228	0.2	381	100.0	37.4	62.6
Chinese, Thiwanese	705	0.4	540	0.6	165	100.0	76.6	23.4
Czechoslovakian	1,695	0.9	794	0.8	901	100.0	46.8	53.2
Danish	1,672	0.9	438	0.5	1,234	100.0	26.2	73.8
Dutch	8,121	4.5	1,362	1.4	6,759	100.0	16.8	83.2
English	40,004	22.3	11,501	11.9	28,503	100.0	28.7	71.3

Table 8.3 Reported Single and Multiple Ancestries
(CONTINUED)

Ancestry	Total	Percent of total	Persons reported single ancestry		Persons reported multiple ancestry	Percent of persons by kind of ancestry response		
			Number	Percent		Total	Single ancestry	Multiple ancestry
Filipino	764	0.4	525	0.5	239	100.0	68.7	31.3
Finnish	616	0.3	255	0.3	361	100.0	41.4	58.6
French	14,047	7.8	3,047	3.2	11,000	100.0	21.7	78.3
French Canadian	1,053	0.6	582	0.6	471	100.0	55.3	44.7
German	51,649	28.8	17,160	17.8	34,489	100.0	33.2	66.8
Greek	990	0.6	567	0.6	423	100.0	57.3	42.7
Hungarian	1,592	0.9	534	0.6	1,058	100.0	33.5	66.5
Iranian	118	0.1	103	0.1	15	100.0	87.3	12.7
Irish	43,752	24.4	9,760	10.1	33,992	100.0	22.3	77.7
Italian, Sicilian	11,751	6.6	6,110	6.3	5,641	100.0	52.0	48.0
Jamaican	184	0.1	158	0.2	26	100.0	85.9	14.1
Japanese	680	0.4	529	0.5	151	100.0	77.8	22.2
Korean	265	0.1	230	0.2	35	100.0	86.8	13.2
Lebanese	322	0.2	179	0.2	143	100.0	55.6	44.4
Lithuanian	832	0.5	317	0.3	515	100.0	38.1	61.9
Norwegian	4,120	2.3	1,232	1.3	2,888	100.0	29.9	70.1
Polish	8,421	4.7	3,498	3.6	4,923	100.0	41.5	58.5
Portuguese	946	0.5	493	0.5	453	100.0	52.1	47.9

Rumanian	335	0.2	132	0.1	203	100.0	39.4	60.6
Russian	3,466	1.9	1,496	1.6	1,970	100.0	43.2	56.8
Scandinavian	340	0.2	110	0.1	230	100.0	32.4	67.6
Scottish	14,205	7.9	1,615	1.7	12,590	100.0	11.4	88.6
Slavic	722	0.4	300	0.3	422	100.0	41.6	58.4
Spanish	12,493	7.0	9,762	10.1	2,731	100.0	78.1	21.9
Colombian	117	0.1	101	0.1	16	100.0	86.3	13.7
Cuban	675	0.4	558	0.6	117	100.0	82.7	17.3
Dominican	119	0.1	107	0.1	12	100.0	89.9	10.1
Mexican	6,682	3.7	5,889	6.1	793	100.0	88.1	11.9
Puerto Rican	1,333	0.7	1,107	1.1	226	100.0	83.0	17.0
Other Spanish	3,566	2.0	2,000	2.1	1,566	100.0	56.1	43.9
Swedish	4,886	2.7	1,216	1.3	3,670	100.0	24.9	75.1
Swiss	1,228	0.7	312	0.3	916	100.0	25.4	74.6
Ukrainian	525	0.3	231	0.2	294	100.0	44.0	56.0
Vietnamese	198	0.1	177	0.2	21	100.0	89.4	10.6
Welsh	2,568	1.4	455	0.5	2,113	100.0	17.7	82.3
West Indian	193	0.1	129	0.1	64	100.0	66.8	33.2
Yugoslavian	467	0.3	283	0.3	184	100.0	60.6	39.4
Other specified ancestry groups	4,942	2.8	2,372	2.5	2,571	100.0	48.0	52.0

— Represents zero or rounds to zero.

[1] Number and percent by ancestry groups do not add to total, as persons may be counted in more than one ancestry group.

Since 1820 the federal government has recorded annually the number of persons migrating to this nation. Note carefully the peak years of 1905, 1906, 1907, 1910, 1913, and 1914 when more than one million persons entered in each of those years. What were the reasons for the mass migration? Why did immigration decline in the 1930s? Identify other significant trends.

Table 8.4 Immigration to the United States 1820 – 1978[17]

[From 1820 to 1867, figures represent alien passengers arrived; from 1868 through 1891 and 1895 through 1897, immigrant aliens arrived; from 1892 through 1894 and 1898 to the present time, immigrant aliens newly arrived and persons who adjust to permanent resident status.]

Year	Number of persons	Year	Number of persons	Year	Number of persons	Year	Number of persons
1820–1978[1]	48,664,965						
1820	8,385						
1821–1830	143,439	1861–1870	2,314,824	1901–1910	8,795,386	1941–1950	1,035,039
1821	9,127	1861	91,918	1901	487,918	1941	51,776
1822	6,911	1862	91,985	1902	648,743	1942	28,781
1823	6,354	1863	176,282	1903	857,046	1943	23,725
1824	7,912	1864	193,418	1904	812,870	1944	28,551
1825	10,199	1865	248,120	1905	1,026,499	1945	38,119
1826	10,837	1866	318,568	1906	1,100,735	1946	108,721
1827	18,875	1867	315,722	1907	1,285,349	1947	147,292
1828	27,382	1868	138,840	1908	782,870	1948	170,570
1829	22,520	1869	352,768	1909	751,786	1949	188,317
1830	23,322	1870	387,203	1910	1,041,570	1950	249,187

1831–1840	599,125	1871–1800	2,812,191	1911–1920	5,735,811	1951–1960	2,515,479
1831	22,633	1871	321,350	1911	878,587	1951	205,717
1832	60,482	1872	404,806	1912	838,172	1952	265,520
1833	58,640	1873	459,803	1913	1,197,892	1953	170,434
1834	65,365	1874	313,339	1914	1,218,480	1954	208,177
1835	45,374	1875	227,498	1915	326,700	1955	237,790
1836	76,242	1876	169,986	1916	298,826	1956	321,625
1837	79,340	1877	141,857	1917	295,403	1957	326,867
1838	38,914	1878	138,469	1918	110,618	1958	253,265
1839	68,069	1879	177,826	1919	141,132	1959	260,686
1840	84,066	1880	457,257	1920	430,001	1960	265,398

1841–1850	1,713,251	1881–1890	5,246,613	1921–1930	4,107,209	1961–1970	3,321,677
1841	80,289	1881	669,431	1921	805,228	1961	271,344
1842	104,565	1882	788,992	1922	309,556	1962	283,763
1843	52,496	1883	603,322	1923	522,919	1963	306,260
1844	78,615	1884	518,592	1924	706,896	1964	292,248
1845	114,371	1885	395,346	1925	294,314	1965	296,697
1846	154,416	1886	334,203	1926	304,488	1966	323,040
1847	234,968	1887	490,109	1927	335,175	1967	361,972
1848	226,527	1888	546,889	1928	307,255	1968	454,448
1849	297,024	1889	444,427	1929	279,678	1969	358,579
1850	369,980	1890	455,302	1930	241,700	1970	373,326

1851–1860	2,598,214	1891–1900	3,687,564	1931–1940	528,431		
1851	379,466	1891	560,319	1931	97,139	1971	370,478
1852	371,603	1892	579,663	1932	35,576	1972	384,685
1853	368,645	1893	439,730	1933	23,068	1973	400,063
1854	427,833	1894	285,631	1934	29,470	1974	394,861
1855	200,877	1895	258,536	1935	34,956	1975	386,194

Table 8.4 Immigration to the United States
(CONTINUED)

Year	Number of persons	Year	Number of persons	Year	Number of persons	Year	Number of persons
1856......	200,436	1896......	343,267	1936......	36,329	1976......	398,613
1857......	251,306	1897......	230,832	1937......	50,244	1976, TQ	103,676
1858......	123,126	1898......	229,299	1938......	67,895	1977......	462,315
1859......	121,282	1899......	311,715	1939......	82,998	1978......	601,442
1860......	153,640	1900......	448,572	1940......	70,756		

[1]From 1869 to 1976, the data is for fiscal years ended June 30. Prior to fiscal year 1869, the periods covered are as follows: from 1820–1831 and 1843–1849, the years ended on September 30–1843 covers 9 months; from 1832–1842 and 1850–1867, the years ended on December 31–1832 and 1850 covers 15 months. For 1868, the periods ended on June 30 and covers 6 months. The transition quarter (TQ) for 1976 covers the 3-month period, July–September 1976. Beginning October 1, 1976, the fiscal years ended on September 30.

Since 1820 the official annual count of immigrants entering the United States has been recorded. The extent of the volume of that immigration and the large numbers of nationality groups reflect the ethnic foundations of the nation. Cite the major numerical groups and give reasons for their large numbers. Also, compare immigration from the various continents. Examine the two columns at the right listed under "Percent." What conclusions can be drawn from reading these columns?

Table 8.5 Immigrants, by Country of Last Permanent Residence: 1820 to 1977[18]

[In thousands, except percent. For years ending June 30 except, beginning 1977, ending September 30. Data prior to 1906 refer to country from which aliens came. Because of boundary changes and changes in list of countries separately reported, data for certain countries not comparable throughout. See also *Historical Statistics, Colonial Times to 1970*, series C 89–119]

Country	1820–1977, total	1951–1960, total	1961–1970, total	1972	1973	1974	1975	1976	1977	Percent 1820–1977	Percent 1961–1970	Percent 1971–1977
Total	47,960	2,515.5	3,321.7	384.7	400.1	394.9	386.2	398.6	462.3	100.0	100.0	100.0
Europe	36,108	1,325.6	1,123.4	86.3	91.2	80.4	72.8	73.0	74.0	75.3	33.8	20.4
Austria[1]	4,314	67.1	20.6	2.3	1.6	.7	.5	.5	.5	8.9	.6	.3
Hungary		36.6	5.4	.5	1.0	.9	.6	.6	.5		.2	.2
Belgium	202	18.6	9.2	.5	.4	.4	.4	.5	.5	.4	.3	.1
Czechoslovakia	137	.9	3.3	1.2	.9	.4	.3	.3	.3		.1	.2
Denmark	364	11.0	9.2	.5	.4	.5	.3	.4	.4		.3	.1
Finland	33	4.9	4.2	.3	.3	.2	.2	.2	.2		.1	.1
France	747	51.1	45.2	2.9	2.6	2.2	1.8	2.0	2.7	1.6	1.4	.6
Germany[1]	6,968	477.8	190.8	7.8	7.6	7.2	5.9	6.6	7.4	14.5	5.7	1.8
Great Britain[2]	4,879	196.5	210.0	11.5	11.9	11.7	12.2	13.0	14.0	10.2	6.3	3.1
Greece	646	47.6	86.0	10.5	10.3	10.6	9.8	8.6	7.8	1.3	2.6	2.6
Ireland[3]	4,722	57.3	37.5	1.4	1.6	1.3	1.1	1.0	1.0	9.9	1.1	.3

Table 8.5 Immigrants, by Country of Last Permanent Residence
(CONTINUED)

Country	1820–1977, total	1951–1960, total	1961–1970, total	1972	1973	1974	1975	1976	1977	Percent 1820–1977	Percent 1961–1970	Percent 1971–1977
Italy	5,285	185.5	214.1	22.4	22.3	15.0	11.0	8.0	7.4	11.0	6.4	3.9
Netherlands	358	52.3	30.6	1.0	1.0	1.0	.8	.9	1.0	.8	.9	.2
Norway	856	22.9	15.5	.4	.4	.4	.3	.3	1.8	.5	.1	
Poland[1]	510	10.0	53.5	3.8	4.1	3.5	3.5	3.2	3.3	1.1	1.6	.8
Portugal	432	19.6	76.1	9.5	10.0	10.7	11.3	11.0	10.0	.9	2.3	2.6
Spain	254	7.9	44.7	4.3	5.5	4.7	2.6	2.8	5.6	.5	1.3	1.0
Sweden	1,271	21.7	17.1	.7	.6	.6	.5	.6	.6	2.7	.5	.2
Switzerland	348	17.7	18.5	1.0	.7	.7	.7	.8	.8	.7	.6	.2
U.S.S.R.[14]	3,367	.6	2.3	.4	.9	.9	4.7	7.4	5.4	7.0	.1	.7
Yugoslavia	111	8.2	20.4	2.8	5.2	5.0	2.9	2.3	2.3	.2	.6	.9
Other Europe	304	10.8	9.2	.6	1.9	1.8	1.3	2.0	2.0	.6	.3	.4
Asia	2,573	153.3	427.8	116.0	120.0	127.0	129.2	146.7	150.8	5.4	12.9	31.7
China[5]	510	9.7	34.8	8.5	9.2	10.0	9.2	9.9	12.5	1.0	1.0	2.4
Hong Kong	[6]169	15.5	75.0	10.9	10.3	10.7	12.5	13.7	12.3	.4	2.3	2.8
India	140	2.0	27.2	15.6	12.0	11.7	14.3	16.1	16.8	.3	.8	3.5
Iran	[6]33	3.4	10.3	2.9	2.9	2.5	2.2	2.6	4.2	.1	.3	.7
Israel	[6]80	25.5	29.6	3.0	2.9	2.9	3.5	5.2	4.4	.2	.9	.8
Japan	400	46.3	40.0	5.0	6.1	5.4	4.8	4.8	4.5	.8	1.2	1.3
Jordan	[6]34	5.8	11.7	2.4	2.1	2.5	2.3	2.4	2.9	.1	.3	.6
Korea	[6]211	6.2	34.5	18.1	22.3	27.5	28.1	30.6	30.7	.4	1.0	6.1
Lebanon	[6]46	4.5	15.2	3.0	2.6	3.0	4.0	5.0	5.5	.1	.5	.9
Philippines	[7]343	19.3	98.4	28.7	30.2	32.5	31.3	36.8	38.5	.7	3.0	8.1

Turkey	384	3.5	10.1	1.5	1.4	1.4	1.1	1.0	1.0	.8	.3	.3
Vietnam	26[8]	2.7	4.2	3.4	4.5	3.1	2.7	2.4	3.4	.1	.1	.8
Other Asia	197	9.0	36.7	13.0	13.5	13.8	13.2	16.2	14.1	.4	1.2	3.4
America	8,740	996.9	1,716.4	173.2	179.6	178.8	174.7	169.2	223.2	18.2	51.7	45.4
Argentina	89[9]	19.5	49.7	2.5	2.9	2.9	2.8	2.7	3.1	.2	1.5	.7
Brazil	55[9]	13.8	29.3	1.8	1.8	1.6	1.4	1.4	1.9	.1	.9	.4
Canada	4,077	378.0	413.3	18.6	14.8	12.3	11.2	11.4	18.0	8.5	12.4	3.9
Colombia	133[9]	18.0	72.0	5.2	5.3	5.9	6.4	5.7	8.2	.3	2.2	1.5
Cuba	490[10]	78.9	208.5	19.9	22.5	17.4	25.6	28.4	66.1	1.0	6.3	7.2
Dominican Rep.	194[9]	9.9	93.3	10.8	14.0	15.7	14.1	12.4	11.6	.4	2.8	3.2
Ecuador	80[9]	9.8	36.8	4.4	4.2	4.8	4.7	4.5	5.2	.2	1.1	1.2
El Salvador	38[9]	5.9	15.0	2.0	2.0	2.3	2.4	2.4	4.4	.1	.4	.6
Guatemala	36[9]	4.7	15.9	1.7	1.8	1.6	1.9	2.0	3.7	.1	.5	.5
Haiti	76[10]	4.4	34.5	5.5	4.6	3.8	5.0	5.3	5.2	.1	1.0	1.3
Honduras	31[9]	6.0	15.7	1.0	1.4	1.4	1.4	1.3	1.6	.1	.5	.3
Mexico	2,015	299.8	453.9	64.2	70.4	71.9	62.6	58.4	44.6	4.2	13.7	15.1
Panama	43[9]	11.7	19.4	1.6	1.7	1.7	1.7	1.8	2.5	.1	.6	.5
Peru	42[9]	7.4	19.1	1.5	1.8	2.0	2.3	2.6	3.9	.1	.6	.6
West Indies	684	29.8	133.9	24.2	21.6	24.4	22.3	19.6	27.1	1.4	4.0	5.9
Other America	657	99.2	106.2	8.3	8.8	9.1	8.9	9.3	16.1	1.3	3.2	2.5
Africa	119	14.1	29.0	5.5	5.5	5.2	5.9	5.7	9.6	.3	.9	1.5
Australia and New Zealand	116	11.5	19.6	2.6	2.5	2.0	1.8	2.1	2.5	.2	.6	.6
All other	304	14.0	5.7	1.2	1.3	1.4	1.8	1.9	2.2	.6	.2	.4

[1]1938–1945, Austria included with Germany; 1899–1919, Poland included with Austria-Hungary, Germany, and U.S.S.R. [2]Beginning 1952, includes data for United Kingdom not specified, formerly included with "Other Europe." [3]Comprises Eire and Northern Ireland. [4]Europe and Asia. [5]Beginning 1957, includes Taiwan. [6]Prior to 1951, included with "Other Asia." [7]Prior to 1951, Philippines included with "All Other." [8]Prior to 1953, data for Vietnam not available. [9]Prior to 1951, included with "Other America." [10]Prior to 1951, included with "West Indies."

1. Reprinted from Henry Cabot Lodge, "The Restriction of Immigration," *North American Review* 150, no. 11 (January 1891):27–36.

2. Woodrow Wilson, *A History of the American People*, Vol. 5 (New York: Harper & Brothers, 1901), pp. 212–13.

3. Reprinted from *Reports of the Immigration Commission*, vol. 1 (reprint ed., New York: Arno Press, Inc., 1970), pp. 13–14, 42.

4. Reprinted from Oscar Handlin, *Race and Nationality in American Life* (Boston: Atlantic-Little, Brown, 1957), pp. 94–95.

5. Reprinted from U.S., Congress, Senate, *Congressional Record*, 68th Cong., 1st sess., 1924, pp. 6355–57.

6. Reprinted from Helen F. Eckerson, "Immigration and National Origins," *The Annals* of the American Academy of Political and Social Science 367 (September 1966): 7,8.

7. Shirley Hune, "U.S. Immigration Policy and Asian Americans: Aspects and Consequences," *Civil Rights Issues of Asian and Pacific Americans: Myths and Realities*, U.S. Commission on Civil Rights (Washington, D.C., 1979), p. 284.

8. *Ibid.*, pp. 284–87.

9. The Select Commission on Immigration and Refugee Policy, *Our Immigration Law* (Washington, D.C.: Government Printing Office, n. d.), pp. 6–8.

10. Select Commission on Immigration and Refugee Policy, *Semiannual Report To Congress* (Washington, D.C.: Government Printing Office, 1980), pp. 13–14.

11. *1978 Annual Report of the Immigration and Naturalization Service*, p. 15.

12. *1977 Annual Report of the Immigration and Naturalization Service*, p. 5.

13. Committee on the Judiciary, U.S. Senate, 96th Congress, 2nd Session, *Review of the U.S. Refugee Resettlement Programs and Policies* (Washington, D.C.: Government Printing Office, 1980), p. 37.

14. U.S. Congress, *Hearings Before The SubCommittee on Immigration Refugees, and International Law of the Committee On The Judiciary*, House of Representatives, 97th Cong., 1st sess., Serial No. 30 Part 1. pp. 198–99.

15. Committee on the Judiciary, House of Representatives, *Hearings Before The Sub-Committee on Immigration, Refugees, and International Law*, 97th Congress, 1st Sesstion, 1981 (Washington D.C.: Government Printing Office, 1982). pp. 553–54.

16. U.S. Bureau of The Census, Current Population Reports, Series p-23, No. 116, *Ancestry and Language in the United States; November 1979* (Washington, D.C.: Government Printing Office, 1982), p. 7.

17. *1978 Annual Report of the Immigration and Naturalization Service*, p. 41.

18. U.S. Immigration and Naturalization Service, *Annual Report*.

KEY QUESTIONS

1. Two United States Senators from Massachusetts present their views on immigran policy in this chapter. Summarize their views and evaluate the reasons they used to justify their views.

2. What was the relationship of the Dillingham Commission Report of 1910 to the restrictive immigration policy of the 1920s?

3. Explain fully three reasons why "nativism" intensified in the decade preceding World War II.

4. What was unique about the Immigration Law of 1965?

5. Has there been any new development in the ethnic composition of the nation resulting from the 1965 Immigration Law? Explain.

6. Is there any relationship between American foreign policy and United Stated immigration policy? Explain.

7. Trace the historical development of United States immigration policy.

8. Explain recent trends in American immigration events.

9. Why was the Select Commission on Immigration and Refugee Policy created in 1978?

10. Detail the latest recommendations of the Select Commission on Immigration and Refugee Policy.

Bibliography

CHAPTER 1

Abbott, Edith. *Historical Aspects of the Immigration Problem.* Chicago: University of Chicago Press, 1926.

Bradford, William *Of Plymouth Plantation 1620-1647.* Reprint. Edited by Samuel Eliot Morison. New York: Alfred A. Knopf, Inc., 1952.

Catlin, George. *Letters and Notes of the Manners, Customs, and Conditions of the North American Indians.* Vol. 1. London, 1811. Reprint. New York: Dover Publications, 1973.

Colton, Calvin. *Manual for Emigrants to America.* Reprint. New York: Arno Press, 1969.

Conway, Alan. *The Welsh in America.* Minneapolis: University of Minnesota Press, 1961.

Donaldson, Gordon. *The Scots Overseas.* London: Robert Hale, 1966.

Dunaway, W.F. *The Scotch Irish of Colonial Pennsylvania.* Chapel Hill: 1944.

Eddis, William. *Letters from America. Historical and Descriptive Comprising Occurrences from 1769 to 1770 inclusive.* London: 1772.

Ford, Henry Jones. *The Scotch-Irish in America.* Reprint. New York: Arno Press, 1969.

Goodwin, Maud Wilder, ed. *Historic New York.* Vol. 2. Reprint. Port Washington: Ira J. Friedman, 1969.

Graham, Ian Charles Cargill. *Colonists from Scotland, Emigration to North America, 1707-1783.* Ithaca: Cornell University Press, 1956.

Handlin, Oscar, ed. *This Was America.* New York: Harper & Row, 1964.

Hartmann, Edward G. *Americans from Wales.* Boston: The Christopher Publishing House, 1967.

Hirsch, Arthur Henry. *The Huguenots of Colonial South Carolina.* Hamden, Conn.: The Shoe String Press, 1962.

Hoff, Rhoda. *American Immigrants.* New York: Henry Z. Walck, 1969.

Irving, Washington. *The Sketchbook.* Philadelphia: Henry Altemus, 1895.

Kraus, Michael. *Immigration, The American Mosaic: From Pilgrims to Modern Refugees.* New York: Litton Educational Publishing, Inc., 1963.

Larabee, Leonard W., ed. *The Papers of Benjamin Franklin.* Vol. 4. New Haven: Yale University Press, 1961.

Leyburn, James G. *The Scotch-Irish.* Chapel Hill: University of North Carolina Press, 1962.

Lucas, Henry S. *Dutch Immigrant Memoirs and Selected Writings.* Vol. 1. Seattle: University of Washington, 1955.

Mulder, Arnold. *Americans from Holland.* Philadelphia: J.P. Lippincott Company, 1947.

Thernstrom, Stephan, ed. *Harvard Encyclopedia of American Ethnic Groups.* Cambridge: Harvard University Press, 1980.

Tocqueville, Alexis de. *Democracy in America.* Reprint. New York: Alfred A. Knopf, Inc., 1961.

Wabeke, B.H. *Dutch Immigration to North America, 1821-1860.* New York: 1944.

CHAPTER 2

Adams, William F. *Ireland and the Irish Emigration to the New World from 1815 to the Famine.* 1832.

Babcock, K.C. "The Scandinavian Element in the American Population." *The American Historical Review* 16 (1911).

Barthold, Richard. *From Steerage to Congress, Reminiscences and Reflections.* Philadelphia: Dorrance and Co., Inc., 1930.

Benson, Adolph B., and Hedin, Naboth, eds. *Swedes in America.* New Haven: Yale University Press, 1938.

Blegen, Theodore G. *Land of Their Choice.* Minneapolis: University of Minnesota Press, 1955.

—. *Norwegian Migration to America, 1825–1860.* Northfield, Minnesota: Norwegian-American Historical Association, 1931.

Faust, Albert B. *The German Element in the United States.* Vol. 1. 1909. Reprint. New York: Arno Press, 1969

Gibson, Florence Elizabeth. *The Attitudes of the New York Irish toward State and National Affairs, 1848-1892.* New York: Columbia University Press, 1954.

Hansen, Marcus Lee. *The Mingling of the Canadian and American People.* New Haven: 1950.

Hawgood, John A. *The Tragedy of German America.* New York: G.P. Putnam and Sons, 1940.

MaGuire, John Francis. *The Irish in America.* 1868. Reprint. New York: Arno Press, 1969.

Mittleberger, Gottlieb. *Journey to Pennsylvania in the Year 1750 and Return to Germany in the Year 1754.* Edited and translated by Oscar Handlin and John Clive. Cambridge, MA: Harvard University Press, 1960.

O'Connor, Richard. *The German Americans, An Informal History.* Boston: Little, Brown and Co. 1968.

Osland, Birger. *A Long Pull from Stavanger, The Reminiscences of a Norwegian Immigrant.* Northfield, Minn.: Norwegian-American Historical Society, 1945.

Qualey, C.C. *Norwegian Settlements in the United States.* Northfield, Minn.:

Norwegian-American Historical Society, 1938.

Riis, Jacob A. *The Making of an American*. New York: Macmillan, 1901.

Rolvaag, Ole. *Giants in the Earth*. New York: Harper and Row, 1927.

Schrier, A. *Ireland and the American Emigration, 1850-1900*. New York. Russell & Russell, 1970.

Schurz, Carl. *The Reminiscences of Carl Schurz*. Vol. 3. New York: The McClure Co., 1908.

Tocqueville, Alexis de *Democracy in America*. Reprint. New York: Alfred A. Knopf, Inc., 1961.

Unonius, Gustav. *A Pioneer in Northwest America, 1841-1858*. Vol. 2. Minneapolis: University of Minnesota Press, 1960.

Wittke, Carl. *German-Americans and the World War*. Columbus: 1936.

Wright, Tobert L. *Swedish Emigrant Ballads*. Lincoln, Nebraska: University of Nebraska, 1965.

Works Progress Administration. *The Swedes and Finns in New Jersey*. Bayonne, N.J.: 1938.

CHAPTER 3

Balch, Emily G. *Our Slavic Fellow Citizens*. 1910. Reprint. New York: Arno Press, 1970.

Buczek, David S. *Immigrant Pastor*. Waterbury, 1974.

Cahan, Abraham. *The Rise of David Levensky*. New York: Harper and Row, 1960.

Capek, Thomas. *The Czechs (Bohemians) in America: A Study of Their National, Cultural, Political, Social, Economic and Religious Life*. 1920, Reprint. New York: Arno Press, 1969.

Davis, Jerome. *The Russian Immigrant*. 1922. Reprint. New York: Arno Press, 1969.

Davis, Jerome. *The Russians and Ruthenians in America*. New York: George H. Doran Co., 1922.

Fox, Paul. *The Poles in America*. 1922. Reprint. New York: Arno Press, 1970.

Gold, Michael. *Jews Without Money*. New York: Liveright Publishers, 1930.

Goldstein, Sidney. *Jewish Americans: Three Generations in a Jewish Community*. Englewood Cliffs, NJ: Prentice-Hall, 1968.

Halich, Wasyl. *Ukrainians in the United States*. Chicago: University of Chicago Press, 1937.

James, E.J., ed. *The Immigrant Jew in America*. New York: 1907.

Joseph, Samuel. *Jewish Immigration to the United States from 1881 to 1910*. New York: Columbia University Press, 1914.

Kezierska, Anzia. *Children of Loneliness*. New York: Funk and Wagnalls Co., 1923.

Kutak, Robert I. *The Story of a Bohemian-American Village: A Study of Social Persistence and Change*. 1933. Reprint. New York: Arno Press, 1970.

Leibbrandt, George. "The Emigration of the German Mennonites from Russia to the United States and Canada, 1873-1880." Part Two. *The Mennonite Quarterly Review* 7 (1933): 36-37.

Miller, Kenneth D. *The Czechoslovaks in America.* New York: Doran, 1922.

Roberts, Peter. *The New Immigration: A Study of the Industrial and Social Life of Southeastern Europeans in America.* 1914. Reprint. New York: Arno Press, 1970.

Sheridan, Frank J. *Italian, Slavic and Hungarian Unskilled Laborers in the United States.* 1907. Reprint. New York: Jerome S. Ozer, 1971.

Thomas, William I., and Znaniecki, Florian. *The Polish Peasant in Europe and America.* 5 vols. 1920. Reprint (5 vols. in 1). New York: Dover Publications, 1958.

United Hebrew Charities. *Twentieth Annual Report.* New York: 1886.

Warne, Frank J. *The Slav Invasion and the Mine Workers: A Study in Immigration.* 1913. Reprint. New York: Jerome S. Ozer, 1971.

Wischnitzer, Mark. *Visas to Freedom.* Cleveland: World Publishing Co., 1956.

CHAPTER 4

Covello, Leonard. *Social Background of the Italo-American School Child.* Leiden, Netherlands: E.J. Brill, 1967.

DeConde, Alexander. *Half Bitter, Half Sweet, An Excursion into Italian American History.* New York: Charles Scribner's Sons, 1971.

Engel, Madeline, and Tomasi, Sylvan M. *The Italian Experience in the United States.* New York: Center for Migration Studies, 1971.

Fairchild, Henry P. *Greek Immigration to the United States.* New Haven: Yale University Press, 1921.

Felici, Ecilio. *Father to the Immigrants, Life of John Baptist Scalabrini.* New York: P.J. Kenedy and Sons, 1955.

First Annual Report with Constitution and By-laws of the Syrian Society of the City of New York. New York: May, 1893.

Foerster, Robert F. *Italian Emigration of Our Times.* Cambridge, MA: Harvard University Press, 1924.

Giovanetti, Alberto. *The Italians of America.* New York, 1979.

Hitti, Philip K. *The Syrians in America.* New York: George H. Doran, 1924.

Iorizzo, Luciano J., and Mondello, Salvatore. *The Italian Americans.* New York: Twayne Publishers, 1980, Revised Edition.

LaGumina, Salvatore J., ed. *Ethnicity in Suburbia: The Long Island Experience.* Garden City, 1980.

Leder, Hans Howard. "Cultural Persistence in a Portuguese-American Community." Doctoral thesis, Stanford University, 1968.

Miller, Randall M. *The Kaleidoscopic Lens—How Hollywood Views Ethnic Groups.* Englewood, NJ: Jerome S. Ozer, 1980.

Moquin, Wayne; Van Doren, Charles; Ianni, Francis A.J. *A Documentary History of Italian-Americans*. New York, 1974.

Neff, Alixa. "Belief in the Evil Eye Among the Christian Syrian-Lebanese in America." *Journal of American Folklore* (January 1965): 46-47.

Rolle: Andrew F. *The Immigrant Upraised*. Norman, Oklahoma: University of Oklahoma Press, 1966.

Saloutos, Theodore. *The Greeks in the United States*. Cambridge, MA: Harvard University Press, 1964.

—. *They Remember America, The Story of the Repatriated Greek-Americans*. Berkeley, CA: University of California Press, 1956.

Schiavo, Giovanni. *Italians in Chicago*. Chicago: Italian American Publishing Company, 1928.

—. *The Italians in Missouri*. Chicago: Italian American Publishing Company, 1929.

Taft, Donald. *Two Portuguese Communities in New England*. New York: Arno Press, 1969.

Weiss, Bernard, ed. *American Education and the European Immigrant, 1840-1940*. Urbana: University of Illinois Press, 1981.

Xenides, J.P. *The Greeks in America*. New York: George H. Doran Co., 1922.

CHAPTER 5

Buaken, Iris B. "You Can't Marry A Filipino." *Commonweal* 41 (1945): 534-537.

Buaken, Manuel. *I Have Lived with the American People*. Caldwell, Idaho: The Caxton Printers, 1948.

Chen, Jack. *The Chinese of America*. San Francisco: Harper & Row, 1980.

Coolidge, Mary Roberts. *Chinese Immigration*. New York: Arno Press, 1969.

Daniels, Roger. *The Politics of Prejudice*. New York: Atheneum, 1968.

Girdner, Audrie, and Loftis, Anne. *The Great Betrayal*. London: Macmillan, 1969.

Grant, Bruce. *The Boat People*. Harmondsworth, England: Penguin Books, 1978.

Hosokawa, Bill. *Nisei, The Quiet Americans*. New York: William Morrow, 1969.

Houston, Jeanne Wakatsuki, and Houston, James D. *Farewell to Manzanar*. Boston: Houghton Mifflin, 1973.

Kawakami, Kiyoshi Karl. *The Real Japanese Question*. New York: Macmillan, 1920.

Kitagawa, Daisuke. *Issei and Nisei, The Internment Years*. New York: The Seabury Press, 1967.

Kitano, Harry H. L. *Japanese Americans*. Englewood Cliffs, N.J.: Prentice-Hall, 1969.

Kwong, Peter. *Chinatown, New York; Labor and Politics*. New York: Monthly Review Press, 1979.

Lasker, Bruno. *Filipino Immigration*. Chicago: University of Chicago Press, 1931.

Lyman, Stanford M. *The Asian in North America*. Santa Barbara, California: ABC-Clio, 1977.

McCunn, Ruthanne Lum. *An Illustrated History of the Chinese in America*. San Francisco: Design Enterprises, 1979.

Melendy, Brett. *Asians in America: Filipinos, Koreans, and East Indians*. Boston: Twayne, 1977.

Miller, Stuart Creighton. *The Unwelcome Immigrant, The American Image of the Chinese, 1785-1882*. Berkeley, CA: University of California Press, 1969.

Park, No-Yong. *An Oriental View of American Civilization*. Boston: Hale, Cushman, and Flint, 1934.

Spicer, Edward H.; Hansen, Asael T.; Luomala, Katherine; and Opler, Marvin K. *Impounded People, Japanese-Americans in Relocation Centers*. Tucson: The University of Arizona Press, 1969.

Sung, Betty Lee. *Mountain of Gold*. New York: Macmillan, 1967.

Tachiki, Amy. *Roots: An Asian American Reader*. Los Angeles: Regents of the University of California, 1971.

Thomas, Dorothy Swaine, and Nishimoto, Richard S. *The Spoilage, Japanese American Evacuation and Resettlement*. Berkeley, CA: University of California Press, 1969.

U.S. Department of State. "Indochinese Resettlement in the United States." Special Report No. 68, February, 1980.

Wain, Barry. *The Refused: The Agony of the Indochinese Refugees*. New York: Simon and Shuster, 1981.

War Relocation Authority. "A Nisei Who Said 'No.'" *Community Analysis Notes* 1 (January 15, 1944): 1-9.

—. "Nisei Report on Their Adjustment to Tule Lake." *Community Analysis Notes* 7 (December 20, 1944): 1-3.

CHAPTER 6

Acuña, Rodolfo. *Occupied America: A History of Chicanos*. New York: Harper & Row, 1981.

Alexander, Tom. "Those Amazing Cuban Emigres." *Fortune Magazine* 74 (1966): 144-149.

Davidson, John. *The Long Road North*. Garden City, New York: Doubleday, 1979.

Forbes, Jack. *Hearing Before the United States Commission on Civil Rights*. Hearing held in San Antonio, Texas, December 9-14, 1968. Washington, D.C.: Government Printing Office, 1968, pp. 25-31.

Gamio, Manuel. *Mexican Immigration to the United States*. Chicago: University of Chicago Press, 1930.

Garver, Susan. *Coming to North America: from Mexico, Cuba, Puerto Rico*. New York: Delacort Press, 1981.

Glazer, Nathan, and Moynihan, Daniel Patrick. *Beyond the Melting Pot.* Cambridge, MA: The MIT Press, 1963.

Grebler, Leo; Moore, Joan W.; and Guzman, Ralph C. *The Mexican American Peoples, The Nation's Second Largest Minority.* New York: The Free Press, 1970.

Halsell, Grace. *The Illegals.* New York: Stein and Day, 1978.

Ham, Edward E. "French Patterns in Quebec and New England." *The New England Quarterly* (December, 1945): 435-447.

Holbrook, Sabra. *The American West Indies.* New York: Meredith Press, 1969.

Kessner, Thomas, and Caroli, Betty Boyd. *Today's Immigrants, Their Stories,Hopes.* New York: Oxford University Press, 1981.

Lewis, Gordon K. *Puerto Rico, Freedom and Power in the Caribbean.* New York: Harper & Row, 1963.

Lewis, Oscar. *La Vida.* New York: Random House, 1965.

Lewis, Sasha Gregory. *Slave Trade Today: American Exploitation of Illegal Aliens.* Boston: Beacon Press, 1979.

McWilliams, Carey. *North from Mexico.* New York: Greenwood Press, 1968.

Meier, Matt S., and Rivera, Feliciano. *The Chicanos.* New York: Hill and Wang, 1972.

Moore, Joan W. and Cuellar, Alfredo. *Mexican Americans.* Englewood Cliffs: Prentice-Hall, 1970.

Moquin, Wayne, and Van Doren, Charles, eds. *A Documentary History of the Mexican Americans.* New York: Praeger, 1971.

Nava, Julian. *Mexican Americans: Past, Present and Future.* New York: American Book Company, 1969.

Portes, Alejandro. "Dilemmas of a Golden Exile: Integration of Cuban Refugee Families in Milwaukee." *American Sociological Review* 34 (1969): 505-518.

Pousner, Michael. "Haitians: The Invisible Minority." *New York Daily News,* January 11, 1971, p. 32.

Rand, Christopher. *The Puerto Ricans.* New York: Oxford University Press, 1958.

Rodriques, Clara E.; Korral, Virginia Sanchez; and Alers, Jose Oscar, eds. *Essays on Survival in the United States.* New York: Puerto Rican Migration Research Consortium, 1980.

Samora, Julian. *Los Mojados: The Wetback Story.* Notre Dame, Indiana: University of Notre Dame, 1971.

Senior, Clarence. *The Puerto Ricans, Strangers—Then Neighbors.* Chicago: Quadrangle Books, 1965.

Stillwell, Hart. "The Wetback Tide." *Common Ground* 9 (1949): 3-44.

Thomas, Piri. *Down These Mean Streets.* New York: The New American Library, 1967.

Wakefield, Dan. *Island in the City.* Boston: Houghton-Mifflin, 1959.

Wessel, Bessie Bloom. *An Ethnic Survey of Woonsocket, Rhode Island.* New York: Arno Press, 1970.

CHAPTER 7

Barrett, S. M., ed. *Geronimo, His Own Story.* (Introduction and Notes by Frederick W. Turner.) New York: E. P. Dutton, 1970.

Breitman, George, ed. *Malcolm X Speaks.* New York: Grove Press, 1965.

Brown, Dee. *Bury My Heart at Wounded Knee.* New York: Holt, Rinehart and Winston, 1970.

Carmichael, Stokely, and Hamilton, Charles V. *Black Power: The Politics of Liberation in America.* New York: Random House, 1967.

Chaput, Donald. "Some Repatriement Dilemmas." *The Canadian Historical Review* 49:4 (1968): 400-412.

Clark, Kenneth B. "Sex, Status, and Underemployment of the Negro Male." In *Employment, Race and Poverty,* edited by Arthur M. Ross and Herbert Hill. New York: Harcourt, Brace and World, 1967.

Debo, Angie. *A History of the Indians of the United States.* Norman, Oklahoma: University of Oklahoma Press, 1970.

Ellison, Ralph. *The Invisible Man.* New York: The New American Library, 1952.

Hagan, William T. *American Indians.* Chicago: University of Chicago Press, 1971.

Josephy, Alvin M. *Red Power.* New York: McGraw-Hill, 1971.

Katz, William L. *Eyewitness: The Negro in American History.* New York: Pitman Publishing Co., 1967.

King, Martin Luther, Jr. "Letter from Birmingham City Jail." In *Black on Black,* edited by Arnold Adoff, New York: Macmillan, 1968.

Leach, Douglas Edward. *Flintlock and Tomahawk, New England in King Philip's War.* New York: W. W. Norton & Company, Inc., 1958.

Lomax, Louis. *The Negro Revolt.* New York: Harper and Row, 1962.

Mebane, Mary E. "Daddy Wasn't a Numbers Runner." *The New York Times,* February 18, 1971, p. 35.

Northup, Solomon. *Twelve Years a Slave.* Edited by Sam Eakin and Joseph Logsdon. Baton Rouge: Louisiana State University Press, 1968.

Osofsky, Gilbert, ed. *Puttin' On Ole Massa, The Slave Narratives of Henry Bibb, William Wells Brown, and Solomon Northup.* New York: Harper & Row, 1969.

Pinkney, Alphonso. *Black Americans.* Englewood Cliffs, NJ: Prentice-Hall, 1969.

Randolph, A. Philip. "March on Washington Movement Presents Program for the Negro." In *What the Negro Wants,* edited by Rayford W. Logan. Chapel Hill: University of North Carolina Press, 1944.

Snellings, Roland. "Sunrise." In *Black Fire,* edited by LeRoi Jones and Roy Neal. New York: Morrow, 1968.

Vogt, Evon. "The Acculturation of American Indians." *The Annals of the Academy of Political and Social Sciences* 311 (1957): 137-146.

Wax, Murray L., *Indian Americans.* Englewood Cliffs, NJ: Prentice-Hall, 1971.
Wilkins, Roy. "Integration." *Ebony* 25 (1970): 54-60.

CHAPTER 8

Civil Rights Digest, Vol. 9, Fall 1976.
Civil Rights Issues of Asian and Pacific Americans: Myths and Realities. U.S. Commission on Civil Rights, Washington, D.C., 1979.
Committee on the Judiciary, U.S. House of Representatives. *Immigration and Nationality Act, With Amendments and Notes on Related Laws.* 5th edition. Washington, D.C.: Government Printing Office, 1966.
"Controversy Over U.S. Immigration Policy." *Congressional Digest* (May, 1965).
Eckerson, Helen F. "Immigration and National Origins." *Annals of the American Academy of Political and Social Sciences* 366 (1966): 5-15.
Graham, Otis L. "Illegal Immigration and the New Reform Movement." Fair Immigration Papers No. 2, Feb. 1980.
Grant, Madison. *The Passing of the Great Race.* New York: Charles Scribner's Sons, 1921.
Handlin, Oscar. *Race and Nationality in American Life.* Boston: Little, Brown and Co., 1957.
Higham, John. *Strangers in the Land, Patterns of American Nativism 1860-1925.* New York: Atheneum, 1971.
Kraut, Alan M. *The Huddled Masses, The Immigrant in American Society, 1880-1921.* Arlington Heights, Illinois: Harlan-Davidson, Inc., 1982.
LaGumina, Salvatore J. "The New Deal, the Immigrants, and Congressman Vito Marcantonio." *The International Migration Review* 4:11 (1970): 57-74.
Liebman, Lance, ed. *Ethnic Relations in America.* Englewood Cliffs, NJ: Prentice-Hall, 1982.
Lodge, Henry Cabot. "The Restriction of Immigration." *North American Review* 152 (1891): 27-36.
—. *Reports of the Immigration Commission.* Vol. 1. Reprint. New York: Arno Press, 1970.
Morrison, Joan, and Zabusky, Charlotte Fox. *American Mosaic, The Immigrant Experience in the Words of Those Who Lived It.* New York: E.P. Dutton, 1980.
Parillo, Vincent N. *Strangers to These Shores.* Boston: Houghton Mifflin, 1980.
Schroeder, Richard C. *Refugee Policy.* Washington, D.C.: Congressional Quarterly, 1980.
Seller, Maxine. *To Seek America.* Englewood, NJ: Jerome S. Oer, 1977.

Shawcross, William. "Refugees and Rhetoric." *Foreign Policy.* Fall, 1979.

Sowell, Thomas. *Ethnic America: A History.* New York: Basic Books, 1981.

Steinberg, Stephen. *The Ethnic Myth: Race, Ethnicity and Class in America.* New York: Atheneum, 1981.

U.S. Bureau of the Census. Current Population Reports, Series P-23, No. 116, *Ancestry and Language in the United States; Nov. 1979.* Washington, D.C.: Government Printing Office, 1982.

U.S. Bureau of the Census. *Race of the Population by States, 1980.* Washington, D.C.: Government Printing Office, 1981.

U.S. Committee for Refugees. *1981 World Refugee Survey.* New York, 1981.

U.S. Senate, Committee on the Judiciary, 96th Congress, First and Second Sessions. *Review of the U.S. Refugee Resettlement Programs and Policies.* Washington, D.C.: Government Printing Office, 1979 and 1980.

Walsh, David I. *Congressional Record.* 68th Congress, 1st Session (April 15, 1924): 6355-6357.

Watson, Barbara M. "Immigration Today." *The International Migration Review* 4 (1970): 47-51.